Dinosaurs or

The United Nations and the World Bank
at the Turn of the Century

by

Helge Ole Bergesen
Leiv Lunde

Earthscan Publications Ltd, London

First published in the UK in 1999 by
Earthscan Publications Ltd

Copyright © Helge Ole Bergesen, 1999

A catalogue record for this book is available from the British Library

ISBN: 1 85383 632 X paperback
       1 85383 647 8 hardback

Typesetting by PCS Mapping and DTP, Newcastle upon Tyne
Printed and bound by Creative Print and Design (Wales), Ebbw Vale.
Cover design by Yvonne Booth

For a full list of publications please contact:
Earthscan Publications Ltd
120 Pentonville Road
London, N1 9JN, UK
Tel: +44 (0)171 278 0433
Fax: +44 (0)171 278 1142
Email: earthinfo@earthscan.co.uk
http://www.earthscan.co.uk

Earthscan is an editorially independent subsidiary of Kogan Page Ltd and
publishes in association with WWF-UK and the International Institute for
Environment and Development

This book is printed on 50 per cent recycled paper

Contents

Figures, Tables and Boxes

FIGURES

TABLES

BOXES

Acronyms and Abbreviations

AIDS	Autoimmunodeficiency Syndrome
CEC	Commission of the European Community
CFF	Compensatory Financing Facility
CSIS	Center for Strategic & International Studies
DAC	Development Assistance Committee
ECOSOC	Economic and Social Council
EDI	Economic Development Institute (World Bank)
EEC	European Economic Community
EPTA	Expanded Programme of Technical Assistance
FAO	Food and Agriculture Organization
GATT	General Agreement on Tariffs and Trade
GEF	Global Environment Facility
GNP	Gross National Product
GSP	Generalized System of Preferences
HABITAT	UN Conference on Human Settlements
IBRD	International Bank for Reconstruction and Development
ICAO	International Civil Aviation Organization
IDA	International Development Agency
IFC	International Finance Corporation
IGO	Intergovernmental Organization
ILO	International Labour Organization
IMF	International Monetary Fund
IMO	International Maritime Organization
IPCC	Intergovernmental Panel on Climate Change
IRO	International Refugee Organization
ITO	International Trade Organization
ITU	International Telecommunications Union
JIU	Joint Inspection Unit
MDB	Multilateral Development Bank
MDI	Multilateral Development Institution
NATO	North Atlantic Treaty Organization

NAM	Non-Aligned Movement
NEAP	National Environmental Action Plans
NGO	Non-Governmental Organization
NIEO	New International Economic Order
NORAD	Norwegian Agency for Development and Cooperation
NWICO	New World Information and Communication Order
ODA	Official Development Assistance
ODA	Overseas Development Administration
OECD	Organization for Economic Cooperation and Development
OPEC	Organization of Petroleum Exporting Countries
SA	Specialized Agency
SAL	Structured Adjustment Lending/Loan
S&T	Science and Technology
SF	Special Fund
SIDA	Swedish International Development Agency
SUNFED	Special United Nations Fund for Economic Development
TA	Technical Assistance
UN	United Nations
UNCDF	United Nations Capital Development Fund
UNCED	United Nations Conference on Environment and Development
UNCTAD	United Nations Conference on Trade and Development
UNDA	United Nations Development Authority
UNDP	United Nations Development Programme
UNEP	United Nations Environment Programme
UNESCO	United Nations Educational, Scientific and Cultural Organization
UNFPA	United Nations Population Fund
UNHCR	United Nations High Commissioner for Refugees
UNICEF	United Nations Children's Fund
UNIDO	United Nations Industrial Development Organization
UNRRA	United Nations Relief and Rehabilitation Administration
UNRWA	United Nations Relief and Works Agency for Palestine Refugees in the Near East
UPU	Universal Postal Union
WFP	World Food Programme
WHO	World Health Organization
WIPO	World International Property Organization
WMO	World Meteorological Organization

Acknowledgements

This study is the result of a research project entitled 'Multilateral Development Institutions at a Cross-roads' carried out jointly by the Fridtjof Nansen Institute and Econ, Centre for Economic Analysis, with financial support from the Research Council of Norway. Our intention has been to explore what role, if any, there is for the two most prominent of these institutions – the UN development system and the World Bank in the critical times they face in the post cold war era.

The final outcome of a collaborative process that began in 1994, this work has included a number of supporters and critics along the way: Kjell Roland has offered inspiration and vision throughout the project. Henrik Harboe and Knut Aarhus have contributed invaluable assistance in fact-finding and in rewriting parts of the text. Gaudenz Assenza has offered both constructive advice and practical support in critical phases. Raino Malnes helped the authors out of analytical dead ends. In addition, sincere thanks are due to Christer Jonsson, Regine Andersen, Leif Christoffersen and Poul Engberg-Pedersen for constructive criticism, as well as encouragement on a number of occasions. Stein Hansen and Jerry Warford contributed their experience at the initial, formative phase of the study. Stian Reklev compiled data and produced figures very efficiently in the concluding stage. The librarians of the Nansen and the Nobel Institutes – Kari Lorentzen and Anne Cecilie Kjelling – responded promptly to numerous requests for documentation. Arne Brimi and the other staff of Fossheim Turisthotell ensured a wonderful atmosphere for our regular gatherings.

Finally, I wish to thank my co-author, Leiv Lunde, for his never failing optimism and stamina over these years and for the friendship that has developed during our common efforts. In the final stage of writing up this book, his talents were discovered by the Government of Norway as he was promoted to State Secretary for Development and Human Rights. This meant that he could not take part in the formulation of the conclusions, for which neither he, nor the Government, bears any responsibility. Nevertheless, I presume he might share my hope that one day they could have an impact on the policies of major donors.

Finally, my warmest thanks go to my wife Nina for never bothering me with questions of what this book is all about.

Helge Ole Bergesen
Stavanger/Oslo, November 1998

Introduction

'This is the age of the United Nations'
                                        Kofi Annan

'This is a God-given enterprise'
                                  James D Wolfensohn

'The United Nations is a noble experiment in human co-operation. In
a world that remains divided by many and diverse interests and attributes, the United Nations strives to articulate an inclusive vision:
community among nations, common humanity among peoples, the
singularity of our only one earth.' So reads the opening lines in the
reform programme published by Secretary-General Kofi Annan on 16
July 1997.[1] In presenting the 'most extensive and far-reaching
reforms in the fifty-two year history of (this) organisation',[2] he
declared: 'Reinvigorated, reformed and recommitted, the UN could
carry the hopes and dreams of all the world's peoples into the next
millennium and make them reality.'[3]

   Only a couple of weeks earlier, his counterpart, World Bank
President James D Wolfensohn had presented his vision for that institution in equally solemn terms under the banner 'People First':

> 'So our role ... is to assist countries in trying to get the
> mechanisms in place – to get a justice system, to get a
> legal system, to have a system of property rights, to have
> roads, to have education, to have health, to stop street
> crime, to enable people to invest and to develop these
> countries ... what we [Bank staff] are all about is trying
> to improve the human condition. This is not a job; this is
> a God-given enterprise.'[4]

If rhetoric of this kind is taken seriously, the current mission of these
two organizations – the United Nations (UN) and the World Bank –

is all encompassing and their ambitions virtually without limits. Nevertheless, both belong to this mundane world. Rhetoric aside, they are bureaucracies that produce paper and governing bodies that make decisions, just like any other intergovernmental organization. But given their visionary aspirations for the world and its peoples, outside observers like us are left with a puzzle: which are the appropriate standards for making a judgement of their performance? What are they to be compared with – a church, a state, a company, a charity? The fundamental question we want to explore in this book is, to put it crudely, what kind of creatures are the UN and the World Bank? More precisely; which roles can and should they be expected to play in world development; which functions can they constructively undertake; and what kind of governing structures are suitable for such roles and functions?

In search of answers to these fundamental questions, we must first analyse how the UN and the World Bank have evolved as development institutions over the last half century, given the dramatic changes in their political environment in the post-war era:

- The world is no longer centred on the Atlantic. UN membership has grown from the original 51 to 185. The founding fathers never envisaged more than 70 member states.[5]
- The optimistic belief in international development cooperation has been replaced by aid fatigue and shrinking financial contributions.
- The notion of central economic planning has vanished.
- The cold war no longer justifies development assistance as a means to win over developing countries to one or the other side.

To arrive at a better understanding of the profound changes that have taken place in the World Bank and the development side of the UN system, we shall develop in Chapter 1 a framework of analysis based on insights from organization theory and studies of international organizations. On this basis, we shall formulate hypotheses on the critical relationship between organizational functions and structure.

In Chapters 2 and 3 we shall present our analysis of the evolution of the UN and the World Bank in the first 50 years of their history. We shall focus on changes in the development agenda and on their functions and governing structure in critical phases throughout this period. This analysis is based on a large number of secondary sources and public documentation from the organizations involved. In Chapter 4, we return to the hypotheses in order to make a judgement of their current predicament and to compare their development with each other.

In Chapter 5, we shall start from scratch by asking anew what need there is for multilateral development institutions (MDIs) in the next century; what can they offer and what can they do that others cannot? How does this compare with the functions the UN and the World Bank have undertaken over time? Are they attempting too much or too little, or perhaps both?

Finally, in Chapter 6 we shall turn to the governments that supply funding for multilateral development assistance; which organizations and purposes are they willing to support and what does this imply for the future of the World Bank and the UN development system?

We do not end up with reform schemes or blueprints for the future, of which the literature already abounds. Our purpose is to analyse and uncover the fundamental dilemmas underlying the current predicament of these two institutions, not to point to concrete solutions in the current discussions of organizational reform. We are, however, convinced that our analysis provides sufficient foundation for suggesting in what direction MDIs and donors should move and what pitfalls they should avoid as they pass into a new century. The UN and the World Bank may not be able to fulfil many dreams or improve the human condition significantly, but they can still have a vital role to play in promoting world development provided that their limitations and potential are properly understood. It is to this latter end that we hope to make a modest contribution with this book.

Chapter 1

Framework of Analysis

Students of organizations make a basic distinction between two ideal types – the *action* and the *political* organization.[1] The former corresponds to everyday perceptions that

> '*organisations exist to generate collective co-ordinated action. Organisations, with their systems of rules and authority, can co-ordinate and steer the behaviour of their individual members towards the production of goods and services which could not be produced without such co-ordination.*'[2]

The action organization is justified by its ability to generate collective solutions, which are valued by the environment. It draws support in terms of resources to the extent that it delivers products that fulfil such expectations. Its structure and processes are determined by the necessity to produce organized action. Hence, it is characterized by hierarchy, strong organizational ideology ('corporate spirit'), consistency between ideology and action, specialization (niche production) and, above all, a focus on solutions: 'The action organisation is geared to solutions rather than problems. Only when we have a solution can we act, and shared loyalty to an organisational ideology will make it easier to find solutions.'[3]

The political organization is on all accounts the very opposite. Its raison d'etre and the basis for its legitimacy lies in its ability not to produce action, but to *reflect inconsistent norms in the environment*; 'products are of no particular significance, because neither they nor their environments really know what they are producing'.[4] This kind of organization thrives not on solutions, but on problems, entertaining 'a special affection for tough and insoluble problems' which can be 'endlessly discussed from all sorts of angles and without ever reaching a conclusion'.[5]

Where the action organization tends to specialize, its political counterpart generalizes by incorporating new ideas, new actors and a widening range of topics. Had it been required to deliver solutions, this would have entailed serious difficulties and ultimately raised questions of survival. For the political organization the effect of generalization is the opposite:

> *'[it] does not only trigger growth; it can also enhance the legitimacy of an organisation. The greater the number of ideas the organisation reflects in a wider range of fields, the more important it will be to its environment ... [it] tends to spread into every corner of its environment and to complement events and actions with ideological reflection, symbols and meaning.'[6]*

The typical output from a political organization is talk, decisions[7] and only occasionally tangible products. As there is no demand for organized action, inconsistency is not a problem, on the contrary, it is an asset. It is characteristic of the political organization 'to talk in a way that satisfies one demand, to decide in a way that satisfies another, and to supply products in a way that satisfies a third'.[8] Since decisions need not be implemented, inconsistencies between words and deeds can be maintained over time, to the satisfaction of different parts of the environment. The crux is all the time not to resolve, but to handle the conflicts inherent in the surroundings. The political organization

> *'wins legitimacy and acquires resources not by fighting for a single interest but by associating itself with several interests and demonstrating their incorporation into its own being. The organisation justifies itself as a vehicle for the reflection of these multiple interests. This is politics by justification rather than by exchange.'[9]*

The fundamental differences between the two ideal types of organization can be summarized as shown in Table 1.1.

In order to bridge the gap between this rather general theory of organization, which was developed by Brunsson for entirely different purposes, that is the study of local government in Sweden, we shall elaborate a typology depicting the functions that intergovernmental organizations (IGOs) commonly undertake in international relations

Table 1.1 *Two Models of Organization*

	Action organization	Political organization
Basis for recruitment	uniformity, agreement	diversity, conflict
Typical output	products, solutions	talk, decisions
Basic expectation from environment	fulfilling specific demand	reflecting inconsistent norms
Substantive focus	specialization	generalization
Process focus	finding solutions	cultivating criticism and problems
Structure	integration, coordination and control	dissolution and variety
Word/deeds	consistency	inconsistency

at the end of the twentieth century. We shall argue that these functions, even if located on a continuum, can provide the analytical basis for two ideal types of IGOs, which in turn have conceptual links to Brunsson's dichotomy of organizations. We shall, then, use this typology of functions and the ideal types of organization as the basis for the hypotheses that will guide our empirical investigation of the UN and the World Bank.

THE CONTINUUM OF IGO FUNCTIONS

IGOs are established by governments normally with a specified purpose in mind. The objective can be broad or narrow, but the intention of the founders is some kind of *intervention* either in the relations among the participating countries and/or within their boundaries. For analytical purposes we shall make a crude distinction between two types of interventions; in principle, an IGO can be set up either to influence the perceptions and norms of relevant actors within a given set of issues, leaving actual implementation to them, or to carry action itself into the field following decisions by participating governments (or other actors). In practice, any combination of the two is possible – a complication for our analysis to which we shall return. Here we remain at the conceptual level where things are simpler and under the control of the analyst. We shall start by outlining the most important functions of IGOs, as we conceptualize them, ending up with our interpretation of the crucial link between functions and organization.

IGOs can perform widely different tasks, depending on their purpose, political priorities, demand for their services and a host of other factors. We conceive of their functions as a spectrum ranging from the most 'innocent' – raising an issue – to the most ambitious and demanding – implementing solutions in the field. For the sake of simplicity we envisage the former, to the left and the latter to the right on a continuum of functions, as shown in Figure 1.1.

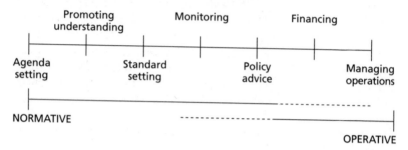

Figure 1.1 *MDI Functions*

Some of the functions correspond to a distinct phase in an international policy-making process, developing in a sequence we shall outline below. We shall also describe which tasks IGOs can be expected to undertake within each function.

Agenda Setting

In a world with a multitude of actors and causes competing for attention, the agenda of political and other decision-makers is never given. The first hurdle to pass for anybody with an issue to present is to get access to the agenda of the relevant bodies. Agenda setting can be defined 'as a process by which demands by various actors at different levels are translated into items vying for the attention of policy-making organs'. As the 'number of potential items far exceeds the capabilities' of these bodies, competition can be fierce.[10] The ability to set the agenda is a question of power and hence on object of study and controversy among political scientists. We shall leave that issue aside as it is not our intention to explain why some actors succeed and others fail in this respect. Suffice it to note that agenda setting ability is by no means confined to state actors. Both non-governmental organizations (NGOs) and scientists have been highly effective in placing issues of their concern on the international agenda. Often the most powerful agenda setting agent is a major, spectacular event that catches the attention of the world media and forces decision-makers to respond. Large oil spills, droughts and nuclear disasters are telling examples – all forcing a large category of issues on to the agenda of both governments and affected IGOs.

Turning an issue into an agenda item is important not only as a prerequisite for official attention, but also because it gives the initiator the opportunity to *frame* the matters at stake in a way that serves its interests, concerns or perceptions. As pointed out by Jønsson et al, the framing of an issue can be as open and as contested as the setting of the agenda. Very few issues, if any, are subject to one, authoritative interpretation. Most can be conceptualized or presented from different angles, invoking various analogies or images and, most importantly, pointing towards different solutions.[11] The latter are, as a rule, not neutral in institutional terms. As a 'solution is somebody's product or idea', there is often an organizational salesperson behind a particular framing of an issue.[12]

So, the agenda setting function includes not only the competition for space in policy-making fora, such as IGOs, but also the first phase of the ensuing discussion and bargaining over competing perceptions of the issues. Formulating an agenda is a question of *which* items to include (and which to exclude), *how* they are to be presented and *where* to handle them. To the outside observer the energy and time invested in negotiating such questions in international fora is astonishing. When disagreement among the states and other actors involved runs high, the struggle over agenda can take years and decades. This underlines the idea that setting the agenda, including the initial framing of the issues, is considered to have considerable impact on the process that follows.

The tasks carried out by IGOs are primarily to serve as the formal forum where the tug-of-war over agenda setting takes place. This can have a passive form, that is simply recording demands for attention in intergovernmental fora made by state and non-state actors, but IGOs can also play a more active and important role by initiating or stimulating the agenda setting process. This is the case, for example, when the UN decides to convene a world conference on a set of issues that has no clearly defined place on the international agenda. This gives IGO secretariats an opportunity to influence both the selection and framing of issues.[13]

Promoting Understanding

Once an issue, or a cluster of issues, is accepted as a legitimate concern for an IGO, substantive discussions can be initiated. Presuming different interests and values are at stake, creating a common understanding among the parties can be a frustrating exercise. It will commonly begin by asking the simple question; what is the nature and scope of the problem? This is in itself often both controversial and difficult. Various actors may hold conflicting views, sometimes reinforced by real scientific uncertainty. Contending perceptions for framing the issues thrive under such circumstances, often carrying over and repeating earlier debates from the agenda setting phase.

Equally difficult and sensitive is the question of cause and effect; which factors produce the problem at hand, and, closely related; which remedies follow? Since such analyses point directly towards both victims and culprits, strong emotions and strong interests, depending on the nature of the issue, can be expected to arise. Whenever high costs are involved, the potential losers are likely to dispute the findings pointing in their direction, demanding a 'sound' basis for action.

Barriers to joint understanding can be concrete and material, for example when those who stand to gain are pitted against those who stand to lose in purely economic terms. But the hurdles can equally well be related to values and ideological cleavages; some actors resist recognizing a problem because it challenges their deeply held moral convictions. Others may be recalcitrant for fear that future action on a given issue will not be defensible on ideological grounds.

The specific role of IGOs in this phase is, first, to provide the forum for such discussions and, second, to supply the factual foundation for debate. This can take the form of fact-finding of a particular problem, studies of relevant practices or a review of available scientific evidence. It is often useful to leave the scientific process to a separate forum shielded from political interference, to the extent possible. In this way, technical experts and scientists can explore the relevant issues in a non-confrontational manner within a forum vested in the legitimacy of the IGO.[14]

However the format, the crux lies in the impartiality of this kind of input. An IGO, or a body established by it, can play a role in promoting common understanding of an issue that the states and other stakeholders involved cannot, but which they badly need. All the actors know and silently acknowledge that most of what they say and most of what everybody else says is coloured by their interest in the issue at stake, whether economic, strategic or ideological, even if this is rarely openly admitted. Every smart negotiator will pretend to be speaking not only for himself, but also for the common good.

Under such circumstances, having a participant that is at the same time impartial, respected and authoritative is of crucial importance. This implies being neutral in terms of interests at stake and considered legitimate by the other actors. Legitimacy can be based on either professional expertise, procedures or both. The position of judges in domestic societies is an analogy, as they draw their legitimacy partly from their professionalism, partly from their commitment to meticulously specified procedures. Just as the parties in court cannot play the role of the judge, the stakeholders in international bargaining cannot play the role of the impartial researcher, fact-finder or mediator. The analogy ends there as the formal authority of the judge has no parallel on the international scene.

Standard Setting

If the actors involved can reach a reasonable level of agreement on the nature of the problem and basic cause–effect relations, they can begin to tackle the thorny question of behavioural response. The material, ideological and other factors mentioned above are likely to come into full play at this stage. Here the actors will watch over every step in the process to make sure that their interests and concerns are taken carefully into account. Hence, negotiating standards in response to an internationally recognized problem can be extremely cumbersome and time-consuming, depending on the complexity of the subject matter and the number of participants.

The specific tasks of IGOs as part of this function are to constitute the forum for negotiations, to supply analytic input, when required, and possibly also to act as a go-between or honest broker. For these purposes, constructive participation by IGOs demands legal/diplomatic experience in drafting international conventions, substantive expertise and, again, recognition for impartiality.

Monitoring

Once international standards have been agreed, in one form or another, the question of implementation will arise. This is normally a closely guarded prerogative of national governments, but if the issues of concern are regarded as having ramifications beyond national borders, international agreements will often include provisions for some kind of review or supervision. The most common form is to commit participants to report regularly on their implementation of agreed standards or other rules of conduct.

This significant task is usually carried out by IGOs; monitoring national implementation.[15] This can be confined simply to collecting and disseminating national reports, but it can also be much more ambitious, including verifying national submissions and data, initiating investigations of follow-up action and analysing the performance reported by governments.[16]

These four functions – agenda setting, promoting understanding, standard setting and monitoring – together constitute the *normative* side to the left of our spectrum. These categories of our typology cover the promotion and creation of norms to be followed by state and non-state actors in dealing with a specified set of international issues.[17]

At the other side of the spectrum, to the right, we have the *operative* functions. Before turning to them, we shall take a brief look at a function in the intermediate position between norms and operations, the provision of advice to governments.

Policy Advice

This function is connected to both the normative and the operative side of our spectrum. As part of the norm creation, governments can reach agreement not only on appropriate standards in legal terms, but also guidelines that should be taken into account by states and other stakeholders. This can take the form of normative principles to be translated into action at the national level.

This, again, opens an interesting room for IGOs. If they possess expertise with international standing and sufficient legitimacy, they can take on the difficult task of turning such principles into recommendations for government policy, for example translating 'sustainable development' into development strategies. This can be the end of a long normative process where national governments take over, or the basis for operations funded and managed by IGOs. In other words, policy advice can be the last of the normative functions, when they develop in sequence, or the first of the operative ones.

Financing

Turning to the operative functions that can be carried out by IGOs, the first prerequisite is money. Without funding, IGOs have no role to play in operations. Whether governments or other donors will commit resources to IGO activities depends, among other things, on the relative attractiveness of a specific organization as a means to channel funds for a particular, or a more diffuse, purpose. Raising finance does not necessarily lead to implementation of operations, even if the link is very close. It is possible for an IGO with access to money to work primarily as a funding mechanism, raising money with the one hand and distributing to operative agents with the other. In that instance, it leaves responsibility for operations to others.

Managing Operations

Under this function the IGO in question undertakes to manage and implement operations in the field through its own channels. It can do so on its own or in cooperation with others. In the latter case, the task is more demanding as operations must be coordinated across organizational lines.

Whether carried out alone or in partnership, operative functions place entirely new demands on an IGO. Formulating principles for a good education policy is one thing, distributing blackboards or running primary schools quite another. Once it is into operations, the environment will ask for quality and efficiency in delivering results of a tangible kind.

FUNCTION AND ORGANIZATION

IGOs can be located at either side of the spectrum, or across the whole or most of it. On paper, its seems logical for them to develop step-by-step from setting the agenda, via formulating standards into operations, but in reality it is much more complex. The original mandate of an IGO may be confined to one specific function, like financing, from which it may extend its activities in either direction. So, an IGO may over time move from left to right on our spectrum or the opposite way. Most important, however, is how widely it casts its net of activities and how it handles the internal tensions that follow from a wide scope. In this section, we shall elaborate the critical relationship between IGO functions and their organization.

Normative Functions

As IGOs have, normally, no recourse to coercive measures, compliance with standards or norms formulated at the international level depends on voluntary cooperation from national authorities. The best way to ensure such collaboration is to allow for broad participation in the normative functions. Even if a norm-creating process may be initiated by a small group of states or by NGOs, to be successful it will over time require general acceptance as to agenda, framing of issues and appropriate responses. Such promotion of broad international understanding is one of the typical functions of contemporary IGOs.

A case in point is the mammoth UN sponsored world conference: governments, NGOs and other stakeholders (depending on the issues) are invited to take part in a multi-year preparatory process, which includes fact-finding, expert analysis, expression of concern and frustration, in addition to diplomatic bargaining. At the end of the day, the conference itself produces a declaration and a programme replete with recommendations of action to be taken subsequently by governments, IGOs and other actors. If successful, this process will produce a common understanding among most participants about an agenda and norms for dealing with the issues identified. If participants have been convinced during the process that the agenda and the proposed solutions serve their interests, they will subsequently pursue action along those lines. When this includes governments, compliance will follow even in the absence of coercive powers at the international level.[18] In this case, the normative functions constitute a *learning process*, which has in itself a lasting impact on subsequent behaviour.

As mentioned above, the normative functions sometimes include scientific assessments in order to foster joint understanding of the underlying issues. In such fora, access may well be limited to technical experts and scientists, but broad participation remains imperative if their findings are to produce consensual knowledge. Legitimacy through participation is linked to both the technical bodies and discussions and to the political/diplomatic organs to which they submit their assessments for consideration and acceptance.

It follows from the above that participation is of utmost importance for the normative functions to be carried out successfully. As national implementation hinges on voluntary decisions to be taken by sovereign states, their participation in the process is essential. Those that have not taken part or feel excluded from the process for whatever reason, do not benefit from the mutual learning and have made no commitment to the normative basis for action along the way.

In addition to broad participation, these functions also require a high level of *equality* among the participating states. Even if everybody knows that in reality some are more equal than others, especially as far as control over relevant resources are concerned, any attempt at introducing a formalized hierarchy will be strongly resented by the less powerful and the smaller states. For them, formal equality among governments is of value in itself and hence a precondition for voluntary participation in such intergovernmental processes. Under these circumstances, universal participation on an equal basis will be the ground rule for intergovernmental relations. Even if cumbersome and time-consuming when membership reaches 185 states, it is difficult to find viable alternatives. The complexity can be reduced, however, if states agree to operate in fixed constituencies (eg regional groups) that elect representatives to decision-making bodies. This will speed up deliberations, as we shall see below, but confines the learning process to the states that participate directly. As the learning and mutual understanding that is the crux of the normative functions can hardly be transferred to those governments that have only indirect representation, these will not be part of the 'normative community' that is ideally the result of the process. As is well known in domestic politics: parliamentarians may reach common understanding of sensitive issues as a result of their deliberations, but their voters may not share this sense of mutuality as they have not been parties to the process.

In short, universal participation on an equal footing among states is the key to the normative functions.

In addition, more and more issues involve actors beyond governments; NGOs and industry are crucial stakeholders in a variety of problem areas confronting the international community. Hence, their participation in norm creation can be as important as that of many governments, which adds to the complexity and unwieldiness of the normative functions.

Operative Functions

The primary purpose of IGOs with a focus on operative functions is to carry out operations in the field, which places emphasis on management and funding. Such organizations need a structure and a culture promoting decision-making capability. They will be judged by the outside world for their effectiveness, which we define as their ability to reach stated goals. An organization is effective to the extent that it realizes the potential for goal achievement that is opened by the resources at its disposal.[19]

There is no standard prescription for an effective organization of this kind (and it is certainly not our intention to give one). Our point is the distinction from the IGO preoccupied with normative functions. A crucial difference lies in the way decisions are reached. The operative IGO must make large and small decisions continuously on allocation of funds, selection of projects and execution in the field. This means that participation, which is a legitimate demand also here, must be tempered by a system of decision-making that is compatible with the need to be effective. This will commonly imply formal recourse to some kind of majority voting, which may not be frequently used, but still exerts pressure on recalcitrant minorities to negotiate compromises within reasonable time limits. Whenever consensus is the ground rule for decision-making, there are no such constraints on procrastination.

In addition, a formal hierarchy with clear division of powers and delegation of authority is required. In IGOs with broad participation, this necessitates a representative system, whereby decision-making rights are explicitly transferred to specific management bodies. These in turn delegate powers over funds and projects to subordinate structures within clearly specified boundaries. Political decisions are separated from day-to-day management by providing strategic guidelines and success criteria for professional managers.

If we summarize the key differences between organizations located at opposite sides of our spectrum of functions, based on the reasoning above, we end up with the ideal types of the normsetting and the operative IGO as shown in Table 1.2.

Table 1.2 *Characteristics of Ideal Type IGOs*

	Normsetting IGO	Operative IGO
Main concern	process	impact
Participation	universal, open-ended	representative, selective
Formal structure	equality	hierarchy
Focus	learning	doing
Decision-making rule	consensus	majority voting
Typical operator	diplomat	manager
Typical tasks	expressive	instrumental
Expected output	joint understanding, normative agreement	solutions

It follows from Table 1.2 that there is a fundamental contradiction between the organizational forms required at the opposite ends of the range of functions. What is an advantage at the left-hand side – broad, participatory learning processes – easily becomes a liability to the right, where decisions must be taken with speed and determination. Conversely, the hierarchical order that produces effectiveness in operations can easily undermine support for the normative basis underlying decisions and hence reduce their impact in the longer run.

In the empirical analysis that follows in the next two chapters we shall pay particular attention to the *governing structure* of IGOs, which we define as the combination of formal structure as stated in the charter or articles of association, and the decision-making pattern that has become standard practice accepted by the states' parties. So, this term includes both the formal rules and procedures and the modus operandi for reaching and implementing decisions in practice, as it has evolved over time.

The core of the reasoning underlying this study is that *the functions of an IGO must be compatible with its governing structure and the governing structure must be supportive of the functions*. The two do not have to fit like hand in glove, but must be in synchronization in broad terms over time. If a serious mismatch develops, the organization will begin to malfunction either in its normative or its operative functions, or both. In the end, incompatibility between functions and structure will put at risk the very legitimacy of the organization.

So, if governments are rational and foresighted when setting up an international organization they will establish, and later maintain, a governing structure that is conducive to (or at least not incompatible with) its purposes which, again in our crude terms, can be either on the normative or operative side of interventions.

- The normsetting IGO, if organized in a rational manner according to its objectives, needs a governing structure marked by formal equality, consensus orientation and wide participation, and a staff reflecting the diverse interests of its membership. Over time, it should open up its processes to an expanding variety of stakeholders in order to secure support for the norms in making.
- The operative IGO, in contrast, needs a governing structure built on hierarchical order among participants, including some kind of majority voting, delegation of powers from political bodies to professional managers, clearly defined success criteria

for operations and consistency between strategy and action. For this purpose it will need a staff that is homogeneous and technically competent.

IDEAL TYPES UNDER CROSS PRESSURE

We can now return to the vantagepoint, the rather general theory of organization developed by Brunsson, in order to compare his categories with our concepts of normsetting and operative IGOs and then develop hypotheses for our empirical investigation. The following quote summarizes the distinction between his two models of organization:

> 'In the action model external effects are in focus: the organisation makes something happen, it solves some important problem, or it changes its environment ... it collects resources, produces consistent goals or ideologies and builds structures and processes which favour agreement, control and consistency. The organisation specialises in fulfilling the demands of a specific part of its environment... The political model is in essential ways the opposite ... instead of having clear boundaries with the environment its borders are so vague, or so general as not to distinguish the organisation from the environment which is going to judge it. This, and not because the organisation produces action for its environment, is why it can appear valuable ... instead of building on the enthusiasm of the few, it builds on the tolerance of the many. Instead of being involved in action, problem-solving and change, the organisation handles important issues and addresses difficult or insoluble problems ... it is the good intentions of the organisation that are important.'[20]

The essential difference lies in the basis for legitimacy. The action organization gathers support because it delivers results, the political organization because it reflects an inconsistent environment. This corresponds very well to the opposite ends of our spectrum of functions: The operative IGO is a typical action organization committed to concrete problem solving. It wins support for its financing and its operations to the extent that it produces solutions on the ground.

The terminology used should not be taken to imply that the action organization is apolitical. Its priorities and purposes can very well be set by political actors from the outset, but politics does not interfere with its running operations.

The normsetting IGO has an entirely different mission. At the extreme to the left on our spectrum, it is confined to endless discussions of agenda, the very essence of Brunsson's political organization. It is considered legitimate to the extent that its discussions mirror the concerns of its participants. It is not expected to produce tangible results and, hence, the whole question of effectiveness that pervades the operative IGO and the action organization becomes elusive. The IGO preoccupied with agenda setting 'produces' little but debate and occasionally decisions on agenda. Consequently, it is hard to find concrete benchmarks for judging its results. Moving to the more demanding normative functions, the question of effectiveness becomes more complicated; an IGO aimed at promoting understanding or standard setting cannot entirely avoid the issue of results. It is not expected to provide action in the field, but still to produce something more than words. Its task is to stimulate changes in the relations among participants, primarily governments, by fostering normative agreement. It is effective to the extent that its activities lead to acceptance of norms that carry what students of international regimes call 'persuasive force'.[21] For this purpose it needs a governing structure that is good at reflecting inconsistent norms in the environment.

As long as an organization, whether on the domestic or the international scene, remains on either side of the spectrum or within any one of Brunsson's two models, it is in smooth waters. The trouble arises whenever an organization attempts to prosper in both worlds at the same time, producing solutions as well as reflecting a chaotic environment. Trying to combine normative and operative functions leads to existential questions concerning the governing structure. 'The demand for action requires an integrative structure; the demand for politics requires dissolution. This is a genuine dilemma, an insoluble problem. It is not possible to be good at both politics and action. It is not possible to solve the problem, only to handle it.'[22] Within well-functioning nation states institutional arrangements to deal with this dilemma have gradually emerged (see Box 1.1), but at the international level no comparable development has taken place.

There are, thus, on paper good reasons for organizations to avoid the cross pressures that arise from undertaking widely different functions and creating expectations of normsetting and operations simultaneously. Nevertheless, in the real world various combinations

---

BOX 1.1 NATIONAL INSTITUTIONS

Within the western model of a nation state what we have here called the normative functions are mostly taken care of by representative bodies, primarily parliaments, in continuous interaction with the public through mass media. Participation and transparency is emphasized in the bodies elected by the people. These are, however, also required to reach decisions on legislation, budgets and other matters of importance to the polity they represent. Hence they have specific decision-making rules and procedures, for example for enacting new laws. Once legislation has been passed by parliament, responsibility for implementation is passed on to subsidiary bodies in the national bureaucracy. They have a defined authority to carry out what we have called operative functions within a mandate given by legislators or the government. The crucial mechanisms applied to handle the trade-off between normative and operative functions in this model are:

- the rules regulating participation and decision-making in bodies with both deliberative and legislative powers;
- the powers vested in parliaments and cabinets to take authoritative decisions;
- the delegation of authority to subordinate bodies responsible for management of public affairs and practical implementation.

---

and mixtures of the two ideal types seem to be quite common.[23] Organizations are not fixed entities following a pre-established logic, but living creatures developing, sometimes, in unexpected and unpredictable ways.[24] As their activities and functions change with time and circumstances, they may easily end up with a combination of functions and expectations that is full of stress or, in the worst of cases, untenable. In the case of our ideal type IGOs, we presume for the sake of analytical simplicity that they either stay with their original functions, which fit their original governing structure or expand into new territory in the following ways:

The Normsetting IGO

This organization can either stay with the typical normative functions or raise its ambitions to expand into policy advice and operations:

- In the former case, we expect it to specialize in agenda setting, which will permit continuous adaptation to shifting concerns in its environment. Any new issue can be incorporated into its agenda if required by its dominant participants or new political fashions. It will thus succeed in reflecting the prevailing, and most likely contradictory, norms in its environment. The main problem for this kind of organization will be the *danger of irrelevance*. It may end up as a talking shop that nobody of significance pays much attention to. We expect this risk to be met primarily with more talk – at international conferences and elsewhere – and occasionally with decisions vague enough to keep everybody satisfied (but nobody happy).[25]

- In the latter case, the organization either deliberately makes a decision to expand the scope of its work or unconsciously drifts to the right on our spectrum. It will then soon face the tension between incorporating different parts of the environment and reaching decisions that lead to action. The stronger the disagreement in its surroundings, the worse the cross pressure. Its governing structure will come under increasing strain as it is required to take on tasks for which it is not intended and ill-equipped. The set-up that was good at handling contradictory demands for the international agenda, turns out to be unfit to provide sound policy advice to governments, not to speak of taking action into the field. After a while, suspicion abounds that the organization has failed in delivering the goods. The response to such criticism is reform and focus on the future. 'Organisations that are strong in politics are unsuccessful, but full of promise.'[26] In addition, the organization will continue to stress its responsibility to a diverse and conflict-ridden environment, that is its original basis of legitimacy.

The Operative IGO

Again, the choice is to 'stay put' or expand, here to the left towards the normative functions:

- If this organization stays within the confines of its mandate, as defined from the outset, it will avoid the painful cross pressures that follows from the combination of widely different functions. Instead it will run the risk of obsolescence in case its original field of work fails to attract interest among its stakeholders. If the external agenda changes, the IGO that remains faithful to its original operative mandate may end up as a loser, as the thrust of international attention and resources moves away to other fields or other functions. Stressing its reputation for effectiveness and business-like behaviour, not running for new opportunities can counteract this risk.

• Another operative IGO may choose or may be led into broadening its original base with changes in its environment. If, for example, its mandate or its operations come under attack it can respond by entering into a broader political debate, thereby taking up agenda setting and other normative functions. This can begin as an attempt to meet a particular situation, gradually developing into a much broader defence of its place in a range of controversies. Once such a process has begun, the organization will need to adapt its governing structure to a more diverse, more contradictory and less predictable environment. It will have to be more open, more transparent and better at handling opposing views. At the same time, it needs to take decisions on operations just as it used to. The stress on its original streamlined, business-like structure from operating in a politicized environment will be very painful. It faces the dilemma of the expanding IGO; its functions and its governing structure become increasingly at odds. If this development continues, it will sooner or later reach the point where they are incompatible. Its response to the growing strain will be much like the normative IGO going in the opposite direction – more talk, continual organizational reform, nebulous rhetoric – and in addition, increasing inconsistency between words and deeds. Actions satisfy one part of its constituency, decisions another – talk perhaps a third.

To summarize we can turn these simplifying assumptions into the following hypotheses concerning the behaviour of our ideal type IGOs (see Table 1.3):

H1: 'Talking Shop'

The normsetting IGO that remains on the normative side of functions will respond to external changes by proliferating its agenda. As a result, it will in turn run into a crisis of irrelevance to which it will respond by further agenda expansion.

H2: 'Never-Ending Reform'

The normsetting IGO that expands into policy advice and operations will experience increasing strain on its original governing structure. As the structure cannot escape from its past, the organization fails to deliver the products expected by the environment. The organization will respond to such crises by promising reform after reform.

H3: 'Obsolescence'

The operative IGO that stays with its business in spite of the changing fashions in its environment will face obsolescence, to which it will respond by stressing its record and scaling up marketing.

H4: 'Overreach'

The operative IGO that expands into normsetting will strain its governing structure as it is required to undertake normative and operative functions simultaneously. It will fail in either or both as it overreaches its resources and respond by either withdrawing back into operations or proclaiming fundamental reform while in practice learning to live with inconsistencies.

Table 1.3 *Four Hypotheses on the Evolution of MDIs*

	Main focus	Problems	Response
Normsetting IGO	agenda setting	irrelevance, talking shop	more talk, new agendas
Normsetting IGO	raise ambitions into operations	failing to deliver	reform and more reform
Operative IGO	stay with business	obsolescence	stress record, better marketing
Operative IGO	expand into normsetting	overreach, inconsistency	1) retreat or 2) reform, talk

EMPIRICAL ANALYSIS: PURPOSE AND SCOPE

Our empirical focus is limited to two specific, albeit very large organizations – the UN and the World Bank – which belong to a subset of IGOs, namely multilateral development institutions (MDIs).[27] They face the same spectrum of functions as other IGOs, and their choices over time are likely to be influenced, among other factors, by the overall development agenda in the post-war era. As we shall describe below, perceptions and political positions on social and economic development have gone through fundamental changes in the latter half of the twentieth century. We expect the two MDIs under study to change with the changing times, which entails pressure and temptation to take up new functions, perhaps discard old ones.

We underline that our ambition is *not* to write UN or World Bank history. That has been done by numerous other analysts, whose work we shall build on in the subsequent chapters. Hence, our framework of analysis has not been constructed for the purpose of identifying systematic explanations for *why* the UN and the World Bank has developed in a particular way in certain periods. That would have required a different theoretical approach. Nevertheless, we shall along the way point, in empirical terms, to driving forces behind critical phases in the evolution of the two organizations.

In spite of the fact that much of this book is devoted to historical description, this study is intended to be forward looking. We want to understand the *present* predicament of the World Bank and the UN development system by way of this framework of analysis, in order to make an assessment of what role these two institutions can constructively play in solving the imminent problems facing the 'global village' on the eve of the twenty-first century. We want to conclude whether they are relics of the past bound for the fate of the dinosaurs or whether they can be dynamos in bridging the gap between the problems in world development and the solutions that are considered feasible for the time being.

More concretely, the empirical questions, to which we shall seek answers are:

1. To what extent do the UN development system and the World Bank, as they have developed over 50 years, fit into our ideal types of normsetting and operative IGOs?
2. Have they run into the problems and responded in the way suggested in our hypotheses about the behaviour of ideal type IGOs remaining within or expanding beyond their original functions? In addition, we want on the basis of such answers to provide our assessment at the end of Chapter 4.
3. How can their current situation be understood by reference to the key concepts in our ideal types – functions and governing structure and the critical relationship between them?

Finally, we want to assess:

4. How such understanding, if indeed a result of our analysis, can contribute to the debate of their future role in solving global problems (Chapter 5) and what conclusions donor governments can draw from this (Chapter 6)?

Chapter 2

The UN from Past to Present

'Who controls this machine?'
                        Sir Robert Jackson, 1969

As the twentieth century draws to a close, the UN is at a crossroads. The world organization goes from crisis to crisis. It is trapped in a seemingly vicious circle: financially squeezed and thus unable to implement reforms required as conditions for releasing more funds. The purpose of this chapter is to understand why the UN arrived at this crossroads in the late 1990s, in a post cold war decade that spelt such promises for international cooperation. To understand why, we will go back in history and analyse different chronological phases that have formed the organization that we see today, or rather the multitude of organizations that are meant to make up 'the UN system'. Focus will be on external developments that have severely conditioned its scope of action, such as the cold war and the proliferation of new member states, as well as various internal UN system dynamics that have contributed to a fragmented organization structure made up of more than a hundred legally independent agencies,[1] creating what already by the late 1960s was considered 'the most complicated organisation in the world'.[2]

We will structure this chapter around the following chronological phases organized along overall changes in the relations among the major groups of countries in world politics. The first phase covers the first decade after the inception of the world organization when the developing world still played a minor role in international relations. The next phase covers the period from 1955 to 1970 characterized by the decolonization process and the struggle between the two main ideological camps of the time for the support of the new states. The next phase from 1970 to 1990 marks the rise and fall of the ambition of a new international economic order as well as the collapse of the Communist bloc and the end of East–West rivalry. The last phase covers the post cold war era from 1990 to the present which started out with renewed aspirations for international cooperation.

THE EMERGING GOVERNING STRUCTURE – ONE NATION, ONE VOTE

The representative nature of the UN's governing structure was considered a unique feature, providing the organization with unrivalled legitimacy in terms of global agenda setting and other norm-creating functions. If new wars were to be avoided, all nations had to be drawn into and progressively integrated in a cooperative forum where all had an equal say. In one sense, at least, it was democracy in one of its more ultimate forms, expected as it was to motivate and discipline nations and convince them to seek cooperative solutions to issues where conflicts were otherwise looming large. In a positive climate for international cooperation, the case seemed convincing for one nation, one vote as the basic principle of UN decision-making.[3] The shared experience and mutual confidence among states that would flow from gradually strengthened cooperation structures constituted the dynamo trusted to move things forward.

Could the founding fathers of the UN have acted otherwise? They did in the security area, and in the central bodies set up to guide international trade and finance (the International Monetary Fund (IMF), the World Bank and the General Agreement on Tariffs and Trade (GATT)). These were policy areas where the dominating powers were not willing to risk being overruled by unruly majorities, and where it was generally acknowledged that decision rules had to match the real power structures. In the economic and social sphere of the UN proper, however, ambiguity of the mission and modest interest in the subject matter go a long way to explain why an egalitarian decision-making system was acceptable to major powers.

The governing structure of the UN was designed neither for a world divided by the cold war, nor for a world in which the emerging score of new states created an ever widening gulf between formal UN authority claims on one hand, and the real power structures of the outside world on the other. Whether assigning the UN with a system of 'weighted voting light' (closer to formal equality than the World Bank, but still more attention paid to existing political power structures) would have worked better is another question. Scholars like

David Mitrany, an influential wartime political analyst who worked with the Royal Institute of International Affairs in London, tended to warn against formal equality as the governing principle for bodies like the coming UN. He held that nations should exercise control over an organization in proportion to their ability to contribute to its activities; only benefits would be common. In the political climate of the time, however, it proved difficult, if not impossible, to compromise on the demand for formal equality among the states signing the UN Charter.

Organizational Design

A range of analysts have tried almost from the very inception of the UN to explain its performance problems by virtue of the uneasy hybrid that emerged between central control and coordination on one hand, and decentralized anarchy on the other. Various models were on the table in the years leading up to the 1945 San Fransisco conference. From one perspective, there were arguments for a strong body that could provide unified leadership and clear-cut lines of command throughout the new organization – including the specialized agencies that were to be brought into some kind of relationship with the UN. Such views were rooted not least in perceptions of what made the ill-fated League of Nations falter – states were not willing to provide it with sufficient authority. Integration along one line of command was the answer, requiring an integrated top-down mode of organization.

Such a design ran into opposition on several grounds. Many, including functionalists like Mitrany, believed that a sectoral, decentralized approach was the most rational way to organize international cooperation. Overly optimistic as they may look in hindsight, functionalist beliefs in the merits of functional cooperation commanded strong support at the time:

> 'As meteorologists, doctors, labour leaders and agriculturists increasingly collaborated in evidently indispensable tasks, the habits of international co-operation would gradually spill over into political arenas, crowding out the dangerous antagonisms and cross-purposes of competing sovereignties.'[4]

Polycentric, autonomous agencies would also be better insulated from political tensions, according to supporters of these views. Others were mainly driven by fears that an integrated organization at global level would develop into an overblown and ineffective bureaucracy impossible for states to govern. Another challenge arose from the fact that some of the UN specialized agencies-to-be had already been in operation for more than 50 years. Integrating them within a tight organizational structure would touch vested interests and thus meet with strong resistance, both in the international secretariats and in the respective national government agencies meeting on their governing boards.

On the face of it, the end result within the economic and social field came out as a compromise between integration and decentralization. Formally, though, the Economic and Social Committee (ECOSOC), a 'Charter' body, legally on a par with the Security Council, was established to function as the force of integration for all UN work in the social and economic area. Specialized agencies, including the World Bank and the IMF, were expected to develop so-called 'mutual agreements' with ECOSOC, spelling out the pattern of cooperation between each particular (and fully autonomous) agency and the central UN organ.

In spite of the integration-prone rhetoric existing and emerging specialized agencies were given virtual independence, with separate mandates and governing boards and only formal and unbinding reporting requirements to central UN bodies like the General Assembly and ECOSOC.[5] The problem was and has been since the UN's inception, that the whole idea of ECOSOC coordination of UN economic and social action was well meant but virtually void of any real content. Specialized agencies, including the new ones created after World War II in the fields of agriculture, health and education, were simply not made accountable to ECOSOC or other parts of the 'political UN'.

Thus, to a large extent the UN that emerged after San Fransisco 1945, was a decentralized and sectorally divided set of autonomous agencies with very loose relationships to the new world organization. A constant source of confusion, however, as framed succinctly by Rosemary Righter, came to be that

> 'the Charter endowed the infant United Nations with the
> fiction that these links constituted a system, by devising
> a nonbinding formula under which the agencies would be
> co-ordinated from the centre by the UN General
> Assembly and ECOSOC. This fiction was justified on
> the perfectly sensible ground that some central body must
> set broad priorities for international co-operation and
> provide a policy forum capable of cutting across different

sectoral interests. Yet means were not matched to ends. *Both the General Assembly and ECOSOC (whose representative roles were so loosely defined that each could, and did, make recommendations to each other in a circular ritual) were intended to fulfil these functions. They were expected to co-ordinate the agencies' activities, although the agencies were not accountable to them. They were given the power to initiate special programs, conferences and reports on particular issues that they felt the agencies were not addressing, but they had no powers to make the agencies pay any attention to what was proposed. The "centre" was thus positively encouraged to expand into the realm of functional co-operation – a temptation to which it was to succumb all the more readily because it was indeed not a centre.'*[6]

BIG SHOCKS, BROKEN DREAMS, ADAPTING TO NEW REALITIES (1945–55)

External Developments

As already indicated, a strong belief in international cooperation and world governance was building up among the allies during the war. Paradoxical as it may seem, the UN's formative years saw an unrivalled optimism on behalf of international cooperation. We have picked three authoritative sources in order to illustrate that particular mood:

> *'At the time the Charter was drafted (1943–45) the atmosphere of public opinion and government policy was extremely favourable to international co-operation for welfare purposes.'*[7]

> *'In the mood of the time, however, the obstacles to effective collaboration were for the most part viewed through a golden haze, and few appeared insuperable. The UN and the specialised agencies, it was assumed by the general public, would play a major role in repairing the ravages of war, in preventing depression, in developing respect for fundamental human rights, and in promoting*

the *"conditions of stability and well-being which are necessary for peaceful and friendly relations among nations".'*[8]

'The San Fransisco Conference, taking place as it did at the background of daily revelations of Nazi and Japanese atrocities, revealed what a profound shift the experience of economic crisis, total war and the Holocaust had produced in the demands made on international organisations.'[9]

This is the perspective within which the following quote from the UN ambassador of the US should be interpreted, as he addressed the inaugural ECOSOC meeting in 1945:

'Seldom before in human history has an organisation been created with greater opportunity to save mankind than has been given to the Economic and Social Council under the Charter of the United Nations.'[10]

Neither ECOSOC nor its thick underbrush of commissions and committees, were given any real chance to live up to such expectations. The onset of the cold war, with its devastating effect on the early development of UN affairs, sealed the fate of any large scheme vision of global governance. The most immediate casualty, though, was the security role of the new world organization, and ECOSOC probably received some of the initial political energy that could otherwise have gone into security cooperation. However, it soon became clear that the serious cleavage between the two emerging superpowers, and the subsequent division of the world in two rivalling camps, buried for good internationalist visions of global governance through consensual UN policy-making.

This first decade saw both the peak in external expectations on the UN as World War II ended in 1945, and the adverse geopolitical developments that severely limited its scope of action. As of 1950, the cold war had already spread to Asia, where the 'loss of China' in 1949 spelt danger for western policy-makers eager to anchor the post-war world in democratic and market-friendly political structures. For the social and economic wings of the UN, the main victim was the global norm-creating functions that required at least approximate consensus among major powers. The very same developments, however, implied a growing impetus for the emerging operative functions of UN bodies. The emergence of multilateral as well as bilateral aid programmes from the late 1940s and onwards were very much motivated out of US and other western countries' urge to save developing countries from the threat of communism.

With a divided world already in 1946, and a host of new and demanding UN members in the making, the political will and courage to submit important strategic issues to UN policy-making, soon subsided. In terms of international problem solving, the world came out far more bilateral in nature than the initial UN rhetoric would have us believe. Reconstruction of Europe and other war-torn areas – a formidable task – was conceived as a multilateral task but ended up squarely on the table of the American President.

Developments Along the Normative Functions

Rhetoric aside, it became clear very early that the US and its major allies were not prepared to develop any global, representative body like the UN into a supra-national organization. Issues of pressing national interest that required international coordination were to be taken care of by institutions that the US and its close allies could control and which reflected the economic and political power structures of the day. In assessing the record of the first post-war decade of multilateral cooperation, Robert Asher did not see a very prominent UN role:

> 'The most notable multilateral initiatives of the last decade, moreover, have, with a few exceptions, been taken outside the UN framework. In the economic field, these include three concomitants of the Marshall Plan, the Organisation for European Economic Co-operation, the European Payments Union (EPU), and the European Productivity Agency; three associations involving Benelux, France, Germany and Italy, the European Coal and Steel Community (ECSC), the European Economic Community (common market), two other European groupings, the proposed free trade area, and the proposed Nordic Customs Union; and a peculiar arrangement that includes participants from several continents and has both multilateral and bilateral features, the Colombo plan.'[11]

Even within what Asher called the UN framework, the most important norm-creating institutions were not part of the UN family proper. They both experienced a tough start-up period, though, but the IMF and the World Bank came out by the mid-1950s as comparatively robust organizations, with the former having the most clear-cut norm-creation role. The remains of the withered International Trade Organization (ITO) concept, GATT, had not yet gained the important position it was later to carve out for itself. Even if ECOSOC received some of the tasks that the ITO was assumed to take care of (and the United Nations Conference on Trade and Development (UNCTAD), was to be created in the early 1960s), the dominating western governments never really considered to provide the UN with a serious norm-creating nor regulatory role in the area of international trade.

In short, the combination of 'un-friendly' external events and the political inevitability of formal equality (one nation, one vote) as the decision-making principle, reduced significantly the scope of UN action in the areas (normative functions) where it was supposed to be best equipped. The conditions for shaping or moving global consensus on economic and social issues in one particular direction, appeared to be limited – although with a couple of interesting exceptions. Below, we will first look at these exceptions to shed light on the preconditions for meaningful normative UN functions, before some of the developments that served to erode UN credibility in normative questions are discussed.

Decolonization

During the first two post-war decades, an unprecedented geopolitical revolution took place. Completely transforming the political map of the world, hundreds of millions of people went from dependent status under colonial rule to become citizens of independent countries. It came out in most cases as a peaceful revolution, although with a number of violent exceptions. Decolonization became a key testing ground for the new world organization. Particularly for the peoples and regions striving to get rid of colonial intruders, the UN emerged as an invaluable political opportunity – both as a favourable arena for political contest and a vehicle of technical assistance (TA) to fragile new states. The UN played an important, and in most regards positive, role in this (not always) velvet revolution. A major assessment of the first decade of UN contributions to decolonization concludes as follows:

> '*Nevertheless, it is clear that the United Nations, in intangible as well as tangible ways, has significantly influenced the post-war efforts that have been made to deal with the colonial problem.* It undoubtedly has contributed to the formation of world opinion that has spurred constitutional advances in most of the eighty-odd pre-war territories.'[12]

In an otherwise devastating critique of the UN, Maurice Bertrand, long time head of the prime UN watchdog, the Joint Inspection Unit (JIU), confirmed this largely positive verdict in a 1985 assessment: '...The United Nations made a positive contribution to this operation (decolonisation), and while it was not able to prevent a number of conflicts, it certainly reduced them in number.'[13] To Bertrand, this relatively isolated success story of the UN was due to two main factors:

1   The fact that the two major world powers, the USA and the Soviet Union, were in favour of decolonization, and the general transformation in world consensus, which reflected the new power relationships, marked in particular by the economic and political decline of the former great European powers.
2   The fact that the interests of colonized peoples coincided with the main principles relating to human rights and the rights of peoples to self-determination, as recognized by the West and already used politically in Europe and other parts of the world in the nineteenth century to set up new states.

These were, though, relatively unique conditions that allowed for strong and often confrontational demands from underprivileged parties to go along with dominant geopolitical trends. The UN was lucky to function as a catalyst for an increasingly legitimate but still very controversial decolonization agenda. It contributed to shape global consensus, even if the main driving forces were found outside UN auspices. The new world organization provided an arena for flagging of concerns and criticism of laggards, a forum for negotiation on terms of transfer of authority, permanent institutional set-ups for monitoring and mediation (the Trusteeship Council), and, gradually, technical aid programmes to the poor majority of the emerging countries.

   This relative success of the UN must be put in perspective, however. In Robert Asher's final summary assessment of the first ten years of UN performance in this area, he claims that 'to an astonishing degree, the Organisation has been flogging a dying horse',[14] implying that the 'colonial problem' would have withered away even in the absence of UN contributions – given the strong alliances to that effect referred to above. Also, he regrets that the ambiguities of the UN Charter, which, again according to Asher, 'was responsible for much of the dissatisfaction with the record of the organisation in this field', and time and again 'involved the United Nations in problems for which it was ill-equipped to solve'.[15] The main problem, which had clear parallels to situations where the UN has basically failed, was considered to be the use of the politically fragile and consensus-sensitive global fora as platforms for confrontational and often nationalistic propaganda. Not to say that the concerns uttered in this way were not legitimate, but the process of using UN fora in such a manner could well have backfired had decolonization not constituted such a 'benign' political case.

Human Rights

Up to a point, the evaluators of UN performance in this formative period identified similar, albeit more mixed, signs of relative success in the area of human rights. Rooted in admittedly western, liberal thinking, the first post-war decade saw a comprehensive framework being built up for the promotion of human rights through various levers of UN policy-making. The painstakingly negotiated Universal Declaration of Human Rights of 1948 is a landmark in this regard, although it is in no way a treaty but a statement of goals. The positive judgement is clearly restricted, however, to the 'negative' political and civil rights that were already about to receive official recognition by most governments, at least outside the Communist bloc. Bertrand (1985) confers that 'systematic violations of these rights have been made more difficult in certain cases'. It is probably fair to assume, though, that the relatively high regard to the UN's normative functions here were due to the dominance by western powers, particularly the US, in defining the relevant policy parameters.

The main criticisms of initial UN human rights performance centred on the following allegations:

1   Even if agreement was reached on the 1948 Declaration, the bulk of time and energy spent on human rights issues in UN fora was consumed by rivalry and controversies rooted in fundamental conflicts. There was often a virtual absence of discipline with respect to ensuring a certain level of (at least prospective) consensus on world view as well as more specific goals, measures and

policy implementation. This was evident not least in the extension of the concept to economic and social rights, which over the
first decade, and since, have consumed a tremendous amount of
energy – but with extremely meagre results.[16]

2   Serious misunderstandings (as judged by the evaluators) arose
almost immediately as to the very nature of the UN as an organization and decision-making forum. Again to quote Asher et al,

> *'In the field of human rights, the concept of the United
> Nations as a forum for voluntary co-operation among
> sovereign states has to a considerable extent been
> replaced by the delusion that the United Nations is a
> legislative body capable of imposing a majority will upon
> recalcitrant minorities. All members must be brought to
> recognise again* that co-operation among sovereign
> governments depends of a meeting of minds, not a
> mustering of votes. *None of the major powers is prepared
> in the human rights field – or in most other fields – to
> accept treaty obligations that would require significant
> changes in its own laws and practices.'*[17]

3   Here, as well as in other policy areas, fragmentation and lack of
coordination between different parts of the emerging system very
soon threatened to paralyse and delegitimize UN fora. The same
issues were discussed in a range of fora unclearly related at best.
Also, action in other subject areas was 'polluted' by rights issues
that may well have been legitimate in their own right, but which
served to unduly politicize UN affairs across the board. Proposals
for radical organizational reform in order to accommodate for
such deficiencies were launched already in the early 1950s, but
met with fierce resistance:

> *'It is very difficult to make organisational changes in the
> machinery of the United Nations for dealing with human
> rights because every proposal is likely to be interpreted
> as an attack on the rights themselves... It is safe to
> predict that no streamlining will be undertaken until the
> General Assembly attains sufficient sophistication to
> recognise that organisational changes need not involve
> abandonment or even reduction of United Nations inter-
> ests in the field in question.'*[18]

To summarize, sufficient common ground existed for the UN to play a meaningful agenda setting role on human rights. It did so by virtue of constituting an arena for the formulation and aggregation of general, albeit vague and uncommitting policy goals, and the set-up of institutions. Still, many years did not pass before the malign combination of organizational weaknesses and ambiguities on one hand and lack of government discipline on the other seriously hampered the usefulness of UN activities in this field.

Redistribution of Wealth

Poverty and economic inequality were concerns that governments of poor countries immediately brought to the UN negotiation table. Initially, there was nothing to say about the legitimacy of their demands, as most nations of the world sought the US and its (relatively few) wealthy allies for support in reconstruction and development. They also had a solid ally in the wording of the Charter and the rhetoric surrounding the first meetings in the General Assembly and ECOSOC, committing the UN to promote 'higher standards of living, full employment and conditions of economic and social progress'. Efforts to utilize UN fora to extract financial resources from rich countries were easily understandable and had the support of many developed states. The first specific steps to prod the UN itself into aid provision came during the first General Assembly session in 1946, through a proposal tabled by Lebanon.[19]

From then on, General Assembly and ECOSOC sessions saw a steadily intensifying use of the UN as a platform for demands for redistribution of wealth from rich to poorer parts of the world. Approaching 1950, the acknowledgement that European countries (and Japan) were receiving the overwhelming share of Marshall Plan and other bi- and multilateral funds during the first post-war years created frustration and served to consolidate developing country positions on North/South transfers in UN fora. Accordingly, the UN stage was set for a sustained effort at many levels to force rich countries in general and the US in particular to extend the Marshall Plan to the poor world:

> 'From 1950 till at least 1960, "financing economic devel-
> opment" *was the most passionately debated economic issue
> in the United Nations. The less developed countries, led
> primarily by Chile, India and Yugoslavia, showed extraor-
> dinary ingenuity in keeping the issue alive and inching*

forward toward their goal. Their campaign splashed over from United Nations channels into other channels and then back again, creating waves and ripples in Washington; in European, Asian, and Latin American capitals.'[20]

The UN fora formed the core of developing country strategies to this effect in two main ways. First, the UN was an ideal platform for aid transfer pledges and demands to set up programmes for technical assistance – within as well as outside UN auspices. Even if the cold war and various domestic factors (altruistic traditions, the colonial guilt complex) clearly mattered, the UN and the arenas it provided for developing world lobbying undoubtedly influenced the speed and volume of the emerging aid programmes.

The second and related strategy, to be more vigorously pursued in decades to come, was to use UN fora in attempts to change the power structures in the international economy to the benefit of countries in the developing world. An initial expression of such a strategy was the efforts to make the World Bank subject to UN control, in order for the General Assembly majority to influence the terms of overall development financing.[21] As this did not succeed, developing country governments from the late 1940s and onwards, brought the UN into fierce competition with the Bank for hosting and designing the terms of soft financing facilities. They basically lost this battle also because the US and most other western countries were simply not prepared to let poor countries, or organizations dominated by them, control the purse strings (see below for our account of the IDA versus the Special United Nations Fund for Economic Development (SUNFED) over battle). The pressures in ECOSOC and the General Assembly were kept up, though, while the strategy gradually shifted towards building organizations within UN auspices with broader and more system-challenging mandates (see 1955–70 period below).

Already by 1955, the main protagonists seemed to have lost sight of the 'close to consensus-criterion' that is so crucial for moving global economic policy-making forward. Developing countries, already constituting a solid UN majority, consolidated their position within UN bodies. They were also in the process of voting through new ones and used every opportunity (read every UN arena) to press for rich country concessions. Industrialized countries, led by the US, were already about to give up the UN as a serious forum for global economic dialogue. They adopted an essentially defensive 'damage limitation' attitude in UN fora, and consciously moved any issue of strategic importance requiring international coordination to institutions offering weighted voting or other ways to marry formal organizational authority to 'real world' power structures (the IMF, the World Bank, GATT, among others).

Logical and understandable as the confrontational developing world drive was, and notwithstanding at least a minimum level of consensus on the case for North/South transfers, there is little doubt that it very rapidly served to alienate the US and major allies from discussions of economic and social issues in UN fora. This is not the place to blame any particular party for the stalemate that already by 1955 threatened to paralyse any meaningful dialogue on international economic policy. Would developing countries have chosen a less confrontational strategy if western countries were more receptive? Had the US considered a more constructive UN approach if developing countries had been perceived as more 'responsible'?

Developments Along the Operative Functions

Throughout the wartime UN planning efforts, little attention was paid to the option of engaging the new organization as an operator for direct promotion of social and economic development. The extensive operations at country level that were a central trademark of UN action already by the early 1950s, were far beyond the imagination of those who drafted the Charter. Reconstruction of war-torn societies was an exception, though, as this naturally was a serious concern at the time of preparing the Charter. Paradoxically, however, the UN was almost immediately left out of the reconstruction picture, due to the cold war and the emerging conviction of the major western powers that this was too great a task to put on the shoulders of the new and vulnerable global body. Partly as a way to fill a critical void in expectations to the UN, demands arose almost immediately for channelling resources for development through the global body and its affiliated specialized agencies.

Emergency Relief and Reconstruction Activities

The UN was never trusted with an important role in post-war reconstruction, nor in emergency aid operations throughout this decade. The very size of the reconstruction task, the decision (basically by the US) to make this a bilateral affair, the political divisions among key players (East-West, but also eg in the Middle East context) and the immaturity of the existing institutional apparatus and financing mechanisms, all worked as restraints on the potential for effective UN action in this area.

The facility set up by the allied powers in 1944, the United Nations Relief and Rehabilitation Administration (UNRRA), led a short life and was closed down in 1946. Neither was it integrated in the UN machinery; it remained an ad hoc body run by a number of governments – again with the US in the lead. UNRRA played an important role, however, in that it set precedents and raised expectations for UN action in the post-war era. For instance, the United Nations Children's Fund (UNICEF), established by the General Assembly as a relief organization for children in December 1946, was a direct descendant of UNRRA.

Apart from UNICEF, three other UN bodies for emergency relief, refugees and reconstruction were set up before 1955: the International Refugee Organization (IRO, 1946–52), the UN Relief and Works Agency for Palestine Refugees in the Near East (UNRWA, 1949–) and the United Nations Korea Reconstruction Agency (UNCRA, 1950–55). Assessments of the time are positive with regard to UNICEF's performance, although framed with an important reservation: 'The relative success of UNICEF has been due not so much to the management or character of the machinery as to the fact that the objectives of UNICEF are universally supported, the concept is simple, and the cost is low.'[22] The other bodies received a more mixed judgement by expert assessments. A major reason for their problems was seen to be member state conflicts and financing problems as the US indicated that they were not willing to shoulder the majority of costs for each new UN programme.

The Emerging UN Structure for Operative Action

> 'The UN Charter provided in some detail for the methods and processes to be used in the maintenance of international peace and security. But in the promotion of general welfare, particularly in the solutions of problems of an economic, social, cultural and humanitarian character, the Charter specified only the general objectives to be achieved and authorised the use of a variety of methods and processes to attain those objectives.'[23]

As brought out in this quotation, the institutional development of UN economic and social operations was a largely unplanned step-by-step process. With one exception (the Technical Assistance

Administration), the early operative initiatives were designed as temporary, but became permanent by virtue of the momentum they created in this era of UN expansion, and because the magnitudes of the tasks embarked upon were generally gravely underestimated. New bodies were launched within the UN proper (under ECOSOC and the General Assembly), as well as outside (eg new specialized agencies), as responses to new demands from member governments. A major impetus for this steep increase in activities was 'new and insistent pressures connected with the emergence of 600 million people from colonial status'.[24] The following quote illustrates the speed and rather accidental manner in which UN operative action developed:

> *'Thus, by the time the General Assembly convened in late 1948, the United Nations was engaged at all levels in furnishing technical assistance to underdeveloped countries,* but without any specific budget for the purpose... *Without waiting, however, for the reaction of intermediate levels, the General Assembly adopted a resolution introduced by Burma, Chile, Egypt and Peru instituting a program of technical assistance for economic development.'*[25]

ECOSOC's fourth session in 1947 formally agreed on the necessity of establishing special machinery within the UN Secretariat for furnishing TA to poorer member countries. Two years later, in 1949, the UN Expanded Programme of Technical Assistance was established, with the launching of the first US aid programme (Point IV) in January the same year. In 1950, the first UN Conference on Technical Assistance was convened in New York, to stimulate donor contributions by UN member governments. The result: a total of US$20 million was pledged to cover operations during the first 18 months of the programme, 60 per cent of which came from the US.

By 1955, a large and heterogeneous group of UN organizations were providing development assistance to poor countries. Already by then, observers found it difficult to grasp the full reach of UN operative action, even if the overall volume of transfers was limited indeed. The following is an effort to describe the main categories of UN bodies (most of which were set up in direct response to General Assembly or ECOSOC resolutions) involved in aid projects of the time:

- TA programmes covered by the UN's regular budget, carried out by the Bureau of TA Operations under the UN Department of Economic and Social Affairs.
- TA funds and programmes financed more or less by voluntary contributions, such as UNICEF, set up in 1946 and the Expanded Programme of Technical Assistance, EPTA, launched in 1949, to work in close cooperation with a range of specialized agencies (as implementing bodies).
- ECOSOC commissions were basically charged with what we call normative functions, but many of the eight New York-based commissions in existence already before 1950 were undertaking operative action within their respective areas of activity – like the Commissions for social affairs, transport/communication and population problems.
- Regional economic commissions for Latin America, Asia and Europe were set up in this first decade, while the one for Africa came in 1958. Reporting to ECOSOC, and although mainly designed to fall within the norm-creation realm, they all launched small-scale operative TA projects from the very start.
- Following the UN's inception in 1945, specialized agencies, some of which had been in existence from the nineteenth century, immediately came under pressure to solve pressing problems in poorer parts of the world. Even if this first decade only saw the small beginnings of specialized agencies love affair with operative action, the launching of EPTA was a major impetus in this direction.

Even if the overall verdict on their first decade of performance tended to be rather positive, observers were already highly critical of the uncontrolled and seemingly uncontrollable institutional developments in this area:

> *'The economic programs of the United Nations have been jogging along for some time now. The pace, one fears, is not quite fast enough to get anywhere by sundown. Moreover, the road map, if it ever existed, has been mislaid and a thick growth of underbrush has sprung up to obscure the pathway.'*[26]

The same author saw ominous implications of such developments for the level of support for UN operative action, only one decade after its inception:

'Although continuing to allege that support for the UN is the cornerstone of their foreign policy, the major Western powers are no longer inclined to nominate their own best men for UN posts, nor indeed to accept outstanding and independent men of other nationalities in key posts.'[27]

SUPERPOWER STRUGGLE FOR THE SOUL OF EMERGING STATES (1955–70)

External Developments

With 'the loss of China' in 1949 and the ensuing Korean crisis, the global nature of the cold war was evident to all. Throughout this whole period, the world remained split in two major camps. Cuba, Indonesia, North Vietnam, to mention just a few of the more ardent challengers of western ideological supremacy, duly demonstrated that there was no free lunch along the road towards a global market-oriented economy. The superpower rivalry for the political soul of the emerging poor nations had begun, and were intensifying all through this period.

Decolonization took off from the early 1950s and onwards. New, independent but vulnerable states emerged, for whom the UN came to be regarded as a projection and protection of their sovereignty; and increasingly, a source of funding for development projects. By 1955, developing countries already constituted a solid UN majority. The emergence of new states put a heavy strain on the vulnerable institutional machinery set up since 1945, and adaptations were made to allow for formally equal representation of all states in UN fora. While this constituted an important form of adaptation to external pressures, it meant the opposite of adaptation to the economic and political power structures outside UN auspices. It reduced, gradually, developed country motivation to play the game in these fora. Apart from the utility of granting multilateral aid and keeping the dialogue with poor countries open to save them from communism, developed countries increasingly came to view the UN as 'a mechanism for compromising their freedom of action and extracting financial aid from them'.[28]

Implications for UN Normative Functions – the Sources of Confrontation

The very existence of the UN, and the global fora it provided, had an invaluable impact on the forming of common identity for poor developing countries. They first organized as a bloc, though, independently of UN auspices in the form of the Non-Aligned Movement (NAM) established in the wake of the first 'developing world conference' in Bandung, Indonesia in 1955. From then towards 1970 a gradually stronger and more coherent developing country front evolved, inside as well as outside UN fora. The UN developed into a crucial catalyst of developing world unity and cooperation, building on the majority developing countries had secured in all main UN bodies for social and economic affairs.

It is important to note that the build-up of developing world unity, that eventually took on a very confrontational shape, was a gradual process. The launching of the NAM implied no revolution of international affairs, as it was, initially, explicitly against using the concept of the 'bloc'. Its formative phase and the early signs of emerging regional developing world groupings, were logical responses to the rapid expansion of UN membership and could well have developed into useful forms of collective organization – had western countries reacted more constructively. Such initiatives offered, in the words of Righter,

> *'the West opportunity for dialogue that, through hostility or the conviction that it interfered with bilateral treaty systems and was irrelevant to multilateral treaty systems, it chose to ignore. Non-alignment was treated in Western capitals with a mixture of distrust and indifference that nourished in it the spirit of militancy.'*[29]

Developing countries, as we have already indicated, sought a number of ways to capitalize on this new momentum of unity and assumed strength, often with the UN as the centre of attention. One was the continuous strive for greater financial transfers from the rich world. Another, which partly was a means to achieve the former, was to vote in new UN institutions both at the norm-creation and operative levels – making up a gradually more coherent drive for structural change to their favour. UNCTAD launched by virtue of a 1962 General Assembly resolution and held in 1964 (first assumed as a one-time affair), became the main institutional expression of this trend. This organization, and its agenda that was in the making in UN fora already from the late 1950s, prepared the ground for what came to be the dominant and finally fully crystallized developing world UN strategy from the late 1960s and onwards: global redistribution of wealth through the imposition of a New International Economic Order (NIEO).[30]

Group of 77

The strategy was born out of the simple fact that this was the only global organization they controlled, and where they could seriously influence the agenda. Their influence in the IMF, GATT and the World Bank was very limited (they are more powerful today, even if the Organization for Economic Cooperation and Development (OECD) governments still dominate). Add to this the general political weakness and vulnerability of their own states – UN representation and the building up of developing world 'power' in UN fora functioned as a welcome distraction from domestic problems.[31]

This build-up of confrontational positions by the developing country majority strongly conditioned the scope for UN action along the norm-creating functions. The ground rule of at least approximate consensus as a precondition for meaningful normative work through global bodies appeared to fade into the background.

The response of western governments to the upsurge in developing world unity and resultant confrontational positions was hesitant and in many ways contradictory. On one hand, poor country aspirations for more power and wealth played on the post-colonial 'guilt complex' and related emergence of altruist-driven concern in the rich world. On the other hand, there was a strong resistance from particularly the US, but also many other countries, to give in to increasingly tougher financial and institutional demands from what emerged from the 1964 UNCTAD conference as the Group of 77. Two broad-based (and interrelated) strategies were at hand:

The first one was to resist demands for setting up new and potentially important developing world-dominated agencies under UN auspices. In the SUNFED case (see Box 2.1), western countries led by the US first rejected the proposed goals of such an agency all together (provision of grant or soft loan-based investment support), and then, as pressures built up and the case for such a fund won more adherents also in the West throughout the 1950s, chose to set up the International Development Agency (IDA) under World Bank auspices as an explicit institutional alternative to SUNFED.

BOX 2.1 FIGHTING OVER SUNFED: THE POTENTIAL AND LIMITATIONS OF EARLY DEVELOPING WORLD POWER

The struggle over SUNFED, the Special UN Fund for Economic Development, started very soon after the UN's inception. As a fight to launch a major UN financing scheme, it lasted for more than ten years and subsided first when the International Development Agency (IDA) was set up under World Bank auspices in 1960. Virtually all central UN fora were used in increasingly intensive efforts to convince developed countries to furnish the UN with a major grant- or soft loan-based development financing scheme. The rationale came forward as follows:

- The fight for SUNFED was a fight for increased North/South transfers. Developing countries felt left out as the overwhelming bulk of (the mostly grant based) post-war reconstruction money went for Europe and Japan. They found World Bank loans at close to market rates, and limited in volume until the early 1960s, gravely insufficient.
- Functionally, it was an effort to convince policy-makers in rich countries that 'loans only' simply did not add up. The World Bank also soon realized that lack of soft feasibility – and prefeasibility – funds meant lack of fundable projects. As such, developing countries gradually won a conditional victory – soft funds started flowing, but they did not win control over their use.
- SUNFED can be seen as probably the first sustained effort to use collective strength by a UN majority to force through structural change in the world economy to the benefit of poor countries. The spectre of voting through aid transfers by UN majority rule was as scaring to rich countries as it promised a bright future for developing world governments.

Continuous lobbying through the General Assemby and ECOSOC notwithstanding, the SUNFED proposal was unacceptable to the US and its western allies. Developing countries tested the potency of their UN majority, and lost – at least in the first round, as the IDA of 1960 was placed squarely under World Bank auspices. More indirectly, however, their struggle for SUNFED can be said to have paid off. It undoubtedly strengthened the overall case for aid transfers – through bilateral as well as multilateral sources. By 1960, everybody came to agree that loans were not enough and that soft development financing – an unacceptable bastard to conservative US policy-makers a decade before – was legitimate. Both the creation of the IDA and that of the World Bank's International Finance Corporation (IFC) in 1956 were at least partly seen as compensation for SUNFED. And finally, the set up in 1958 of the UN's Special Fund (far more limited than the original SUNFED proposal), and its eventual merger with EPTA into the UNDP, in 1966, was at least a partial victory – even if the UNDP has never become the central aid financing body that G-77 hoped at that time.

A similar strategy was pursued as western governments sensed that the planning for the 1964 UNCTAD conference won increasing support for redistribution of wealth through rewriting the rules of the game of the emerging market-based world economy in general, and commodity trade in particular. In 1963, they decided to set up a Compensatory Financing Facility (CFF) under the IMF, to help exporters of commodities deal with sudden price fluctuations. Contrary to what happened in the SUNFED case, however, the CFF functioned as a lubricant rather than an obstacle to further developing world institution building under the UN umbrella. It reflected a considerable leap in developing world bargaining power in the decade from 1955 and onwards.

The same can be said of the Generalized System of Preferences (GSP) that was negotiated under UNCTAD auspices and accepted by developed countries as a complement to the emerging GATT free trade regime (UNCTAD II, 1968). To cut short, GSP is a scheme that ensures 'special and differential treatment' for developing countries, allowing them to retain some of their own trade barriers while gaining access to developed country markets. The GSP compromise was a conditional developing world victory in many ways: it demonstrated the utility of newly established UN bodies under their control, and it signalled an acknowledgement by the rich countries that the global economic system worked against the interests of developing countries, and that at least limited corrective action was legitimate. It was fully integrated with GATT by 1971, and has been subject to extension through negotiations in GATT and UNCTAD ever since – although with only moderate success.

A second strategy to meet rising demands of the developing world considered adverse to western interests, was to widen the purse and provide more money for development assistance – bilaterally as well as multilaterally. To quote Paul Mosley,

> 'This decade [the 1960s] was the high water-mark of
> idealism concerning what overseas aid could achieve... It
> was the decade in which most countries first began to
> formulate a policy towards the third world, and in which
> an institution, the Development Assistance Committee of
> the OECD, was set up to co-ordinate the efforts and
> policies of the Western donor nations. It was a period of
> substantial multilateralization of aid... It was the end of
> the 1960s before one saw any signs of the feedback (as
> failures implanted the beginnings of doubt).'[32]

The extent to which increasing (bi- and multilateral) aid budgets was a conscious move to deflect developing world attention away from promoting structural economic change through existing and new UN fora, varied across western countries. Apart from 'colonial guilt' and related altruism-driven motivations, the main force driving up aid transfers in this period was the scramble for the political soul of developing country governments. Liberation wars spread throughout Africa, with both the western and the Communist bloc as more than passive bystanders. Global politics was edging towards an assumed major stand-off between the two superpowers. It was not difficult, therefore, for smart developing world governments to play them and their respective allies out against each other. In asking for more aid, they were pushing at an open door.

However, the concessions implicit in rising aid budgets throughout the 1960s seemingly did little to defuse the build-up of a confrontational developing world stance in UN fora. The failure to avoid such confrontation led to a protracted 30 years war of the trenches over the UN normative functions. Whether confrontation was unavoidable or not is an open question, which we will discuss in some detail in the next section (UN 1970–90), but the result was rather unambiguous. By 1970, the UN world was divided in three camps: G-77, the OECD countries and the Soviet bloc, who were all at cross purposes.

Other Normative Functions – the Merits of the Functional SAs

The politicization and resulting North/South confrontation made an increasingly clear mark on normative UN functions throughout the 1960s, with paralysis and virtual western abdication from many fora as discouraging results. It would not be fair, however, to present an entirely bleak picture of UN performance in the normative field. First, UN secretariats were still seen by observers to deliver work of high quality, although politicization and skewed recruitment patterns started to make their impact. Moreover, the growing number of specialized agencies performed tasks that were in high demand – in developing countries but also in a global context.

What we may call the functional specialized agencies had mandates then, and still have today, that are essentially global in nature. Their missions are basically technical, and North/South confrontation was never allowed to permeate in significant ways the agendas of their governing bodies. Neither were their original functions compromised by the scramble for operative action to the extent realized for bodies like the World Health Organization (WHO), the Food and Agriculture Organization (FAO) and the United Nations Educational Scientific and Cultural Organization (UNESCO). Some of the functional agencies in fact date back to the nineteenth century: ITU, the International Telecommunications Union (1865), WMO, the World Meteorological Organization (1873), UPU, the Universal Postal Union (1875).[33] Others came into being after 1945 in response to increasingly complex global coordination challenges: ICAO, the International Civil Aviation Organization (1947) and IMO, the International Maritime Organization (1959). WIPO, the World International Property Organization, followed as late as 1970, although taking on functions covered by the Bern and Paris Conventions of the 1880s (protecting artistic work and industrial property rights respectively).

It is, thus, more than a hundred years since governments recognized the demands for international, and in many areas, global coordination. Their work seldom makes the headlines, but these specialized agencies perform indispensable services without which the world would have been a far more chaotic and dangerous place to live. In addition to the direct benefits stemming from coordination and the systematization and distribution of information, it is probably fair to assume that they have had a broader political impact in terms of enhancing discipline and the cooperative spirit in global society. Tensions often run high, though, in their governing bodies, since there are considerable commercial and even geopolitical implications of the rules and standards developed in these specialized agency fora, and therefore distributional issues that require very careful handling to avoid protracted conflict. So why have they succeeded?

No overall evaluation is available of the performance of functional specialized agencies, neither in the period assessed here nor in general. Nevertheless, analysts tend to give largely positive verdicts on their achievements, and the role they play in international society.[34] If not a very precise indication, these agencies come as exceptions in the otherwise extremely critical assessments of UN performance by Jackson (1969) and Bertrand (1985). To Bertrand, a major reason for their relative success in norm-creation was *their foundation in at least approximate consensual views on the (carefully delimited) subjects under scrutiny and the overall mission of the respective bodies.* Along with such consensus flows the motivation to participate and to ensure the relevance and focus of the organization's agenda. The same could not be said at this point in time of the other main parts of UN norm-creating machinery, where developed countries had already voted with their feet (in practice if not formally) and moved the important strategic issues to other institutional arenas. Bertrand also noted another significant feature: the functional agencies, and the norm-creation parts of the WHO and UNESCO's work, represented less than 7 per cent of total UN system expenditure.[35]

The Emerging Strains on the 'Big Four' Specialized Agencies

The 'big four' specialized agencies cared for many of the same kind of services as the functional bodies just presented. Their mandates were also genuinely global, and they perform tasks in just as high demand 50 years after their inception. The four are made up of UNESCO, (1946), the FAO (1946), the WHO (1948) and the ILO (1946, though originally established in 1919 under the League of Nations). UNIDO, the UN Industrial Development Organization, is also often put in this category. It first became a specialized agency in 1986, but was set up under UN auspices by virtue of a General Assembly resolution 20 years earlier, in 1966.

Even if this period (1955–70) saw sustained growth in the budgets and range of activities of these agencies, we can identify sources of strains that were soon to threaten their performance and very legitimacy.

1   Politicization, growing out of the increasingly confrontational character of UN deliberations, rapidly permeated the governing bodies and general assemblies of these specialized agencies, making it difficult to keep a sharp thematic focus.
2   Already by 1955, steadily increasing shares of agency resources were devoted to operative projects in the developing world; competing all the more critically with attention to their original norm-creation tasks.
3   Resulting from the two former developments, the quality of recruitment procedures, and of the personnel recruited, deteriorated, as pointed out in the 1969 Jackson report.[36]
4   Their unsystematic growth contributed to the coordination crisis that was the main target of the highly critical judgement made by Jackson.

Operative UN Action, 1955–70

A major implication of the overall thrust of UN action in the normative field, was, as can be seen in Figure 2.1, an increase in resources devoted to operational activities for development, and, in fact more pronounced in this particular period: in the number of UN organizations 'going operational'. The process had started already in the late 1940s, but did not take on significant proportions until the mid-1960s. From then on the world saw two decades of rapidly increasing aid transfers to developing countries – through both bilateral and multilateral sources. The trends in official development assistance (ODA), multilateral aid and UN contributions to developing countries are shown in Figure 2.2. The UN share of total ODA is shown in Figure 2.3.

A range of different categories of UN institutions got deeply involved in development assistance: specialized agencies, regional commissions, functional commissions, secretariat bodies and financing schemes. Some of the more important institutional developments can be summarized as follows.

With regard to aid financing and programming, EPTA, founded in 1950, was complemented in 1959 with the limited UN Special Fund

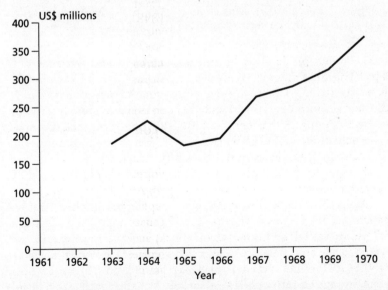

Source: OECD/Development Assistance Committee (DAC) Annual Reports

Figure 2.1 *Total ODA Flows to Developing Countries Through the UN 1963–70 (current US$ millions)*

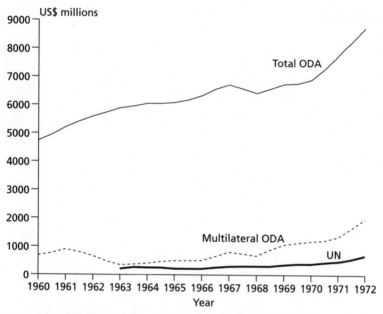

Source: OECD/Development Assistance Committee (DAC) Annual Reports

Figure 2.2 *Total ODA, Multilateral ODA and ODA Through the UN 1960–72 (current US$ millions)*

(SF). Various proposals were also tabled and fought over since the late 1950s for a more investment-directed UN Capital Development Fund (UNCDF). Due to ensuing North/South rivalries, however, it did not get into operation until 1971, and on a modest level with pledges of only US$3 million. By 1965, however, the General Assembly decided that EPTA and the SF should be merged into the UN Development Programme (UNDP), which was to become, at least on paper, the main body for financing and coordination of UN operative activities.

Many different UN bodies were developing implementation capacities in response to the funding made available through EPTA/SF/UNDP and other channels. Among the more important were the 'big four, then five' specialized agencies: the FAO, the WHO, UNESCO, the ILO and UNIDO. This period (1955–70) saw a significant expansion into operations for all of them. Other specialized agencies, including some of the functional agencies discussed above, also engaged in operations, but on a far more modest level and without compromising their original mandates. In addition, the

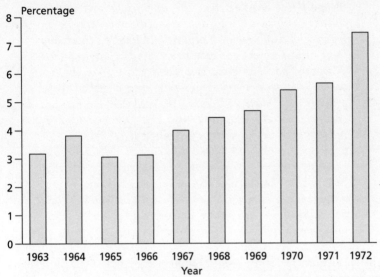

Source: OECD/Development Assistance Committee (DAC) Annual Reports

Figure 2.3 *ODA Through the UN as Percentage of Total ODA, 1963–72*

regional UN Economic Commissions, with the African one joining the other three in 1958, also took on operational roles – in spite of largely normatively oriented mandates.[37]

Organizational complexity and lack of coordination

The Jackson report of 1969 can, at least up to a point, be meaningfully compared to the major 1957 Brooking Institution assessment drawn on in discussing the first decade of UN operational action.[38] As such, the 15 years that had passed since this first major evaluation had revealed some disturbing features that threatened to undermine the effectiveness of UN services to poor countries. The main concern of the Jackson report, in trying to adopt a systems perspective on the challenges to UN operative action, was the apparent anarchic structure of the whole system. What Jackson and his compatriots wanted to see was a well managed system with clear incentive structures and in which the different components were designed to complement each other according to an overall design from top to bottom in the system. The contrast to what they did see, however, is revealed in the following quote from the report:

> *'Below [UN] headquarters, the administrative tentacles thrust downwards into an extraordinary complex of regional and sub-regional offices, and finally extend into field offices in over ninety developing countries. This 'Machine' now has a marked identity of its own and its power is so great that the question must be asked, Who controls this "Machine"? So far, the evidence suggests that governments do not, and also that the machine is incapable of intelligently controlling itself. This is not because it lacks intelligent and capable officials, but because it is so organised that managerial direction is impossible. The machine as a whole has become unmanageable in the strictest sense of the word. As a result, it is becoming slower and more unwieldy, like some prehistoric monster.'*[39]

The sheer quantity of different UN bodies aiding individual developing countries has been described as follows:

> *'This system of allocation of funds means that in a single country which is recipient of aid, about 15 different organisations intervene simultaneously to organise their projects there. Added to these will be one or more of the 13 independent bodies directly attached to UNDP, or other independent (UN) bodies. The aid channelled through the UN system can thus be proposed to one and the same country by some 30 bodies of the most varied types and completely independent.'*[40]

The result was a largely uncontrolled proliferation of UN organizations, and of subdivision under them again. Precise data of what was going on was difficult to get hold of even for the most experienced insiders. The Jackson study complains about the dearth of reliable facts and figures:

> *'In many cases, records apparently do not exist. In others, they are incomplete or contradictory. This unsatisfactory state of affairs was probably inevitable, the price paid for the very rapid expansion of the UNDP. But it is a major drain on capacity. No one today in the UN development system is fully informed about all aspects of the present operation.'*[41]

Not that anybody had acknowledged the problems before, or not tried to create some order out of the seemingly chaotic situation. The period in question saw many coordination initiatives added to the UN machinery: in 1962; the Committee on Programme and Coordination was set up, as main subsidiary organ both of ECOSOC and the General Assembly for planning, programming, evaluation and coordination; in 1964, the Committee for Development Planning, a group of experts appointed in their personal capacity to 'consider and evaluate the programmes and activities of the organs of the UN and of the specialized agencies relating to economic planning and projections', and in 1968, the JIU, whose members have the broadest powers of investigation in all matters having a bearing on the efficiency of services and the proper use of funds, and who have been given the task 'of achieving greater co-ordination between organisations'.

These efforts, and a range of new ones instituted over the coming decades, have not significantly improved the situation, as we will return to below. Bertrand's verdict is negative indeed:

> *'The extreme decentralisation of the system, deliberate at the outset and then aggravated by the establishment of dozens of new organs, has not been able to be made up by 'co-ordination' imposed on agents who did not want to be co-ordinated.'*[42]

THE RISE AND FALL OF NEW WORLD ORDERS (1970–90)

External factors

The early 1970s displayed a range of disparate and conflicting signals about where organized global society was heading. One implication for the UN was a marked increase in expectations and ambitions for developing world-inspired UN influence on world economic structures. Another was substantial increases in the availability of aid money to be channelled through the UN and other organizations: total aid increased from US$7 billion in 1970 to 55 billion in 1990. External factors of relevance for the UN scope of action in the period from 1970 to 1990 can be summarized as follows.

The Cold War Continues

With the Vietnam War raging till 1975, the Soviet invasion of Afghanistan in 1980 and a range of other developing countries still undecided about main ideological leanings, cold war shadows were hanging over much of this period. Approximate consensus, the major condition for meaningful economic or political norm creation, was non-existent – right up to crumbling of the Berlin Wall in 1989. The paralysing implications for UN normative functions seen in the previous periods – in peace and security but also in economic and social affairs – therefore prevailed throughout the two decades under scrutiny here. Changes were in the making, though, not least due to the gradual dissipation in NIEO support from the early 1980s and onwards.

Disintegration of the Monetary System – Uncertainty and Volatility

The collapse of the Bretton Woods system of fixed exchange rates in 1971 marked the culmination of many years of considerable unrest and volatility in global currency markets. The US government had built up a huge trade deficit, and saw no alternative to devaluation (first in 1971 and then in 1973) and thus delinking the US dollar from the gold standard. It implied, moreover, the transition from US domination of global macro-economic management, to a more pluralistic OECD-based financial power structure. A rethink also became urgent for the role of the IMF, and the ensuing exchange rate turbulence in the early 1970s created a general sense of uncertainty about the future of global economic governance. The main implication of these developments for UN fora and functions, was to strengthen the case for structural changes in the world economy, a UN role therein, and G-77 ambitions with regard to influencing such change. Seen from another perspective, NIEO demands would probably have been far easier for western countries to deflect had they themselves had full confidence in the existing world economic regime. They had not, and 'the "old order" seemed ripe for a decisive attack'.[43]

The First OPEC Oil Shock and Developing World Radicalization

OPEC's oil price shock in 1973 sent shock waves into the world economy, and contributed to the first serious post-war round of recession in oil-importing western countries. Oil-dependence and related politico-economic vulnerabilities of the rich world were exposed for all to see. It represented, on the other hand, a major encouragement for poor commodity-exporting countries that sensed a unique opportunity for increased earnings. Add to this the broader political impetus OPEC's power demonstration implied for G-77, the developing world's negotiation block in the UN – which is important to understand the political energy fuelling demands for a NIEO.

The radicalization of the developing world agenda started in many ways with Libya's unilateral decision in 1970 to extract higher oil prices from foreign companies, and to increase them on several occasions in the absence of reaction from western powers. UNCTAD III in 1972 reflected an increasing self-confidence of developing countries, as Mexico's president Luis Echeverria called for, and was able to force through, the elaboration of a Charter of the Economic Rights and Duties of States. The fourth non-aligned summit in Algiers in September 1973 became 'the catalyst that fused the disparate elements of third world radicalisation into a militant political platform'. The summit crystallized the demands for a NIEO, developed a programme of action for how to implement it and decided to give the Rights Charter top priority at the following UN General Assembly. What matters about the Algiers summit 'is not whether the propositions formulated there were coherent – they were not – but that it established Third World solidarity as a galvanising political principle and provided it with sacred texts'.[44]

The Second OPEC Oil Shock and the Emerging Debt Crisis

The second oil shock of 1979 further challenged battered western economies and helped energy security (and diversification of energy imports) remain at the top of the international political agenda for some more years. It also introduced, however, what came to be seen as the 'lost decade' for the majority of (oil-importing) poor countries. 'Lost' in terms of general development performance, and lost in terms of getting bogged down in a vicious debt crisis circle. Moreover, the recession in OECD countries strengthened protectionist interests and led to reduced demand for developing country exports. Accordingly, while the first oil shock raised unrealistic expectations for significant developing world economic and political advances, the second one touched off developments that effectively killed any ambition of unified G-77 advances towards a new world order. It gradually became clear that the debt crisis, and subsequent development crisis, from which many developing world countries were suffering, was partly a result of the actions of oil producers in the developing world.

A Relative Decline of US Leadership

As already indicated in the field of macro-economic management, this period saw a beginning to the downturn of the US leadership. The intransigence (as judged by the US) of France in NATO and related fora symbolized the 'grown-up' and increasingly independent attitude of European countries, who were no longer willing to follow the US lead in international fora. Developments like the humiliating defeat in Vietnam (1975) dealt a further blow to its geopolitical stature – the US did no longer rule the world. This point should not be overstated, though. The US government continued to play a dominant role in framing the potential and limits of global governance, which not least the UN itself came to experience as US support for the world organization came under increasing domestic scrutiny.

Developments Along the Normative Functions

The NIEO Era of the 1970s and UN Institutions

Political developments outside the UN, reinforced by clever but shortsighted G-77 utilization of UN organizations, created the drive for a NIEO. A range of UN fora were available for exploitation:

- The annual sessions of the General Assembly and ECOSOC, which both constituted important arena and forum roles where NIEO advocates could make their imprints on the global political agenda. Given G-77 majority, there was no effective opposition from western countries – despite strong misgivings in countries like the US.
- UNCTAD launched in 1964 and placed under the General Assembly, rapidly developed into a key developing country stronghold in the UN system, and a very effective NIEO catalyst. Regular UNCTAD conferences, particularly UNCTAD III in 1972 and UNCTAD IV in 1976, represented month-long sessions where G-77 attempted to make NIEO proposals for structural economic change subject to global negotiations – in fora where the cards were stacked against those effectively in charge of world economic management (and those who paid 98 per cent of overall UN expenses).

- The governing bodies of UN funds, programmes and specialized agencies, where developing countries with varying degrees of intensity aimed to add substance to NIEO claims. UNIDO is a case in point, where G-77 voted through, against the entire OECD, a resolution that called for a US$300 billion fund for industrial development, to be managed by the developing countries, and for good measure condemned capitalism as responsible for colonialism, racism and imperialism.[45]
- The secretariats of the various UN bodies mentioned above, as well as those serving the broad range of committees and commissions under the General Assembly and ECOSOC. These bodies, and those of UNCTAD and the central UN in New York in particular, became important, and gradually more independent, actors in the unfolding NIEO drama. They were charged with elaborating programmes to reflect the NIEO platform, sometimes, according to critics, going beyond anything formulated in the intergovernmental debate. Secretariats were no doubt prodded in a NIEO-legitimizing direction by radical developing world governments, as witnessed by the claim by the president of the 1974 General Assembly, Algiers' foreign minister Abdelaziz Bouteflika, at the end of that session in New York that 'the battle of the agenda was won', and that 'the only thing left now to decolonise was the UN secretariat'.[46]

There are exceptions to the trend of confrontational developing world politics seemingly immersing every bit of UN normative functions throughout this period. Most functional agencies, as presented in the previous section, were to a large extent shielded from such pressures – even if polarization over for example Middle East politics could paralyse the most genuinely technical of agency deliberations. The overall picture in the 1970s, however, was one of profound polarization and ensuing confrontation over global economic issues in UN fora; the implications of which we will briefly summarize in what follows.

Whatever perspective applied, the quest for a NIEO as forced through by way of bloc negotiation, failed. It failed conclusively if the result is compared to the stated objectives of developing countries. Judging the actual outcome according to more down to earth assessments provides some nuances, of which the increase in absolute (if not relative) aid flows is a case in point. The overall picture, however, remains very bleak. This holds whether one looks at proposed changes in global decision-making structures, modifications in global production structures, stabilization of commodity prices, system-wide improvements in market access or more specific NIEO demands.

Volumes have been written about the NIEO outcomes or lack of such.[47] Our task here is to assess what the implications of NIEO strategies and tactics meant for the ability of UN bodies to fulfil global normative functions. The following implications are worth noting.

Decreasing Developed Country Support for UN Institutions

From the UN's very inception, temptations abounded to force through decisions by way of confrontational (majority voting power) tactics, thus risking minority walkouts and disintegration of the fora in question. The NIEO decade implied the peak of this strategy, which culminated, according to many observers, with the confrontational and virtually fruitless bargaining at UNCTAD V in 1979 (Manila) and UNIDO III in Vienna in 1980 – 'where the positions of the North and South had become entirely irreconcilable'.[48] The result was a progressive decline in confidence and support for UN fora handling economic and social issues, on behalf of industrialized countries but also, increasingly, of many developing countries. It was thus not accidental that 1981 marked the occasion on which the Reagan administration decided to undertake a comprehensive survey of US participation in UN organizations. A tangible output of this process was the Kassenbaum-Solomon amendment of 1985 to the US Foreign Relations Authorization Act, implying drastic cuts in US contributions to the world organization.

Further Institutional Sprawling

NIEO confrontational strategies stimulated further institutional and agenda sprawling within the UN, reflecting, among other features, strong G-77 beliefs that their institution-building strategy of the 1960s – the launching of UNCTAD and UNIDO in particular – had been a success.[49] This was evident not so much in the rise of big new organizations, as it was in the proliferation of issues to be subject to elaboration in new committees or commissions under ECOSOC and/or the General Assembly. The 1970s saw a wealth of what we later discuss as 'agenda sprawling', including a growing number of UN conferences and 'years' and 'decades' of various kinds. More or less ad hoc fora like these were just as vulnerable to politicization as regular UN sessions. For instance, the UN Conference on Human

Settlements (HABITAT) Conference in Vancouver in 1976 spent a lot of political energy on fighting over resolutions concerning the rights of Palestinians and the struggle against racism, 'and the Western experts on low-cost solar energy and slum upgrading dispatched to Vancouver were ill equipped to cope'.[50]

Add to this that the belief in structural change through the wielding of (majority vote-based) institutional strength was so strong, as to effectively block any attempt at serious organizational adaptation to changing external environments. Such adaptation, especially if it meant downsizing, merging or other ways of reducing certain institutional functions, came to be seen as attacks at the very core of developing world ambitions. Hence, NIEO politics resulted in both uncritical organizational proliferation and the virtual impossibility of adapting existing ones to new demands – making the system even more unmanageable.

Declining Quality of Secretariat Services

Ensuing NIEO-related confrontation progressively deflated the value of central UN norm-creating fora, not least through the politicization and gradual decline in quality of secretariat services. Incentive structures of UN staff were skewed towards aiming to sustain a set of ultimately indefensible policy prescriptions. The following quote from an old US UN hand is probably rather representative evidence of how western governments came to view the relevance of UN action in global economic affairs, and indirectly, then, the quality of services rendered to this effect by the central secretariats:

> '*It would not be an appropriate use of the State Department's limited human and political resources for that agency to encourage other federal agencies and major governments to take more seriously the macroeconomic debates in ECOSOC and the General Assembly's Second Committee.* The sceptical and often hostile attitudes toward ECOSOC in finance ministries, central banks, and other government circles are too deep seated and too well founded to be overcome in present or foreseeable circumstances.'[51]

This period of confrontational North/South politics harmed the credibility of UN secretariat services through their uncritical adoption of G-77's NIEO agenda. Probably more important, however, was the more indirect impact in terms of deflating developed country interest in UN secretariat output. Maurice Bertrand, in the 1985 JIU report cited earlier, stresses this point in referring to the 'shortcomings of the countless documents and reports that clutter delegates' desks day after day have often been criticised but never remedied. Major policy documents such as the International Development Strategies, to which a great deal of time and effort is devoted, reflect in their superficial character the inadequate equipment of the United Nations in the sphere of economic and sociological thought.' He attributes a main reason for this situation to 'the average inadequacy of qualifications of the personnel, which in this field in fact is extremely bad'. Several related explanations are examined, before Bertrand concludes that 'the UN secretariats are regarded at present by the member states as areas over which they have to exert political influence so as to gain maximum control over operations and install the largest possible number of their nationals.' In his opinion, governments had ended up caring more for such narrow positioning than for the actual value of secretariat outputs: 'The mediocrity of the outputs does not strike them, in most cases, as a major concern, since the benefit they derive is negligible.'[52]

Declining Focus and Quality of Specialized Agency Services

NIEO-related confrontation spread, as we already have seen, to a range of specialized agencies, implying increasing waste of time and resources and further depreciation of their image among donor countries. Among the specialized agencies, UNIDO, UNESCO and the ILO were among those most liable to become submerged in 'new order politics' or politicization in more delimited forms (Palestine, racism, peace and disarmament, etc), significantly widening and in many cases obscuring the focus of their initially rather targeted agendas. UNESCO, for instance, for long a body under criticism for lacking sufficient focus, spent a wealth of resources on preparing the ground for a New World Information and Communication Order (NWICO). NWICO is probably among the most telling examples of how unclarity of focus of UN deliberations allow for the build-up of positions and policies by the contending parties that are so funda-mentally at variance as to render real negotiations impossible.

The quality of services provided by the big five specialized agencies (the FAO, UNESCO, the WHO, the ILO and UNIDO) were further challenged by their vastly increasing level of operational activities in developing countries. The growing volume of resources made available for operative action through UN agencies from 1965 into the early 1980s, is attributed much of the blame for a steadily decreasing quality of their core mandates as specialized agencies: to function as centres of excellence within their (delimited) fields of expertise, to systematize research and statistics, help develop targeted norms and standards and provide policy advice on the basis of assumedly unique competence. May be partly because an erosion of focus had already started, the agencies gave in willingly to the 'projectitis temptation' (see below for details), functioning as a further disincentive with respect to concentration on the normative concerns they were created to care for. In concluding a comprehensive survey on specialized agency performance, Edgren and Møller conclude as follows:

> '*But it is also true that the shift in emphasis to a large degree has taken place outside the control of the agencies' governing bodies, and that the current orientation of work in many ways deviates considerably from the original objectives for which the specialised agencies were created.* The most important undesirable effect is the declining quality level in almost all activities of the agencies. *This is true for the normative and informative functions of the agencies, which over the years have had little appeal to external funding sources.*'[53]

1980s – Back to Square One and New Beginnings?

By the early 1980s, the quest for a NIEO was rapidly waning. Although structured according to the agenda of the 1970s, at UNCTAD VI in Belgrade (1983) and even more so UNCTAD VII in Geneva (1987), only lipservice was paid to the NIEO demands. The failure of the NIEO programme was clear for all to see, with ramifications of UN proceedings in the political world outside UN auspices virtually non-existent. Apart from the 'failure effect' itself (and a related decreasing utility of UN fora as bargaining platforms), other factors also contributed to a marginalization of the UN in terms of economic-political debate. As pointed out above, the second oil shock of 1979 and the debt crisis unfolding from 1982 and onwards, dealt serious blows to developing country economies. Even if impacts were primarily economic in nature, they probably also served to further weaken G-77 unity that had kept the NIEO high on the agenda for more than a decade.

With the cold war still keeping UN security functions close to the freezing point, and the Reagan administration up in arms against

UN spending, the mid-1980s saw support for the UN reaching record low points. North/South stand-offs in UN fora had come to be regarded as an exercise in futility by the world's major powers. Even if efforts to reform or streamline the UN machinery were still broadly seen by G-77 as harmful to developing country interests, they could no longer withstand pressures from OECD countries to commission comprehensive reviews of the functioning of the UN system and its diverse institutional sub-structure. US spending cuts and withdrawals from UN bodies (eg UNESCO in 1984) created shockwaves. They were signs of things to come – increasingly tougher scrutiny of the effectiveness of UN performance. ECOSOC (among others) came under increasing pressure, with questioning of its contributions both in terms of its agenda function, its substantive policy advice and its role in coordination of overall UN activities in the economic and social domains.

A result of the post-NIEO void in UN imprints of the international economic debate, was soul-searching for new areas where the 'normative UN' could make a difference. One challenge as of the mid-1980s was to adapt UN agendas and services so as to make them more attractive to western governments. Forty years of developing country mobilization in UN fora had shaped the world organization in ways that alienated rich countries and made them search elsewhere for international problem solving. Was it possible, in a world of increasing interdependence between states, to identify political challenges that called for common action beyond what bodies like the World Bank, the IMF and GATT could deliver, and where rich and poor countries had matching interests? The late 1980s were not without developments that pointed towards a revitalized UN charged with genuinely global problem-solving tasks.

We shall round off this review of normative functions since the 1970s by taking a closer look at UN initiatives and achievements in environmental protection and climate change, which we shall briefly contrast to its effort to promote science and technology. Finally, we shall summarize some of the characteristics of the UN as a normsetting organization by finishing the account of its activities in the field of human rights.

Protection of the Environment

The start-up of UN activity on a broad scale in this area was marked by the first conference on the human environment held in Stockholm in 1972. The result of western initiatives, this event was dominated by the western agenda of the day, primarily pollution of air, water and earth, toxic material and protection of endangered species. As the first in the class of mega conferences with wide media coverage, it was successful in placing these issues on the international agenda. The timing was propitious with environmental concern rapidly increasing in both Europe and North America. A new generation of activist NGOs, like Greenpeace and Friends of the Earth, grew up in the early 1970s, capitalizing on a groundswell in public opinion.[54] In this atmosphere, the UN conference captured public attention and reinforced the modern environmental agenda that was in its formative stage in 1972.

In addition, the preparatory work involved numerous scientists across environmental disciplines and led to improved understanding of the nature of important ecological problems and underlying cause–effect relations. In some cases this stimulated political action, like banning DDT, in others, advances in knowledge remained largely within scientific circles for another decade, as was the case with ozone depletion and climate change.

As for institutions, the conference gave birth to the UN Environment Programme (UNEP), which was located in Nairobi in a gesture to developing countries.[55] Despite this attempt to extend the agenda and the concern beyond the western world, developing world governments remained hesitant or sceptical. The North–South divide came to set its mark on international environmental relations in much the same way as the NIEO debacle engulfed UN discussions of economic development in general throughout the 1970s and into the early 1980s. This was basically a dispute over how to define an environmental agenda that carried resonance across the gap between developed and developing countries. The lack of agreement on the fundamental question of approach to the ecological problematique seriously constrained the work of UNEP and other multilateral bodies.[56]

When the ideological climate changed as the NIEO debate petered out in the early 1980s, time seemed ripe for another attempt to bridge the environmental 'agenda gap' between North and South: In 1983 the General Assembly asked the Secretary-General to set up a high level World Commission on Environment and Development, which came to be known as the Brundtland Commission. In its landmark report, 'Our Common Future', published in 1987, the Commission made a bold attempt to merge the environmental agenda of the West and the development agenda of the South into a single concept – 'sustainable development'. The core message was that environment and development 'are inseparable'. Previous efforts to treat them in isolation were discarded and the links between 'poverty, inequality and environmental degradation' forcefully emphasized.[57] The Commission argued that development cum-environment is the solution to the decade old dispute between North and South. The crux lay in the very definition of sustainable development; meeting 'the needs of the present without compromising the ability of future generations to meet their own needs'.[58] The Commission advocated economic growth in developing countries to deal with the challenges of poverty, but also underlined that 'sustainable development (as a minimum) must not endanger the natural systems that support life on Earth: the atmosphere, the waters, the soils, and the living beings'.[59]

This 'dual track' message immediately struck a chord across the North-South cleavage. In the West, the Commission responded to environmental sensitivity in the wake of the Chernobyl disaster. Its call for renewed international collaboration to protect the common environment fell on fertile ground in the late 1980s. In the South, the Commission was widely seen to reopen the stalemated development discourse in a way perhaps more promising than any attempt made since President Kennedy launched development assistance as a 'banner of hope' in the early 1960s. Finally, a meeting of minds based on common interest to replace the antagonism of the 1970s was perceived as a real possibility.[60] The basic idea was as simple as it was appealing: The notion of development within ecological limits should encourage the West to assist developing economies in exchange for environmental protection policies on the part of governments in the developing world. Fifteen years after Stockholm a common agenda seemed within reach.[61]

The Commission concluded its report by calling on the General Assembly to initiate a 'UN Programme of Action on Sustainable Development' and to convene an international conference for this purpose.[62] The stage was set for the Rio Conference.

The UN Conference on Environment and Development (UNCED) held 20 years after Stockholm, attracted much wider participation from governments, NGOs, industry and media. At that time, it was probably the largest political event in UN history. Following a long, inclusive process of preparatory work the Conference itself was successful in setting and propagating around the world through the mass media the sustainable development agenda, as defined by the Brundtland Commission. Its output in terms of standard setting was, however, less impressive: The Rio Declaration added little of substance to its predecessor from Stockholm. Agenda 21, its 'action programme', turned out to be a voluminous listing of everything connected with either development, environment or both.

Both would have suffered the fate of so many previous UN conference statements and resolutions, if it had not been for the timing. Public opinion, certainly in the West and increasingly in other parts of the world, was ripe for the message: Governments must cooperate to save the planet and to improve the lot of the poor. The combination of a receptive audience, activist NGOs and attentive media made UNCED an unprecedented success in terms of promoting understanding for an agenda identified through a UN process. Rio became the focal point that no government could afford to ignore.

The institutional outcome was, however, modest. The legacy from Rio was entrusted to a new Commission on Sustainable Development located under ECOSOC way down the UN hierarchy. The momentum created by the UNCED process was the result of political energy and media attention, both volatile commodities in the late twentieth century. In the years following the Rio gathering, public attention and media coverage of environmental issues declined. Political interest seemed to follow a similar track.[63] As long as political and media attention was on the rise, the tendency to expand the sustainable development agenda was not a problem. New issues, like democratization and the rights of indigenous peoples, just added to the political momentum. After Rio, with dissipating political energy, the accumulation of concerns, issues and demands – as incorporated in Agenda 21 – turned from an asset to a liability. The follow-up process has turned out to be extremely cumbersome and tortuous, even for a UN context. With high-level attention waning, the centrifugal forces have reappeared. The different 'camps' that were held together for a while under the sustainable development umbrella have picked up their old causes – the NIEO veterans, the economic liberalists, the conservationists, the development activists, in addition to the bureaucratic cleavages within the UN system. All their diverging demands and conflicting interests are to be 'coordinated' in an 'integrated' approach to development by a commission meeting for a few weeks once a year at UN headquarters.[64] The result is issue overload. Where the Brundtland Commission succeeded in framing a coherent, if somewhat woolly, concept, the follow-up process has suffered from lack of focus and fragmentation of agenda.

UN debate of sustainable development since 1992 has by and large remained at the general, rhetorical level, often simply recycling the message from Rio, and has therefore gradually lost much of the public interest. With few exceptions, the UN follow-up process after UNCED has not succeeded in going beyond agenda setting and promoting understanding in terms of normative functions. Agenda 21 is much too general to define standards of behaviour and monitoring has been hampered by lack of focus and developing world resistance.[65] However, Agenda 21 as a symbol has had an impact at both the national and local level.[66] The momentum created at Rio has stimulated creativity in industrial circles and among local governments in a large number of countries and has led to major progress in issue-specific UN-sponsored processes, such as the bargaining over climate change.

Climate Change

The rapid emergence of global warming from exotic science to high politics benefited greatly from the catalytic role of the Brundtland Commission. One of its immediate institutional spin-offs demonstrated another promising avenue of normative action for the UN. The Intergovernmental Panel on Climate Change (IPCC) was set up under joint UNEP and WMO auspices in 1988, charged to examine the nature and limits of scientific evidence about climate change.[67] Roughly speaking, the IPCC's task was to frame in consensus terms the scientific component of the decision-making foundation for the world's environmental policy-makers. It did so by engaging leading scientists from all over the world in a multi-year consensus process, which still goes on within the framework of the Climate Convention it helped to create. The IPCC's first main report was presented to the Second World Climate Conference in Geneva in late 1990, and formed a crucial input to the decision to launch negotiations aimed at controlling greenhouse gas emissions – which eventually led to the signing of the Framework Convention on Climate Change at UNCED in 1992.

The IPCC's major achievement was to transform extremely complex scientific material into 'politically readable' information as to what we know and what we don't know about global warming. It provided policy-makers with tools to judge whether the still uncertainty-ridden risk of global warming justified political action or not. The main functions of the UN as such were to provide a universal forum including developing country participants, to mobilize the leading scientific experts around the world, to frame an agenda telling scientists what the outside world wanted from them and to do this in ways that did not compromise the credibility of science. Even if many have questioned, and still do, the role of governments and intergovernmental organizations in this kind of 'scientific consensus production', there is broad support for the conclusion that one of the chief merits of the IPCC process has been to shield the deliberations of scientists from undue politicization from any side.[68] This is no small achievement within an issue area as scientifically complex and politically explosive as climate change.

The Framework Convention set up a procedure whereby first developed country parties, and later their developing counterparts, submit regular reports on emissions of greenhouse gases and policies to deal with them. It also committed the parties to review the adequacy of the commitments undertaken by developed countries to stabilize emissions at the 1990 level by 2000. (Developing countries have accepted no substantive commitments.) Before the meeting of the parties in 1995, the IPCC again warned of indications of global warming trends. On this basis, and following pressures from environmental NGOs across the western world, governments began to seriously consider reduction targets post-2000. When the IPCC in 1996 published its second major assessment strongly indicating a discernible human influence on climate, the political pressures added up to a new momentum in the intergovernmental negotiations, which led to the Kyoto Protocol.

During this process, governments gradually agreed on a political agenda by accepting that climate change is a problem that has to be tackled through international collaboration. In addition, the combination of the scientific credibility of the IPCC and the high-level attention plus media circus of UNCED brought the question of climate change out to policy-makers and opinion leaders in every part of the globe. Within less than a decade, these UN sponsored processes (the IPCC and UNCED) covered the entire range of normative functions with a speed and outreach that has few precedents; from agenda-setting and promoting understanding in the late 1980s and early 1990s to standard-setting in the Kyoto Protocol of 1997 and monitoring established gradually by the Convention secretariat since the middle of the 1990s.

The UN experience in the field of climate change can be summarized as follows:

• Media attention is critical in the initial phase to catch the attention of policy-makers and get the 'snowball' rolling.
• Establishing a credible scientific basis for political bargaining is essential for the process that follows. The more controversial the issue, the more important the legitimacy of science.
• Decoupling the issue-specific process from general discussions in the UN system can be very productive in order to focus attention on practical step-by-step solutions at the expense of political recrimination.

Science and Technology for Development

It is tempting to compare the performance of the IPCC and related (at least relative) UN successes in the ozone depletion area, to the much more mixed record of decades of UN involvement in 'Science and Technology for Development'. Born out of early post-war development and technology optimism, lots of resources and political energy have been wasted on UN efforts to stimulate growth through the application of science and technology (S&T). It is a long and sad history of unclear objectives, lacking groundwork to ensure developed country support, and geared more towards empire-building within and outside the UN than measurable results on the ground. The 1979 Vienna Programme of Action on Science and Technology for Development is a case in point. Building on UN efforts since the Geneva conference on the subject back in 1963 and numerous committees and commissions set up since then, this new 118 paragraph programme document established a US$250 million interim S&T fund (never filled), and framed the challenges in what has come to be seen as typical UN prose: 'strengthening the S&T capacities of the developing countries at national, regional and international level, restructuring the existing pattern of international S&T relations, strengthening the role of the UN in the field of S&T'. The programme also recommends, 'inter alia, that each developing country should establish one or more bodies for science and technology policy-making and implementation, supported at the highest level'.[69]

The verdict on four decades of UN deliberations in this area is generally negative, in that they have been so comprehensive in scope as to become virtually useless, with very vague objectives except in the sense of proposals to build new bureaucracies – in developing countries as well as within the UN system.[70] Typically, the existence of the UN S&T programme and the limited funds that became available through it, developed into a battleground for UN specialized agencies, where, according to Douglas Williams, 'agencies typically saw new worlds to conquer (eg more studies of the problem of undertaking research, conferences, data collections etc), rather than new possibilities for real research to discover new facts that would help development in poor countries'.[71]

Human Rights

As mentioned above, the UN human rights debate became thoroughly politicized at an early stage. Throughout the 1970s and well into the

1980s the intergovernmental fora continued to be a battleground for East-West rivalry. Both sides accused the other of violations and fought eagerly to enlist support from developing world governments. The latter remained deeply sceptical of the human rights agenda; most of them had not participated in formulating the Universal Declaration in the 1940s and had no intention of adopting western standards of civil rights for their citizens. Like the two other camps, developing world leaders used human rights as an instrument in promoting their foreign policy objectives. Apart from a handful a small, primarily neutral countries human rights was not considered an end in itself by most governments, but a stick to use against one's adversaries at convenience.

Under these circumstances, the normative agreement that was set out in the Universal Declaration was largely ineffective. Its 'persuasive force' (cf. Chapter 1) on most governments was negligible. This was the result of underlying disagreement on the nature of human rights, but also followed from its rather general formulation. The Declaration provided few concrete benchmarks for subsequent behaviour and no institutional mechanism for monitoring compliance. There was no scarcity of intergovernmental meetings and bodies, but they remained primarily fora for the manifestation of conflict. The majority of governments were not willing to give either a mandate or the resources necessary to any body entrusted with monitoring national follow-up of the norms enunciated in the Universal Declaration.

Standard setting remained, however, on the UN agenda, but discussions suffered from East–West controversy over political vs economic rights. In the end, after almost 20 years of consecutive bargaining, agreement was reached in 1966 on two separate documents, one covenant on civil and political rights and another on social and economic. It took another decade until the two entered into force, in 1976. During the 1970s, other legal instruments on specific human rights were formulated and in some cases accepted as part of international law. Very slowly, almost imperceptibly, the first elements of impartial fact-finding and monitoring developed from the middle of the 1970s and onwards, often in response to acute crises.[72] Over time, enough precedence was created to pave the ground for a UN role at least in fact-finding in cases of human rights controversies. Setting up ad hoc bodies to study accusations of violations gradually came to be accepted, despite serious misgivings from affected governments and their closest allies. During the 1980s a number of conventions went into effect and procedures for national reporting were set up. So, by the time the major barrier – the cold war – was eliminated, the institutional framework for intergovern-mental collaboration was well established. Consequently, in the 1990s it has been possible to set up a much more systematic and less politi-cized system for monitoring human rights developments in specific cases and in thematic clusters of issues. This includes some of the most controversial matters on the UN agenda, like the fate of disap-peared persons and accusations of torture. The new atmosphere has also facilitated placing human rights monitors in the field, such as in the case of the former Yugoslavia.

On this basis, a long-time student of these affairs has concluded that 'there has indeed been a diplomatic and legal revolution on human rights. The UN in the 1990s is acting for human rights in ways unthinkable in the 1940s', but adds that this 'has yet to lead to a complete and consistent behavioural revolution.'[73]

Returning to our framework of analysis, we can interpret UN efforts to protect human rights in the following manner: The agenda setting began at the San Francisco conference in 1945 with the drafting of the UN Charter and has continued ever since as new concerns and new concrete cases have been added to the general normative vantage point. UN bodies have used all the means at their disposal to disseminate the agenda and catch the attention of governments and civil society; world conferences, human rights days and decades, information campaigns. They have received invaluable support from an NGO community that has undergone remarkable growth in the post-war period. What began as small, narrowly based associations (of lawyers and judges) confined to the West has become probably the best organized mass movement in the world with grassroots organizations around the globe and professional lobbyists in capitals as well as in intergovernmental fora. The human rights 'revolution' is the result of a mutually reinforcing interaction between discussions at the interstate level and activism from non-governmental quarters.

The growing awareness of the importance of human rights, also for economic development, has been stimulated by the UN agenda, but is largely due to fundamental political changes outside its control. The wave of democratization in the developing world since the late 1980s and the fall of the Soviet empire are both clear signs of the universal appeal inherent in the concept of civil rights and political freedom. The normative core that was a distant ideal in the Universal Declaration 50 years ago, has become a standard that no government dares openly defy. This does not mean that all states in practice show respect for human rights, but the fundamental normative dispute between East and West and between North and South that characterized the 1950s, 1960s and 1970s is no longer predominant. The question of the universality of human rights will remain on the agenda, not least following initiatives from Asian governments, but the discussion is much less polarized now.

This has allowed the UN in the 1990s to continue its nitty-gritty standard setting work of codifying normative agreement into legal language and binding conventions. These processes carry a dual importance; they focus the interaction among governments and NGOs on specific issues and lead, if successful, to concrete standards for subsequent behaviour.

In addition, the wide normative agreement has made it possible to extend the monitoring functions of the UN into a territory that its founding fathers never envisaged. In the field of human rights, a number of intergovernmental and expert bodies regularly supervise implementation of international conventions. They receive and review national reports, while maintaining close contacts with NGOs. Some conduct regular question-and-answer sessions with representatives of governments. After a long struggle, the key bodies have been granted the right of initiative; if the situation so warrants, they can organize their own investigation of alleged human rights abuses in a given country and publicize their findings. This stands in stark contrast to the 25 years after 1945, when official UN policy was to take no action on such matters, regardless of the number of complaints and petitions.

Along the operative functions in our framework, UN human rights activity has been marginal. The secretariat through the Centre for Human Rights and more recently the High Commissioner has undertaken limited programmes of TA, like training courses and seminars for the legal professions. Practical assistance and advice has been provided to governments on request, for example on the role of the judiciary. In addition, the UN has assisted a large number of governments with conducting elections. From 1992 to 1996, 91 requests for electoral assistance were received and accepted by the UN.[74] So, the organization is involved in operations also in this field, but in an ad hoc, time-limited fashion, providing concrete services on demand. The main thrust of UN activity has been and remains on the normative side of the spectrum, moving slowly, but systematically from agenda setting and promoting understanding to formulating more and more specific standards and in recent years increasingly into monitoring.[75]

Developments Along the Operative Functions

The Strong and Increasing Support for Development Aid

With the trend taking shape already by the mid-1960s, this period comes out as the high point of development aid from rich to poor countries. Emerging signals of crisis and recession notwithstanding, developed countries' strong growth experience up to 1970 laid the basis for development optimism, altruism and related willingness to help the poor countries join the growth bandwagon. Developing world countries also played their cards well in lobbying for enhanced financial transfers, in UN fora and elsewhere, playing effectively on the ex-colonial powers' guilt complexes. Add to this that continued cold war-dominated aid motives were still important in driving up aid budgets. Figure 2.4 shows the overall developments in official aid (bi- and multilateral) flows in the 25 years from 1975 through 1995.

'Economic' (supply-oriented) explanations of increasing aid budgets particularly from 1970 to 1985 are challenged by the fact that oil-crisis driven recession and squeeze on public spending in OECD countries in the 1970s failed to stem the substantial growth in aid transfers. Were geopolitical (cold war-related) motivations more

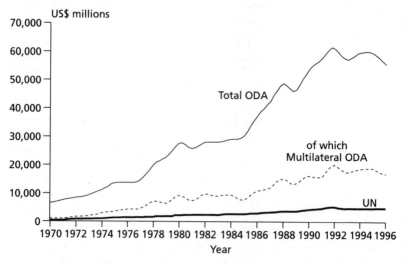

Source: OECD/Development Assistance Committee (DAC) Annual Reports

Figure 2.4 *Total ODA of Which Multilateral and UN, 1970–96 (current US$ millions)*

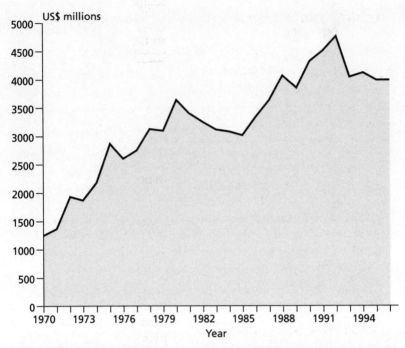

Source: OECD/DAC: *Development Cooperation, 1996 report.* Conversion of current prices to constant values has been done by using the US consumer price index (1992=100)

Figure 2.5 *ODA from DAC Countries to the UN 1970–96, Constant Values (1992 US$ millions)*

important, or were rich countries becoming unprecedently vulnerable to G-77 campaigning in UN fora, with altruistic NGOs in the North as effective amplifiers? One option may be to reckon with *a public policy time lag* in the ups and downs of aid budgets: The 'economic rationale' for aid was laid in the 1950s and 60s, with strong economic growth and belief in state planning (within a market-based economic framework, though) as central characteristics. This paid off in the form of enhanced aid transfers in the 70s and far into the 1980s, notwithstanding domestic OECD country recession and the revelations of failing aid projects. According to this line of thought, the dissipation of cold war tensions coincided with a maturing aid fatigue in the latter part of the 1980s, contributing to the recent downward trends identified since 1991 and documented in Figure 2.4.

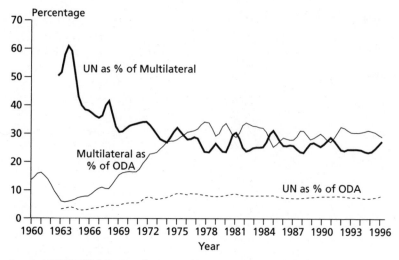

Source: OECD/DAC: *Development Cooperation, Annual reports*

Figure 2.6 *Multilateral and UN Shares of Total ODA, and UN Share of Multilateral ODA, 1960–96*

The UN gets its Share in the Aid Growth

Support for UN operative services was growing rapidly from 1970 through 1985, when its share of total multilateral ODA levelled off and saw a relative decline in the 1990s (see Figure 2.6). This growth is conspicuous when assessed against the confrontational and largely unproductive stand-offs between industrialized and developing countries in the normative realms of the UN, and the deepening scepticism in the West to the way poor countries utilized the UN as a vehicle to extract resources from them. The growth in support for UN operations also strikes the eye in light of the strong criticism in various evaluations citing lack of coordination, focus and decreasing quality of services as indictments against UN assistance. Figure 2.5 shows the ODA to the UN in current prices, while Figure 2.6 shows the relative size of UN assistance (UN funds, programmes and specialized agencies) in the period in question as compared to total multilateral aid (including multilateral development banks (MDBs) and European Union) and overall ODA.

As demonstrated in Figure 2.6, multilateral aid as compared to overall ODA sees a strong relative increase from 15 per cent in the late 1960s to around 30 per cent in the late 1970s, at which level it

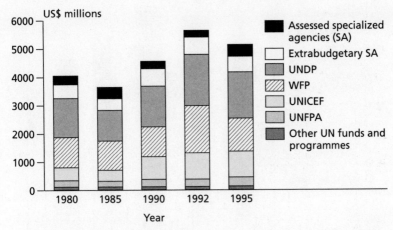

Source: Comprehensive statistical data on operational activities for development for the years 1985, 1993, 1994 and 1995. Conversion of current prices to constant values has been done by using the US consumer price index (1992=100).

Figure 2.7 *Contributions to UN Development Activities, Constant Values (1992 US$ millions)*

has since remained more or less stable up till 1994. The 1970s also sees a considerable absolute as well as relative increase in UN assistance compared to overall ODA, from 5.4 to 8 per cent in that decade. Since the early 1980s, however, the UN share of total official transfers to developing countries falls to 8 per cent in 1990 and further down towards 7 per cent by 1995.[76] The relative decrease in the role of UN bodies as compared to other multilaterals starts already by 1975, however, and falls steadily from 32 per cent then to about 25 per cent in 1994 – loosing out, primarily, to MDBs and the European Union.

In absolute terms, however, support for UN development activities fell from 1980 to 1985, but rose again in the early 1990s. Much of this increase was, however, due to extraordinary contributions to the World Food Programme (WFP) and the United Nations High Commissioner for Refugees (UNHCR) for emergency purposes, as illustrated in Figure 2.7 and Figure 2.8.

Much of the growth in contributions to UN assistance since 1980 has come in the form of earmarked contributions to specific purposes, and not as core or so-called assessed funding. This is but one sign that donors increasingly have wanted to increase their leverage and control

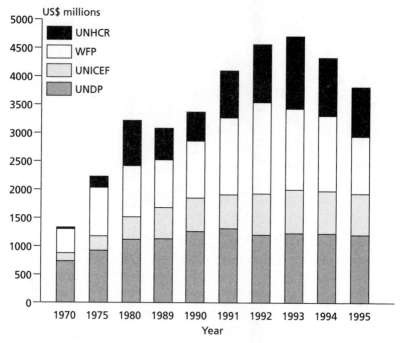

Source: OECD/DAC: *Development Cooperation, 1996 report.* Conversion of current prices to constant values has been done by using the US consumer price index (1992=100).

Figure 2.8 *Disbursements by UNDP, UNICEF, WFP and UNHCR, Constant Values (1992 US$ millions)*

how money channelled through the UN system is spent. These trends are illustrated in Figures 2.9 and 2.10, giving developments in core versus non-core support for the UN as a whole and for the WHO respectively.

The increasing contribution of non-core resources is most conspicuous in the case of the UNDP, where core funding declined in the early 1980s and again after 1992. The relative stagnation in core financing for the UNDP, once meant to become the main multilateral body for financing development activities, is illustrated in Figure 2.11.

As we have seen, UN bodies received their share of the increasing availability of aid money from the mid-1960s and onwards. In the 1970s, the UN also increased its share of total ODA (see Figures 2.3 and 2.6). This growth in aid spending was primarily driven by factors external to the UN, some of which have been discussed above. The

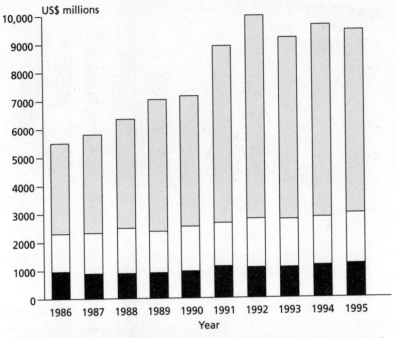

Source: United Nations: *Budgetary and financial situation of organizations of the UN system. Statistical report by the Administrative Committee on Coordination*, various years, (Tables 1 and 8). Numbers for voluntary shares also include contributions from other than states. Conversion of current prices to constant values has been done by using the US consumer price index (1992=100).

Figure 2.9 *Regular and Voluntary Shares of Total UN Budget (Excluding Peacekeeping Operations), Constant Values (1992 US$ millions)*

UN's rise to significance in the aid business throughout the 1970s may also have reflected, however, donor convictions that UN agencies provided a promising aid channel. This growth took place, however, in the absence of structural and organizational reforms like those proposed by the 1969 Jackson report. Thus, what was expanding was not a well-designed system of operations where the different components were

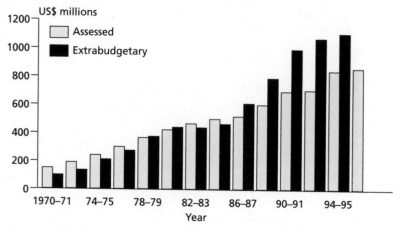

Source: WHO financial statements

Figure 2.10 *Assessed and Extrabudgetary Resources in WHO by Biennium (current US$ millions)*

carefully complementing each other in order to form a coherent approach to UN support for development. Rather, the generous avail-ability of donor funds led existing and some new UN bodies into an unprecedented scramble for new projects and programmes – often, and increasingly, in fierce internal competition over turf and funds.

Since the 1970s an increasing number of UN funds and programmes, in addition to the specialized agencies, established a vast operative machinery with large and small units in every corner of the world, often duplicating one another. By 1995, the number of UN field offices had reached 1125 in all developing regions taken together, up by 60 per cent since 1985.[77] A similar expansion took place at the headquarters of the organizations involved in develop-ment activities, broadly defined, as seen from Table 2.1. The growth is particularly visible in funds and programmes like the UNDP, the United Nations Population Fund (UNFPA), UNICEF and the WFP and in field-oriented organizations like UNHCR. The large special-ized agencies, which with the exception of UNIDO were already well established as large bureaucracies in the early 1970s, have not expanded at all. The staff increase in the UN proper seems to be related to expansion of normative activities in organizations like UNEP, UNCTAD and HABITAT. In total, the staff of the UN devel-opment system, according to this estimate, rose from 31,000 in 1974 to 47,000 in 1994 with the bulk of the increase (11,000 of 16,000)

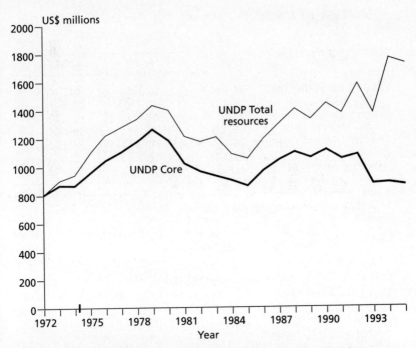

Source: UN A/48/940: Funding Operational Activities for Development within the UN System, May 1994, and UNDP Resource Mobilization Department. Conversion of current prices to constant values has been done by using the US consumer price index (1992=100).

Figure 2.11 *UNDP Core and Non-Core Resources 1972–95, Constant Values (1992 US$ millions)*

taking place outside headquarters, reflecting the corresponding increase throughout most of this period in operative activities in the field all over the developing world. As a further illustration, UNDP currently operates in 174 countries and territories and runs 137 country and liaison offices.[78] This world-wide presence is often pointed to as one of the basic strengths of the UN system.[79] It can also, however, be regarded from a different angle.

Even if the resources available for development purposes within the UN system grew very rapidly in the 1970s and well into the 1980s (and in some cases have continued to grow in the 1990s), the overall volume remains modest in relation to other channels of development assistance. According to DAC (OECD) figures the total net flow of financial resources going through the UN amounted to 4.2 billion

Table 2.1 UN Staffing Pattern 1974–94 (non-headquarters
staff in brackets)

	1974	*1983*	*1994*
UN (including UNCTAD, UNDCP, UNEP etc)*	11,436 (7017)	16,205 (11,171)	14,710 (9056)
Funding organizations (UNDP, UNFPA, UNICEF)	2,151 (1313)	7,941 (6513)	11,287 (9059)
UNHCR, UNRWA, WFP	705 (175)	2673 (2980)	5028 (3647)
Large SAs (FAO, ILO, UNESCO, WHO, UNIDO)	17,273 (8705)	17,133 (8526)	16,551 (7619)

* Not comparable with other field categories due to inclusion of UNEP,
HABITAT etc as non-headquarters stations.

Source: Joint Inspection Unit: *Strengthening Field Representation of the United
Nations System*, Geneva 1997, JIU/REP/97/1.

dollars in 1995, which is considerably less than, for example, the
European Commission (5.3), not to speak of net grants by NGOs
which stand at 5.9 billion.[80] The World Bank expects to lend 22 billion
from the IDA alone over three years from 1997 onwards.[81] Another
way of putting the UN figures into a proper perspective is to compare
them with the large bilateral channels: France 6.4 billion dollars, Japan
10.4 and Germany 4.8. The Swedish and Norwegian bilateral ODA
programmes, the Swedish International Development Agency (SIDA)
and the Norwegian Agency for Development and Cooperation
(NORAD) are larger than the UNDP.[82]

As indicated above, the growth in resources channelled through
UN bodies has, for most of the time covered above, not reflected
ideological convergence among donors and recipients. It seems logical
to expect a reasonable level of agreement on the basic approach to
development as a prerequisite for large-scale cooperation between
North and South on multilateral assistance. In reality, it is hard to find
such compatibility between ideological consensus and the volume of
resources committed to development assistance under UN auspices.
In the 1960s and 1970s, governments of developing countries never
succeeded in winning wider support for their demands for redistribution of wealth (including binding ODA commitments) from the West,
nor for the new economic order. The acrimonious war of words over
development ideology between North and South did not, however,
seem to interfere with the rapid expansion of UN operative activities,
in particular in the 1970s when the 'new order' controversy reached

its peak. Despite the underlying disagreement on ideological funda-
mentals, developed and developing countries found a common interest
in multilateral development assistance through UN (and other)
channels. This situation continued through the 1980s when the
ideological front was dominated by the structural adaptation argument
– this time with the West on the offensive. The explanation for this
paradox – ideological strife yet practical cooperation – may lie outside
the scope of our analysis, in the cold war. Whatever the cause, the
consequence for the UN was constant organizational proliferation, to
which we can now turn.

THE CHALLENGE OF THE 1990S: SPRAWLING UN AND THE PROSPECTS FOR REFORM

We shall now attempt to summarize the current organizational set-up in
the UN system dealing with economic and social affairs. We shall also
seek explanations behind the system that has developed over the
decades. Against this backdrop, we shall discuss implications for UN
reform, briefly reviewing the main lines of thought that have been
presented since the 1960s under this label. It is not our intention to
describe the decades-old negotiations over UN reform, which could
easily fill a book in itself. We will confine ourselves to elaborating the
thrust of the arguments as advanced over the years and noting the main
results achieved. The purpose is to pave the ground for a forward-looking
discussion in Chapter 5; what can be learnt from the reform exercises
that will be of use for the UN in the years to come? Not the least: how
can approaches that have proved futile for decades be avoided?

Institutional Sprawl

As demonstrated above, the part of the UN system that deals with
economic and social development has expanded and diversified
constantly since the creation of the world organization. Much of the
institutional innovation took place in the 1940s and 1950s, but the
tendency to establish new organs has continued into the 1990s. For
example, instead of expanding the UNEP in the aftermath of the Rio
Conference, it was decided to set up another intergovernmental body
under ECOSOC, the Commission for Sustainable Development,
thereby adding to the organizational complexity of the system.[83]

As a result of five decades of institutional fragmentation the development system of the UN, broadly defined as those parts falling outside the remit of the Security Council and the International Court of Justice, today consists of the following main clusters:

- Sixteen specialized agencies (or comparative autonomous bodies affiliated with the UN system). Being formally independent, these have their own constitutions, governing bodies, secretariats and budgets, but they have a reporting obligation to ECOSOC, which in most cases is defined in a formal agreement. Without exception, these agencies carefully guard their financial, administrative and operational independence from the UN interference.
- Eleven functional commissions under ECOSOC, plus the World Food Council.[84] These are all intergovernmental bodies working within designated areas, some narrowly defined, like drug prevention, others very broad like social development, status of women and sustainable development. Member states are normally elected by ECOSOC, and the work of the commissions is serviced by the central UN secretariat in New York.
- Five regional commissions. These are made up primarily of UN member states in each part of the world. They have their own secretariat region by region, financed as part of the UN budget.
- Eleven funds and programmes (including UNCTAD) connected to both ECOSOC and the General Assembly. Many of them have their own governing structure and considerable funding outside the UN budget in the form of voluntary contributions. Executive heads are normally appointed by the Secretary-General of the UN.
- Two High Commissioners (for refugees and human rights). Both are appointed by the Secretary-General and operate within mandates given by the General Assembly. UNHCR has a separate intergovernmental Executive Committee overseeing her programmes, while the High Commissioner for Human Rights works closely with the Commission on Human Rights. Both Commissioners in practice report to the General Assembly through ECOSOC. UNHCR has built up a large, separately funded network of programmes and activities in recent years.
- Five research institutions, plus an infinite number of expert, ad hoc and intergovernmental committees. In 1985 the JIU pointed to more than 100 legally independent entities within the UN development system, including the specialized agencies. It added

that even 'this impressive list gives only an approximate idea of the real complexity'.[85]

Agenda Sprawling

It is not only on the institutional side that the UN has grown and expanded over the decades. The same trend is visible when it comes to issues, both inside and outside established intergovernmental bodies. In the General Assembly and ECOSOC old causes and concerns remain on the agenda from year to year, while new ones are added, bringing the total number of items for the annual General Assembly sessions up to 150. With such wide, repetitive agendas, discussions tend to be superficial, predictable and of little interest to the outside world. Similar ritualized proceedings took place with regular intervals at the UNCTAD conferences in the 1970s and early 1980s. Another telling example is the strategies for the four UN Development Decades, which were first formulated for the 1960s and continue into the 1990s. The last, fourth version of the so-called International Development Strategy is, in essence, an extensive repetition of unresolved grievances in North-South bargaining over the last generation.[86] To call this a 'strategy' is quite a stretch of imagination.[87]

The proliferation of issues and agendas is most vividly seen in the tendency to organize world conferences to deal with new or recurrent concerns. Some of them are ad hoc operations, others are repeated with regular intervals. Taken together, not counting the special sessions of the General Assembly, but including the UNCTAD gatherings, the UN has organized 38 world conferences over the last three decades, that is more than one a year.[88] In the first half of the 1990s, a record high number of 11 world conferences were held under UN auspices.

Another, related instrument for promoting issues on the UN agenda is the proclamation of UN 'decades' and commemorative days. As of 1998, we are in the midst of 14 UN sponsored decades, with objectives ranging from preventing natural disasters to eradicating poverty. The UN calendar now includes a total of 37 'annual days' (plus one week) dedicated to a wide variety of causes and concerns – protection of the ozone layer, press freedom, older persons, African industrialization and abolition of slavery, to name a few.

It is, indeed, very hard to imagine a topic on the comprehensive modern agenda of economic and social issues that has not been made a UN concern. The UN agenda is virtually without limits.

The Forces Behind the Sprawling of Agendas and Institutions

How can we account for this amazing upsurge in UN bodies, conferences, decades and the seemingly endless agenda? First, most issues
originate in one way or another from member states. They bring to
the UN arena the matters that they are for a variety of reasons unable
to deal with within a domestic context. These can be the result of
growing interdependence across borders, but also increasing power-
lessness on the part of governments. The UN agenda can, in any case,
serve as a useful substitute for national measures which governments
may be unable or unwilling to take. As member states are formally
equals, they all have the same sovereign right to articulate their
demands and aspirations in UN fora.

These formal rights to use the UN as a rostrum have been particularly attractive for governments of developing countries which have
come to dominate the UN agenda on economic and social policy from
the 1960s onwards. During the cold war, western governments out of
foreign policy considerations connived at both the rhetoric and the
demands for additions to the UN machinery (studies, funds,
programmes, committees, conferences). The western powers for long
periods left the UN development system as a playground for developing world politicians and diplomats under the safe assumption that
the outcomes would have little, if any, practical consequence.[89]

Second, following this formal equality there is little, if any,
adaptation or aggregation of concerns on the way from the national to
the international level. Every government is entitled to put its items
on the agenda, year after year if it so insists.[90] In a well-organized
national society there will be intermediate-level organizations, such as
political parties and interest groups (unions) that will filter demands
from the grassroots and adapt them to a form or a programme that
makes them amenable to negotiated decision-making, for example in
parliament.[91] In the UN, there are very few such filters, as all participants are sovereign equals and the basic decision-making rule is
consensus. This means that nobody can prevent a member state from
loading the common agenda with concerns that may be of little interest to anybody else. In the name of international understanding, such
issues may wander from arena to arena with no hope of finding a
solution, simply because nobody is in a position to stop it. UN veteran
Brian Urquhart put it bluntly in his autobiography:

'*Cockeyed ideas from member states or other sources begot studies which produced reports which set up staffs which produced more reports which were considered by meetings which asked for further reports and sometimes set up additional bureaucratic appendages which reported to future meetings. The process was self-perpetuating.*'[92]

Third, the organizational structure within the UN system is itself both a result and a cause of the proliferation of bodies and issues. As mentioned above, the sprawling of the UN began right after its creation. In spite of lofty pronouncements of 'coordination' from the very start, the system never had any 'centre' with coordinating powers. Urquhart observed as early as the late 1940s

'*the built-in diffuseness of the United Nations system. There was, and is, as little chance of the Secretary-General coordinating the autonomous specialised agencies of the UN system as King John of England had of bringing to heel the feudal barons... In the co-ordinating section (where he worked at the time) our self-serving documents papered over this ambivalence by being skilfully drafted to give the appearance of saying something while giving offence to no one.*'[93]

It appears that the latter skills have been well preserved within the organization. The similarity with feudal times is also a lasting feature.

The diffuseness that marked the system from the start has been well suited to serve the pervasive agendas of a rapidly increasing number of member states. A government can always find a forum receptive of its ideas or invent one, if necessary. This has stimulated and over time reinforced the institutional sprawl described above. Every intergovernmental body, conference, programme or agenda item develops a constituency of member states that ensures its further expansion. The lack of discipline has, thus, spilt right over into bureaucratic self-interest. To quote Urquhart's early observations again:

'*when bureaucracy becomes involved with more or less abstract ideas, a terrible elephantiasis often sets in, and this happened in the United Nations system... Few senior officials were able to resist the siren call of empire-building in their departments, and governments were insatiable in their thirst for jobs.*'[94]

So, if demands from member states are the impulses that set the machine going in different directions, organizational vested interests have become the engine. Over time, attention moves gradually from substance to procedure. 'The way in which the mill operates becomes much more important than the quality of the flour it produces', as the JIU observed in its 1985 report.

Fourth, the tendency towards fragmentation and the ritualistic, non-substantive, repetitive exercises at the intergovernmental level have undermined staff morale. 'Too many top-level officials, political appointments, rotten boroughs, and pointless programs had rendered the Secretariat fat and flabby over the years, and it clearly needed drastic rehabilitation', Urquhart noted in 1987.[95] Writing as an outside observer with Erskine Childers seven years later, he observed a 'cynicism virtually unknown in the early decades of the organiza-tion... Cronyism has become widely entrenched in secretariats.'[96] If these observations are correct, there is good reason to believe that bureaucracies of low quality, in itself a result of the sprawling process, in turn reinforces the same trends. If secretariats have lost touch with the real issues, they can at least perpetuate the processes that justify the existence of the organization.

The situation we have described above, was captured in the analy-sis presented by Maurice Bertrand, on behalf of the JIU:

> *'The extreme decentralization; the complexity of struc-tures of secretariats and intergovernmental and expert machinery; ...the difficulties of co-ordination; the undue importance of internal problems; ...the general medioc-rity of outputs and the inadequacy of the qualifications of too large proportion of the personnel; the unreal nature of the resolutions and documents describing programmes; and the patchwork nature of activities, all contribute to make a clear picture of what the United Nations System is and does impossible.'*[97]

Implications for UN Reform

As pointed out above, the anarchic nature of the UN system is almost as old as the world organization. Consequently, ever since the 1950s numerous efforts have been made to 'reform' the system, or, in UN jargon, to 'revitalize' and 'streamline' it. Leaving the euphemisms aside, we shall concentrate on four of the major proposals to introduce *structural reform* in the system. By this term we shall mean a) vertical consistency, that is the ability to formulate policy at macro level and implement it at micro in a consistent fashion, and b) horizontal coherence, which points to coordination across sectors and organizations, so that their policies and programmes compliment and support each other. We will briefly review how these issues have been tackled in four reform schemes since the 1960s: The Jackson report of 1969, the Gardner report (or the Group of 24) of 1975, the Bertrand report of 1985 and the Nordic UN Project of 1991. Table 2.2 summarizes the major features of each of these reform schemes. At the end of this chapter we will return to the most recent reform effort, Secretary-General Kofi Annan's 'Renewing the United Nations' of 1997. We are aware that this somewhat arbitrary selection excludes important reform proposals, but are still convinced that our list is fairly representative for the discussion that has taken place over the last 30 years. As mentioned above, we have no ambition of analysing the intricacies of UN reform *proceedings*. We will simply take note of the results achieved over the decades, which is what we need as background in search for proposals for change in Chapter 5.

The Jackson Report

In his landmark report, the so-called 'Capacity Study' referred to above, Sir Robert Jackson underlined the chaotic state of affairs: 'For many years, I have looked for the "brain" which guides the policies and operations of the UN development system. The search has been in vain. Its absence may well be the greatest constraint of all on capacity. Without it, the future evolution of the UN development system could easily repeat the history of the dinosaur' (p13). His prescription for change is to develop 'a strong central co-ordinating organisation' (piv), ideally a single IDA. In practice, he settled for a scheme he considered more realistic given the history of the system by the late 1960s. He envisaged ECOSOC, in the longer run, as a 'one-world parliament' with powers to review and approve the policies of the specialized agencies, which would retreat to their original mandates as 'technical bodies' (p53). This kind of centralization would also require drastic changes in the central UN bureaucracy. For this purpose Jackson proposed a UN director-general equal in rank to the Secretary-General.

On the operational side, the key to coordination would be a greatly strengthened UNDP based on central funding, joint country programmes and a cooperation cycle that 'gathers together in one

comprehensive and integrated pattern all the interdependent
processes which together constitute the development co-operation of
the UN development system' (p25). UNDP would thus become 'the
hub of the UN development system' (p34) with a clearly defined
role vis-à-vis the World Bank. The latter was foreseen to become 'the
chief arm of the UN system in the field of capital investment, while
UNDP should perform the same function for basic technical cooperation and pre-investment' (p 21). Given the power of the purse,
underpinned by a high quality professional corps of experts devoted
to a UN career, the UNDP should be able to take on this leading role,
provided there is sufficient donor support.

The Gardner Report

In 1975 the so-called Group of 24 consisting of government experts
presented its report to the General Assembly, following broadly along
the lines drawn up by Jackson. Again, the main thrust was on
improved central management of the unwieldy system. A new UN
Development Authority (UNDA) should merge all operational units
of the UN proper (except UNICEF) and be governed by a board at
ministerial level. A new top administrator, the Director-General for
development, should be second only to the Secretary-General.
ECOSOC should dissolve most of its subsidiary organs and instead
develop a system of small negotiating groups where representatives of
donor and recipient governments could resolve their differences
behind closed doors under the direction of chairmen working full
time. The group also made sweeping suggestions for streamlining the
'feudal' parts of the system: UNCTAD should be abolished, UNEP
merged with UNDA and the specialized agencies redirected to their
original standard-setting functions.[98]

The Bertrand Report

The report produced by Maurice Bertrand on behalf of the JIU in
1985 was even more critical of the gaps between words and deeds
than Jackson had been. It concluded that the comprehensive efforts at
coordination instituted since the late 1970s had

> *'produced no results..."Joint planning" has remained
> wishful thinking... "country programming and field co-
> ordination" have never been anything more than
> meaningless terms... The notion of an "integrated*

approach to development" … has remained for the United Nations System an empty formula.'[99]

As for recommendations, Bertrand followed the path of his predecessors: ECOSOC having been 'drained of all content' after membership was expanded from 27 to 54 in 1973, should be replaced by an Economic Security Council consisting of the largest countries in terms of economy and population and a limited geographical representation. According to Bertrand, 23 members would do.

As for operational coordination he suggested 'a single, interdisciplinary development agency or enterprise responsible at once for health, agriculture, industry, education etc'.[100] In other words 'a total reconversion of all the operational structures … such as UNDP, WFP, UNFPA, UNICEF etc'.[101] This new enterprise should have integrated operations and offices at regional and sub-regional level.

The Nordic UN Project

In 1991 the Nordic governments jointly presented their analysis and recommendations for UN reform, which also focused on governance of operations and coordination across the system. To improve high level interest and participation in policy-making at the macro level the idea of an International Development Council was floated, in rather general terms. Several arguments in favour of a 'unified structure' for UN operational activities were referred, such as economies of scale, consolidated resources (of 3–4 billion dollars) and consolidated financial management.[102] As for governance, executive bodies of operational organizations should limit membership to around 20 states in order to enhance effective decision-making. UNDP should be strengthened, in particular at country level. The specialized agencies should avoid 'overextention' and concentrate on their normative functions.[103]

Common Elements

These reform proposals, with a time span of 22 years, have one common denominator – the search for order in an anarchic system. Whether it is called a brain (Jackson), a development authority (Gardner), a single enterprise (Bertrand) or a unified structure (Nordics) the ambition is the same; to inject formal hierarchy and thereby produce both vertical consistency and horizontal coherence. The basic message rings through the decades: a centre must be estab-

Table 2.2 *Reform Schemes: Major Features*

Report	Date	Economic policy-making	Operations	Secretariat	Specialized agencies
Jackson	1969	ECOSOC 'parliament' International Development Authority	Central funding through UNDP	UN Director-General equal to Secretary-General	Integrated at country level
Gardner (Group of 24)	1975	Small negotiating groups under ECOSOC	All merged under UN Development Authority	Director-General for development cooperation	Back to original functions, phase out UNCTAD
Bertrand (JIU)	1985	Economic Security Council: 23 members	Single agency and enterprise		Subordinate to agency
Nordic UN Project	1991	International Development Council	'Unified structure'	One official in charge of economic matters	'Centres of excellence'

lished with formal powers to impose policy decisions downwards from top to bottom and enforce a specified division of labour among the competing units in the system.

It follows from the account we have given above, that almost three decades of reform discussion, much of it inspired by these proposals, has produced meagre results. Notwithstanding some reshuffling in ECOSOC subsidiaries and a certain rationalization of decision-making in funds and programmes, the basic structure has survived despite devastating criticism. The fundamental features of the system remain intact. The proliferation, fragmentation and complexity that was observed a generation ago by Urquhart and Jackson and confirmed by Bertrand have rolled on by its own force. Jackson's warning of a machine beyond control seems no less relevant today than it was almost 30 years ago.

A confirmation that the current structure is outdated was given in the report of the Independent Commission on Global Governance. On the role of ECOSOC, purportedly the very centre of UN coordination and policy-making, it concludes briskly that the body 'has not worked' and therefore should be, not reformed, but wound up and replaced by an Economic Security Council. This latter body should have no more members than the Security Council itself.[104]

In our judgement, the reform proposals referred to above and others along similar lines have all fallen victims to the centrifugal forces that pervade the entire UN development system, at two levels – the political and the interorganizational. As noted above, the system was fragmented from the outset. What we need to explain is therefore why further proliferation was allowed, indeed stimulated, and why repeated attempts to establish a system with clearer lines of command and authority have consistently failed.

Political Conflict

A fundamental cause of fragmentation of the UN development system and especially the inability to establish an authoritative centre for decision-making is the fact that governments in North and South have so far not been able to agree on the overall objectives to be pursued by the world organization.[105] Much of the bargaining and rhetoric over 'reform' and 'revitalization', not to speak of 'streamlining', is diplomatic shadow boxing that is made meaningless by the underlying political divide between the West and the developing world.[106] As we have pointed out earlier, the two camps have since the 1970s pursued agendas that are for a large part irreconcilable. It is true that much has changed since the late 1980s and that the meta-ideological controversy over the NIEO now belongs to history. However, an atmosphere of mutual distrust remains with one side fearing a closedown of significant parts of the world organization, the other suspecting economic extortion by the majority if the UN is given real powers in the world economy.

The level of North/South conflict is probably intensified by the virtual independence of many developing world UN delegates in New York and Geneva from their constituencies at home. A culture of confrontation is nurtured that may not reflect the national interest of the respective developing countries. However, this is not only a legacy of a heated political debate, but also a reflection of real conflicts of interest: developing world governments, in particular the poorest majority in the Group of 77, see the UN primarily as a forum in which economic concessions can be won and as a stepping stone to improve their position in economic policy-making in the world. The major western powers, on the contrary, see no interest in giving the UN majority more influence over the money they use for development assistance and in the most important bodies dealing with economic issues, such as the World Bank, the IMF and the Group of 77. Given this stalemate that has not seen much change over the last three decades, it is not surprising that the two sides have not been able to agree on an institutional structure conducive to effective decision-making. Whatever else 'effectiveness' might be taken to mean, it must somehow be related to a goal or a set of agreed objectives which remain elusive in the UN development context.[107]

Interorganizational Conflict

Another permanent feature of UN politics, though not as visible as the North–South cleavage, is the turf fight among the operative agencies, often compared with medieval feudalism (cf. the quote from Urquhart above). Jackson at an early stage underlined the resistance to coordination or centralization that was bound to come from the individual agencies – the 'principalities' of the system.[108] Problems are aggravated by the tendency illuminated by Bertrand for governments to pay scant attention to the output from the various organizations, while being more interested in putting their own candidates, often with questionable qualifications, in the top posts.[109]

Following decades of fragmentation and empire-building by individual organizations, as illustrated by Righter,[110] the bureaucratic vested interests in favour of institutional status quo and against any attempt to centralize authority are stronger than ever. Jönsson has pointed out the difficulties in coordinating international secretariats working in the field of aid, because of institutional jealousy. He recommends informal coordination, since formal hierarchy seems to lie beyond reach for both governments and agencies involved.[111]

Effectiveness and Functions

In Chapter 1, we underlined the critical links between the functions performed by MDIs and their organizational structure. Agencies with operative functions require effective decision-making bodies based on representation, not universal participation. They also need a formal hierarchy with clearly defined powers and responsibility among units at different levels and, most importantly, central control over the purse.

The other kind of MDI, preoccupied primarily with setting norms and standards, thrives from universal participation and broad processes focused on mutual understanding and learning. It does not need formal ordering of operative units as its main outcome is consensus on action to be taken by governments and other actors. The norm setting MDI is more like an academic colloquium than a business enterprise or a national bureaucracy.

In this chapter, we have described how the UN development system, from the outset lacking a clearly defined centre, soon proliferated in different directions to become a conglomerate of intergovernmental bodies, autonomous agencies and semi-independent secretariats which is unique in modern history. There is no political creature that can be compared with the UN development system. It bears no resemblance to the multinational company, the colonial empires or the modern nation state, the main difference being that all of these 'political animals' have one thing in common – a brain that gives direction and orders to the constituent parts. Had the UN confined itself to normsetting functions, this would not have been a problem. When the purpose is to include as many stakeholders as possible in an educative process, the absence of a central command is an asset, not a liability. If, however, the ambition is to move from decisions on general policy to mobilizing funds, coordinating inputs and implementing projects in the field, then a formal and effective decision-making centre is a sine qua non. Large parts of the UN development system have moved in that very direction while the governing structure has not followed suit. Despite numerous attempts to the opposite, the sprawling of the system continues with new bodies, new funds and new items on the agenda.

We can conclude, then, that a growing mismatch has developed over the decades between the governing structure of the UN and the bulk of functions that it is aiming to fulfil. While its comparative advantage as an organization comes with the universal and representative nature of the way it runs its business, UN activities have increasingly moved to operative functions where these features are liabilities rather than advantages.

UN reform, as we have described it above, is an attempt to combine the participatory organization based on universality and formal equality with the requirements of operative effectiveness. This puts enormous strain on the ability to produce both vertical consistency and horizontal coherence. At least four levels of decision-making and implementation have to be carefully coordinated, both 'downwards' and 'sideways':

• establishing overall political objectives and general strategies, often in the General Assembly or in a world conference;

- setting priorities within this framework, eg in a specialized agency or a UN programme;
- giving direction to executive managers, for example at a regional or country level including allocation of funds (operational governance);
- taking decisions on the ground (executive management).[112]

The more diversified the system in terms of new, disconnected units and the more operative tasks it takes on the more difficult this coordination from general decisions to practical implementation. As we have noted above, the major reform proposals, with very few exceptions, have tried to solve this problem by devising an authoritative centre. Invariably, they have failed to produce changes of significance because this approach runs against the political and bureaucratic determinants of the system – the insistence on member state equality, the lack of agreement among governments and the vested interests of bureaucracies. UN reformers since the late 1960s have failed not because their analysis was misconceived or their ideas inappropriate, but because they have tried to reconcile irreconcilable parts. The issue then becomes; is UN reform like trying to square the circle? With this question in mind, we shall briefly review the latest attempt at broad scale restructuring.

'Renewing the United Nations'

In July 1997, Secretary-General Kofi Annan presented 'the most extensive and far-reaching reforms in the fifty-two year history of (the) organisation'.[113] For our purposes the most important points can be summarized as follows:

The Secretary-General proposed a sweeping reorganization of the central UN secretariat with executive committees for each sector, a Senior Management Group, akin to a UN cabinet, and a new post as Deputy Secretary-General.

As for the intergovernmental machinery, his proposal was much more modest: 'The Economic and Social Council needs to be positioned to play more effectively the role envisaged for it in the Charter. In the longer term, fundamental rethinking of the role of the Council may be required...'[114] As for the regional commissions, it was merely recommended that ECOSOC 'initiate a general review'.[115] The Secretary-General underlined that his reform efforts focused on 'the Organisation itself that is, on the United Nations Secretariat, programmes and funds'.[116] The critical issue of system-wide coordination, including also the specialized agencies was left aside with the reminder that 'if the objectives of the United Nations are to be fully realised, a much greater degree of concerted will and co-ordinated action is required among the system as a whole'.[117] By working closely with the executive heads of the entire system through the ACC, the Secretary-General intends to 'rationalise the division of labour within existing structures' in the system.[118]

On the controversial question of coordinating UN development activities, the Secretary-General sought to strike a balance between order and diversity: 'The reform process is designed to maintain and reinforce the distinctive nature of these entities while seeking to facilitate their functioning in a more unified, co-operative and coherent framework as members of the UN family.'[119] In more concrete terms, he proposed the designation of a UN Development Group, consisting of the UNDP, UNICEF and UNFPA with ad hoc participation of other organizations when appropriate. The Group will provide 'concerted directives' to the country level, where a Resident Coordinator appointed by the Secretary-General will act as leader of the UN team.[120] As for funding, however, 'each of these funds and programmes will continue to be clearly identifiable ... full accountability for funds raised will remain vested in the individual entities'.[121] This financial independence will necessarily constrain the coordination efforts at both headquarters and country level.

Of particular interest to us is the Secretary-General's view of UN relations with the World Bank:

> '*The movement of the Bank into areas similar to those hitherto in the purview of the United Nations will bring additional resources to bear on similar objectives. However, this brings added urgency to the task of ensuring an appropriate distribution of responsibilities between the World Bank Group and the United Nations for the benefit of the programme countries. This should take the form of* functional rationalisation *in a complementary and co-operative manner between the work of the United Nations and the World Bank ... (t)his rationalization of functional roles and mandates will require support and endorsement of member states of the World Bank ... (g)overnments play an important role of bringing the United Nations and the World Bank together not just at the intergovernmental level, but at the country level as well.*'[122]

In short, the Secretary-General's approach seems to be based on the assumption that UN reform is primarily a question of management; reshuffling key elements in the secretariat, establishing new coordinating mechanisms (like the UN Development Group) and enforcing 'functional rationalization' on the individual entities. Consequently, the problem of overlap between the UN and the Bank can and should be solved, in his view, by a formalized division of labour based on intergovernmental decisions in the respective governing bodies and implemented from the top to the country level. In Chapter 4, we shall examine whether this approach to reform of the multilateral development system is viable.

Chapter 3

The World Bank from Past to Present

INTRODUCTION

Even if in a far stronger position than the UN, the World Bank is also facing a decisive crossroads. Critics from different quarters question its very existence. Environmental and anti-poverty advocacy groups have claimed that 50 years are enough, and want the Bank closed down. Jesse Helms, chairman of the US Senate's Foreign Relations Committee, although for different reasons, is not far from joining the bandwagon. After numbers of assessments citing decreasing loan performance, the heat is on its current president, James Wolfensohn, to streamline and restructure the organization. Private capital threatens to crowd out the World Bank and the IFC, its private sector affiliate, from their main markets in Asia and Latin America. To many, the increasing flow of private finance to these regions serves to question what remains for the Bank to do, as it may soon find itself competing with rather than facilitating private investment. Better then to focus on environmental protection and poverty reduction, where markets fail to get things right. But is the World Bank, which still is, basically, a bank, the right place to start when the task in question is poverty reduction on a global scale?

In order to understand the potential and limitations of the World Bank we first have to look at how it has coped with the challenges of the past. In particular, we will try to come to grips with how its governing structure and organizational design have influenced its problem-solving capacity. Given our main research question, a logical point of analysis is how the Bank has coped with the dilemma between the demand to produce tangible results on one hand, and the demand for participation, openness and equality on the other. An important dimension of success in these regards is adaptation to rapidly changing external demands, which have challenged the Bank to continuously move into new problem areas. As we will see below, many of these bear little resemblance to the functions for which the Bank was created.

The structure of this chapter is based on six different chronological phases:[1] The first covers the years from 1944 to 1948 where the International Bank for Reconstruction (IBRD) activities were geared towards reconstruction projects in Europe. The next phase is characterized by geographical expansion out of Europe to Japan, Australia and developing countries. The third phase (1958–68) marks the start of the Bank as a development agency in addition to its traditional banking activities with the creation of the IDA and transfer of concessional finance. The fourth phase (1968–80) includes the reign of Robert McNamara as president of the Bank, a radical growth in lending volume and increased attention to poverty alleviation and human resources as contrasted to the previous focus on infrastructure. The fifth phase (1980–90) is the period of increased attention to the policy environment of the projects and a shift towards policy-based lending. Finally, the sixth phase (1990 to the present) is a period of increased strains on project quality, harsh criticism from the outside and continuous efforts to cope with these challenges both politically and organizationally.

HOW THE WORLD BANK CAME INTO BEING

As with the UN, expectations and demands on the emerging new multilateral lending institution were formed in a unique context. On one hand a devastating war was raging, and allied victory was by no means ensured. On the other hand expectations were great for the coming post-war world order, as it seemed only natural for policy-makers to unite around the 'Never Again!' credo: never again should the conditions of the two previous decades be allowed to repeat themselves, with their mass employment, protectionist beggar-thy-neighbour policies, competitive currency devaluations, deflation, collapse of commodity prices and stock exchange crashes.[2] The war was a sufficiently traumatic event to shake and dislodge previous assumptions and force those planning the post-war world to start thinking afresh. According to Hans Singer, among the more radical proposals were:

- a world currency, based on the average price of 30 primary commodities (including gold and oil) which would thus have become automatically stabilized;
- a World Central Bank which would provide unconditional liquidity to balance-of-payment-deficit countries to maintain full employment;
- the penalization of balance-of-payment-surplus countries by means of an international tax on these surpluses (at the rate of 1 per cent a month).[3]

Motivations for launching the Bank were, however, disparate. Importantly, US policy-makers knew that any proposed scheme would have to be put before a sceptical Congress. Right up to the 1944 Bretton Woods conference, it was not at all clear that proposals to launch the Bank would come off the ground. To charge the IMF with the task of guarding the post-war world's monetary matters so as to avoid the pre-war currency chaos and stock exchange crashes provided the key rationale for summoning so many senior policy-makers to Bretton Woods.[4] However, reconstruction of war-torn societies was also, understandably, high on the agenda. Strategic doubts about mandate notwithstanding, governments agreed to give the concept of an IBRD a fair chance.

The dominance of the US is crucial to understand the genesis and early developments of the World Bank. Almost all preparatory work was done within the US government. The first time US policy-makers seriously involved other countries in their thinking was through a Secretary of the Treasury Henry Morgenthau memorandum in November 1943 entitled 'Preliminary Draft Outline of a Proposal for a United Nations Bank for Reconstruction and Development'. The proposal got a chilly welcome among more adventurous British policy-makers; one of whom who saw it as *'stripped, as it had long since been, of all the exciting features, this document was an uninspiring one. The Bank had been dressed, with an eye to Congress, to look as orthodox as possible.'*[5] US policy-makers got so little response on the Bank idea that they were tempted to drop the whole thing from the agenda of the preparatory meeting for Bretton Woods in early 1944. On their way by boat from London to Atlantic City, however, the British and a range of allies (residing, due to the war, in the UK capital) drafted statements that were so clearly in favour of a reconstruction bank that they convinced the US treasury to keep the proposal floating.

So what kind of institution was created, finally, at Bretton Woods? It is worth quoting the summary provided by Brookings Institution historians Mason and Asher:

> '...Its initial, if not primary function, was the financing of reconstruction and only afterward of development; its capital subscriptions were relatively small, but its guarantee fund was intended to be large. Its dependence for funds therefore was mainly on private investors, which underlined the importance of establishing its position on capital markets; and the consent of the concerned government was required to raise funds in particular markets. The Bank was intended to operate mainly by guaranteeing private investors against loss, but it could also lend directly and participate in private loans. It was to lend primarily for specific projects and ordinarily only for the financing of foreign exchange costs; its loans were not to be tied to procurement in any particular countries, and the proceeds of the loans were to be used with due attention to considerations of economy and efficiency. Finally, its loans were to be made solely on the basis of economic considerations.'[6]

What came out of Bretton Woods was a conservative organization in terms of the tasks to be performed, far more conservative than its framers had initially intended. Notwithstanding the participation of more than 25 countries at its inaugural meeting, the international status of the emerging Bank was also in many ways limited. It is probably fair to view the 1944 Bretton Woods creation as first American, second Anglo-Saxon and only third international. The US supplied most of its loanable funds and was by far the predominant market for Bank securities. Even if the British and others argued that the Bank's location should not necessarily be in the US, or at least that location should be viewed in relation to that of the UN headquarters, given the weak political and economic position of war-torn European countries, any alternative suggestions (to US location) were simply non-starters.

THE EMERGING GOVERNING STRUCTURE AND WORLD BANK FUNCTIONS

As indicated in Chapter 1, our definition of governing structure covers the formal structure in the charter or articles of an organization, and the decision-making pattern that has become standard practice accepted by the relevant government parties. It includes, in other words, both the formal rules and procedures and the (informal) modus operandi for reaching and implementing decisions in practice. Below, we will elaborate briefly on formal and informal dimensions of the governing structure established 50 years ago, and make some initial observations as to implications for the emerging pattern of Bank functions.

Formal Structure of Decision-Making

The US dominated, as shown above, the terms under which both the IMF and the World Bank were set up. Plans for the IMF were far more advanced when delegates met at Bretton Woods, and important aspects of the IMF's Articles of Agreement were just copied for the Bank. The boards of governors of both came to consist of one governor and one alternate appointed by each member country, meeting once a year in parallel IMF/World Bank sessions. All powers necessary to the daily operation of the Bank were delegated to the executive directors, but only the board of governors was given the authority to admit new members, increase or decrease the capital stock of the Bank, suspend a member and determine the remuneration of directors.

The Articles of Agreement for the Bank provided initially for 12 executive directors, of whom five were to come from the countries having the largest number of shares, and the remaining seven elected by all the governors other than those appointed by the five 'core' members.[7] The executive directors were expected to function in continuous session at the principal office of the Bank. Article V, section 3, provided that 'a) each member shall have two hundred fifty votes plus one additional vote for each share of stock held,' and 'b) except as otherwise specifically provided, all matters before the Bank shall be decided by a majority of the votes cast'.[8] Subscriptions to the capital of the Bank, which determined voting power, were in effect set by IMF quotas. But while all countries wanted large IMF quotas (since the size determined the volume of drawing rights), the less developed countries pressed for lower subscriptions to the Bank, recognizing that their opportunity to borrow would be independent of their capital contribution. The US agreed to fill the ensuing gap, providing them with a voting power of more than 35 per cent (35.1 per cent in 1947). Following additions of new member states and related increase in capital subscriptions, the US share of the total vote was reduced to around 25 per cent by 1970, and decreased gradually to 17 per cent by 1995 (see Table 3.1).

Table 3.1 *Voting Power of World Bank Part 1 (OECD)*
Members, 1947–95

Number and power	1947	1955	1965	1975	1985	1995
Countries	44	56	102	125	149	178
Board members	12	16	20	20	21	24
Voting power						
G-7	61.7	60.0	54.9	51.3	49.7	43.3
USA	35.1	30.7	26.3	22.7	19.7	17.0
OECD	70.0	71.9	67.6	64.7	63.6	57.5

Source: The World Bank/The Brookings Institution, 1997.

The Role of the Bank President

The Bank president was to be the chief officer 'responsible for the organization, appointment and dismissal of the office and staff, subject to the general control of the executive directors'.[9] The UK delegation, led by Lord Keynes, and many other governments, strongly preferred the executive directors, like the Bank staff, to consider themselves as international civil servants with an allegiance only to the Bank. Such a view, however, was completely unacceptable to the US government, who wanted its representative on the board of directors to be subject to close governmental control. Due to its hegemonic position at the time in almost all respects, the US position prevailed in the early, evolutionary years. Controversy over this issue ensued for five years after Bretton Woods, however, with two presidents resigning at least partly in protest against undue external (US government) interference in 'internal bank affairs'. As we will see later, though, the president and his senior staff soon managed to establish themselves in a strong and quite independent position. This was not least due to the selection of presidents whose management plans and world views were fully shared by the US government (valid particularly from Eugene Black's entry into the president's office in 1949, partly since he was the former US executive director to the Bank).

Recruitment Principles

Contrary to what applied in most (other) UN agencies, the World Bank president met no geographical restrictions when setting out to recruit staff to the new organization. While discussing the IMF Articles of Agreement at Bretton Woods, India pressed for the principle that in recruiting staff, 'due regard shall be paid to the fair representation of the nationals of member countries'. This proposal was rejected in favour of the following text that came to apply for both the Fund and the Bank: 'In appointing the officers and staff the President shall, subject to the paramount importance of securing the highest standards of efficiency and of technical competence, pay due regard to the importance of recruiting personnel on as wide a geographical basis as possible.'[10] According to Mason and Asher, writing in the early 1970s, these discretionary powers of the president 'without question had a great deal to do with the favourable reputation of both the Bank and the Fund as efficient institutions'.

In one of the few departures from IMF regulations, Article V, section 6 provides for an advisory council 'selected by the Board of Governors including representatives of banking, commercial, industrial, labour and industrial interests...'. It was through this medium that other parts of the UN system, which would be consulted in appointing members of the council, hoped to exercise some degree of influence on Bank policy. Although a distinguished group was appointed initially, the council quickly fell into disuse and was never revived, despite clear provisions in the charter that 'it should meet annually and on such other occasions as the Bank may request'. Another practice that made the Bank stand out from the UN was the decision to make English its single working language, a decision that 'saved money and enormously expedited the conduct of business'. Protests from French and Spanish language regions led to some modifications, but the 'English only' policy has all since ruled in Bank operations. As established, it was one of many initial expressions of the Bank as an effectiveness-geared operational body as compared to a UN-type political organizations.

Towards a Highly Centralized Institution

Another provision that was not implemented, was the authorization of the Bank through Article V, section 9, to establish agencies or branch offices in any member country, and in section 10 to set up regional offices to be advised by representative regional councils. Thus the founding fathers clearly gave the Bank the option to become a decentralized agency, with lending operations based in the respective regions. This never did materialize, however, as the Bank grew up to become a very centralized organization, with all important decisions being taken in Washington. Interestingly, in contrast, a major thrust of President Wolfensohn's reform package is decentralization, with a range of country offices already testing out the vision of a more decentralized World Bank.

Initial Limitations to Political Leverage

Finally, another important contrast to the IMF's charter was that the Bank was not authorized to collect information from member states. While the IMF was clearly designed as a regulatory agency, the only leverage given to the World Bank in this respect as linked to specific loans – just as any other bank requiring information to ensure loan security. Such lack of authority to elicit information from non-borrowing members amply illustrates the clearly limited focus on project-specific lending that the Bank was originally designed for. This limitation soon created problems in line with increased demand on the Bank to take on broader development-related tasks in developing countries. For instance, in his 1967 manuscript 'Negotiation History of the Bank', Henry J. Bitterman pointed out that 'this problem arose when the Bank began systematically to collect data on the indebtedness of member countries and the provision of information by the creditor countries had to be arranged on a purely voluntary basis'.[11]

This illustrates the emerging tension between carefully delimited project lending based on strict economic criteria on one hand, and the wider role in terms of policy influence in poorer countries on the other. On paper, the 'economics only' rule was clear enough, as brought out in Article IV, section 10:

> *'The bank and its officers shall not interfere in the political affairs of any member; nor shall they be influenced in their decisions by the political characteristics of the*

member or members concerned. Only economic considerations shall be relevant to their decisions, *and these*
considerations shall be weighed impartially.'[12]

It soon became clear, however that it was more difficult than the
founding fathers may have realized to draw very distinct lines
between economic and political considerations. One thing was the
influence wielded from the very start through (relatively uncontroversial) conditions linked to individual loan agreements. More
difficult to defend as 'pure economics' was the refusal, throughout
most of the early Bank history, to lend to manufacturing enterprises
in the public sector on the grounds that they were unlikely to be
managed efficiently. And with the pressure on the Bank to use its
growing leverage to induce or reward good economic performance,
and punish a bad one, the political dimension to World Bank operations was revealed ever more clearly.

A RECONSTRUCTION BANK (1944–48)

External Environments and Pressures

Like the UN, expectations for what the Bank was supposed to do
crashed with reality – although for somewhat different reasons. As
the initial name of the Bank reads, post-war reconstruction was
considered a main business area for the new world body. Much of the
early planning and business development focused around how to play
an important role in this field. Six of the nine loan applications
received by the end of April 1947 were for European reconstruction,
in Czechoslovakia, Denmark, France, Luxembourg, The Netherlands
and Poland. Its first loan, in the order of US$250 million, was in this
category and went to France in 1947. In real terms, this remains the
largest single loan (worth $2.5 billion at 1994 prices). Other recon-
struction loans followed to The Netherlands, Denmark and
Luxembourg, together matching the size of the French loan.

These reconstruction loans contradicted one of the basic initial
policies, namely to lend to individual projects only. Such flexibility
and pragmatism vis-à-vis 'the demands of the day' was a sign of things
to come, particularly from the 1970s and onwards. The love affair
with programme-type reconstruction loans soon ended, however. This
was not primarily due to objections over how the Bank handled the
loans, but to external forces that also turned UN prospects upside

down. It soon became clear that there was not the political will to entrust fragile multilateral bodies with the task of rebuilding Europe. The size of this task had been vastly underestimated, and the emerging cold war made full US control with European reconstruction a must. Add to this that the world of the time was far more restricted to traditional bilateral affairs than the Bretton Woods participants seemed to acknowledge. Particularly the IMF but also the World Bank long fought an up hill battle due to general malfunctioning of European economies and lack of US/European currency convertibility. Hence, Bank efforts were dwarfed by US Marshall Plan Assistance, through which a massive $13 billion was disbursed from 1948 onwards.

A Slow and Difficult Start-Up Period

In most respects, and partly because of the external factors just touched on, the World Bank came off to a slow start. It opened its doors for business on 25 June 1946. Most observers viewed the early Bank years as inauspicious, with few signs of the enthusiasm at the close of the Bretton Woods meeting back in 1944. Mason and Asher (1973) probably epitomizes widely held judgements in stating that:

> 'the contrast between the fledgling organisation that was testing its wings and striving to get off the ground during the last half of the 1940s and the World Bank of today (around 1970) – self-confident, esteemed, active, and influential – could hardly be greater'.[13]

The Bretton Woods rhetoric notwithstanding, creating new global financial institutions proved an up hill battle indeed. Even if serious efforts went into the two years of preparation following Bretton Woods, the bank that opened its doors in the summer of 1946 was a highly vulnerable creature, still grappling with the most fundamental issues of mandate, governing structure and organizational design. One illustration of this is that it proved difficult to recruit the first Bank president, as a number of candidates reportedly turned down the offer. After Eugene Meyer took office in June 1946, there were many expressions of frustration from the Bank's early management that the demand for reconstruction loans came far too early, and implied too large sums, for the Bank to be able to handle them properly. And already in early 1947, he was leaving a Bank that was, reportedly, at its lowest ebb, its reputation considerably tarnished, its accomplishments nil, and its problems mounting because of the worsening economic situation of western Europe. Far more so than one had realized, launching the World Bank (and the IMF) meant building a structure for international economic cooperation almost from scratch. Practical problems stemmed from the fact that currencies were not convertible. This, together with the precarious state of most post-war economies, required that almost all attention be fixed on winning the confidence of the finance community. At the same time, US domination became close to complete, which was not easy to live with for a president of a presumably global institution.

The Battle Between Management and their Political Masters

1949 is often seen as a watershed year for the Bank. It was not until then that a workable balance was created between the power of the president on one hand, and that of the appointed governors on the other. Even if the rationale for their early abdication was mixed, they grew increasingly impatient with what they saw as US dominance and meddling in internal Bank affairs. Eugene Meyer had a particularly hard time. Appointed in June 1946, he spent much of his time battling with the board for leadership of the organization. His relationship with the executive directors simply did not work, prodding him to resign after less than one year at the helm of the Bank. In February 1947, John J McCloy was elected as the new president, on the condition that he had full support from his political masters (he had previously turned down offers to run the Bank), and their acceptance of a far more independent role of the management vis-à-vis the directors. A report from an informal meeting on the subject brings out the salience of this issue very clearly:

> 'There had been a difference of opinion from the beginning in the Bank as to the role of management and the role of directors... It was understood in conversations with McCloy that the management would actually manage the institution and the directors would play the usual role of general supervision, without interference in the conduct of the business. When we got down there (from New York to Washington), there was still some hesitation on the part of some of the directors to make

> *that position perfectly clear. So we listened to the discus-*
> *sions, and then McCloy finally said that the only*
> *condition under which he felt it was possible to handle*
> *the situation would be a clear declaration as to the power*
> *of the management to manage, that if the directors were*
> *not fully in agreement with that, we would go on back to*
> *New York that afternoon.'*[14]

Importantly, the self-confident and ambitious US executive director, Emilio Collado, was removed in this process and replaced by Eugene Black, who happened to know McCloy from before. With a more harmonious relation between the president and the US director, prospects looked better. It was not full harmony, though, as the tough and independent profile of McCloy obtained, according to observers of the time, only a grudging cooperation from the other executive directors. His appointed deputy, Robert L Garner, was even tougher with the political masters, and it was felt necessary to remind him from time to time that 'the same Articles of Agreement which did not create his position did create the Board's'. McCloy stayed with the Bank for just over two years, a period in which his relations with the executive directors apart from the US one gradually deteriorated. Upon his resignation, Eugene Black, who had served as US executive director under McCloy, was asked to take his job, which he seemed to be happy to do. Black came to run the Bank for more than 13 years. One of the reasons often given for his undoubtable success was that he finally managed to establish a constructive balance between a strong and independent management on one hand, and a group of executive directors who followed Bank activities closely but allowed the president to preside over the rapidly growing organization.

Trying to Overcome Wall Street Scepticism

A key criterion for the selection of presidents, was their ability to mobilize wide support in the international financial community. All three presidents of this early period, as well as their deputies, satisfied this criterion, as their esteem in the important circles was generally good. There is no doubt, however, that the high 'independent banking profile' (at the expense of executive directors) of McCloy from 1947 and Black from 1949 was more positively received at Wall Street than Meyer's early efforts to strike a balance between commercial and polit- ical concerns. For instance, a columnist writing in the *Financial Times* welcomed the McCloy reign from 1947, whom he believed would have far less patience with 'these chatterers who have nothing to do but to sit around and give copious amateur advice'. Observers at the time saw US concerns with political control behind the system of executive directors working in almost continuous session. Many found this active role of the board to create huge administrative problems.

In hindsight, one may see these extremely negative private sector reactions to the public dimensions of the World Bank's mandate as rather exotic. However, the rather messy start of Bank operations made the financial community quite confused as to what kind of creature the World Bank was meant to be. Therefore, agreeing on the basic mission and organizational structure, and then conveying that message squarely to the US bank and financing sector, was a fundamental challenge to the first Bank presidents. By 1946 as it is today, the chief source of the Bank's ability to lend is its ability to borrow. Evidently, the main problem of the Bank was not to find borrowers, but lenders prepared to accept reaasonable terms. As we have already seen, particularly in the first decade, there were no other places than the private financial markets from which to generate the needed capital for reconstruction and then development loans.

Status by the End of the Decade

So, what kind of organization was handed over to Eugene Black in 1949? The first three or four years of operation had been a tough testing time indeed. Handling the tension between political demands and interference on one hand, and the financial community's insistence that it be run according to fully commercial principles on the other, was too much of a task for the Bank's first two presidents. Not only did they have to spend the bulk of their time on outreach to private financiers in order to secure its own financing. This job was all the more difficult since it had to substitute its assumedly chief mission; lending to individual, bankable projects; for vaguely defined programme loans for European reconstruction. The Bank was still a financial fledgling, and it was in desperate need of simple recipes for success – on Wall Street terms. Problems were further compounded by the sky-high expectations and ambitions on its behalf that were born in Bretton Woods and nurtured by national policy-makers eager to lift attention away from severe domestic economic constraints.

Still, the most important building blocks had been put in place, and the private finance community knew far more in 1949 about the

Bank and how it was conceived to operate, than only a year or two back. Even if disappointing and confusing to the first generation of Bank officials, the early departure from general reconstruction loans probably served the new institution well. By the end of the decade, the table was cleared for working towards the Bank's prime goal: leveraging finance for key investment projects in capital-squeezed countries. Much thanks to Black's predecessor, he took over an organization that it was possible to manage. And where McCloy had failed in establishing a constructive working relationship with non-US executive directors, Black's experience from the other side of the table made him uniquely positioned to build up a complementary division of labour between management and the Bank's political masters.

A CONSERVATIVE, BUT SUCCESSFUL LENDER (1948–58)

External Environments

The emergence of the cold war made significant imprints on the early developments of the Bank. It remained for the period in question firmly within the US sphere of influence, and thus sided with one of the two superpowers. The terms of participation and lending were set by the capitalist world, as conceived by Stalin, and thus unacceptable by the countries within the Soviet sphere of influence. Czechoslovakia and Poland handed in applications for loans totalling $1 billion in 1946, and negotiations started in early 1947. The process got stalled in 1948, however, due to the unfolding cold war.[15] Cold war concerns are also likely to have fuelled demands, in the latter half of the 1950s, for the Bank to develop a soft loan window – notwithstanding the strong management (and US government) resistance to that idea from the late 1940s and onwards. For western countries, the Bank never became the prime vehicle of 'saving the poor world from communism', but the creation of the IDA at the end of the decade was at least partly motivated by such concerns.

Importantly, however, the Bank was not paralysed by cold war friction to the extent that the UN was, even if the 1950s saw it rapidly developing into a global institution. Reflecting not only US but also overall shareholder dominance, Bank policy came out more independent of emerging developing country demands than the UN, as illustrated by its unwillingness to comply with UN boycotts of Portugal and South Africa in the 1960s. The Articles of Agreement laying out the governing structure and main functions of the Bank, and the precedents set by Bank management in terms of independence and 'political space' to run the Bank as a bank, made up effective shields against complex external pressures. This is not to say, though, that the Bank was immune to pressures from the increasing number of poor, independent states, as expressed for instance through ECOSOC and other UN fora. The strong growth in new members naturally became a challenge to World Bank operations. While 38 countries joined the Bank at its inception in 1946, the number had increased to 67 by 1958 – and was set to continue growing in line with the decolonization process.

Growing up to Become a Major Global Infrastructure Player

By the end of the 1950s, the World Bank had earned itself the stature of triple A rating, allowing it to borrow money at the best conditions achievable. In less than 15 years, the Bank had grown to become the fourth largest financier of international development projects. While the burden of evidence regarding sustainability rested firmly on Black's shoulders when he took over in 1949, a decade later he already had success stories like Australia and Japan to boast of (see below). Bank lending averaged at $3–400 million up to 1958, when it jumped to a level of $700 million (see Figure 3.1). This may seem inconspicuous by today's standards, but it happened in a period of turbulent reconstruction and capital constraints, and with bilateral (and UN) development assistance still existing on the margins. The Bank also saw organizational proliferation, with the creation of its private sector affiliate (the IFC) in 1956, and the (already introduced) IDA in 1960.

The recipe for success was, at least seemingly, quite simple. As the title of this chapter suggests, the Bank's approach to lending was a very conservative one. The international banking community simply would not have accepted anything else, as they were by no means convinced of the new player's sustainability at the start of Black's presidency. So the Bank's management set out to scrutinize possible project portfolios that satisfied the criterion that it should finance only those projects for which other financing was not available on reasonable terms. This was a rather lax criterion in the early post-war years, as severe capital constraints were seen to hamper development efforts in virtually all sectors of economic activity. Within this very broad landscape, with Wall Street concerns clearly in mind, the Bank set out to help complete

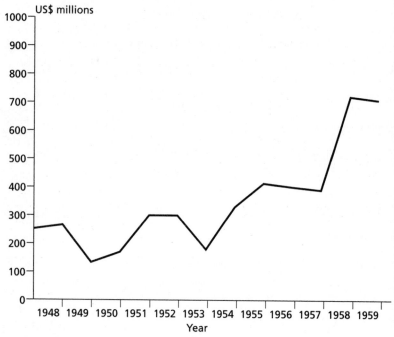

Source: Mason and Asher, 1973.

Figure 3.1 *World Bank Loan Commitments 1948–60*
(current US$ millions)

specific productive projects rather than to make general purpose loans, to secure a guarantee of payment from the governments in project countries, and to go for projects large enough to justify loans from a global agency with headquarters in Washington DC.

These requirements practically assured a heavy concentration by the Bank on power plants, railroad lines, highway networks and similar infrastructure investments. Costly equipment from abroad was seen to be in demand for electric power plants, transportation and communication systems, and related facilities that were not under current circumstances attractive to private capital, while being prerequisites (at least as the Bank saw it) for the attraction of private capital to industry, agriculture and services. Public utilities of the kind now prioritized by the Bank had attracted private capital, also from international sources, in pre-World War II days, but the investments were seen as too large, the returns too low and uncertain, and the prospect of government intervention too great.

However, according to the World Bank historians, it was the early availability of financing for such undertakings that stimulated philosophies about the vital role of economic infrastructure in the development process, rather than the reverse. The Bank drew criticism also in the very early days for eschewing 'social overhead' issues such as sanitation, education and health facilities, as these were widely considered to be as fundamental to development as were physical infrastructure of the type listed above. 'Soft' infrastructure, though, was seen by the Bank to be less measurable, with unclear success criteria and generally solvable, given political will, through domestic resource mobilization. The Bank also feared that 'going soft' would open the door to vastly increased demands for complex loans far beyond its management capabilities, and also knew very well that Wall Street hackles about the soundness of its portfolio would reemerge should the Bank become adventurous in areas like anti-malaria strategies, reduction of illiteracy, building vocational schools or establishing clinics.

Recruitment and Personnel Policies

It is common to relate conceptions of the World Bank's relative effectiveness as compared to, for example, UN agencies to differences in recruitment and personnel policies. As conceived in the early 1970s, Mason and Asher claim that:

> 'over the years, the Bank has acquired a staff unique among the international agencies in terms of its professional competence. Its reports are generally of high calibre, and its staff members are respected for up-to-date knowledge in their field of specialisation, even where they are considered insufficiently aware of, or sensitive to, special problems of particular geographic areas.'[16]

As shown above, great care was taken by the founding fathers, led by the US delegation, to avoid politicization of recruitment processes, and to attract highly qualified expertise to World Bank jobs. Following logically from the Bank's troublesome evolutionary years, recruitment policy started out in an ad hoc catch-as-catch-can manner. People were recommended to the Bank's top management by friends, by staff already employed and by executive directors. Some were borrowed from the US government, while the support staff (of various nationalities) during the Bretton Woods and Savannah conferences made up another fertile ground of recruitment. Still, also as Bank routines in this area grew more standardized, the management firmly resisted demands to make geography and related criteria compromise the established 'competence only' criterion.

Moreover, the president and his men insisted on flexibility regarding salaries and had a generous starting point in these regards due to terms set out at the Savannah conference (the inaugural meeting of the board of governors, March 1946). Here, the US had pressed through, against strong resistance from the UK and other delegations, a very high salary level for executive directors and the Bank president. US delegates emphasized that salaries should be competitive in the international banking community, while European and Canadian representatives were afraid that the US proposals would result in a Washington club of public bankers aloof and estranged from financial affairs in their home countries. The levels originally proposed were modified, but they ended up closer to the US than other positions. From this starting point, the president had the financial scope of action needed to recruit top-level expertise – especially as the salaries of Bank professionals were, and still are, fully tax-exempt.

The 430 Bank staff employed by 1951, and also the 646 within its ranks in 1960, were heavily biased towards the US first, and then the UK and a number of other European countries. This was a natural reflection of political power and availability of expertise. Still, already in the 1950s this dominance was seen as a potential challenge to the overall legitimacy of the Bank as a global player. A familiar plea, therefore, at the board meetings and related occasions, was for faster staff internationalization. Barriers against realizing this were the management's insistence on not compromising on 'quality first-requirements', lack of expertise in developing countries and desperate demand for potential Bank candidates in the management of their own countries' economies. In the early days, the 'mind-sets' of the Anglo-American majority may also have inhibited a fully global perspective in the search for promising candidates. From 1960 and onwards, however, the process of internationalization gained steam. By 1971, although still dominating the higher ranks of the Bank, officials from the US and the UK made up less than 50 per cent of total professional staff.

Anglo-American dominance notwithstanding, the impression seems to have been that Bank staff were thinking and behaving 'internationally'. The first decades saw few documented examples of criticism that Bank officials were overtly or covertly lobbying for national interests or particular government positions. Overall, and reinforced by the independent role of the presidency from about 1950 and onwards, the Bank early earned itself high marks regarding recruitment procedures, quality of competence and integrity. In so doing, it came to stand in clear contrast to the procedures and performance of the much more politicized UN and UN-related organizations. It was, therefore, also logical for Bank management to fend off all attempts to install UN supremacy over the World Bank, or, less radically, to make the Bank report to ECOSOC or other UN bodies.

Independent Role vis-à-vis the UN

Time and again, demands surface for various degrees of UN control over World Bank action. Such demands have intensified throughout the 1990s, particularly as the Bank has met tough criticism over the impact of structural adjustment programmes and perceived failure to take environmental concerns seriously. In that perspective, it is interesting to note that subsumption of the Bank under UN auspices had strong support over the development of the first couple of post-war MDIs. A letter from New York spelling out UN demands on specialized agencies was awaiting participants at the 1946 inaugural meeting of the board of governors at Savannah. UN Charter Article 17, section 3 empowers the Secretary-General to 'examine the administrative budgets of specialised agencies with a view to making recommendations to the agencies concerned'.

At the August 1947 ECOSOC session, Finn Moe of Norway said that it was impossible for his country to accept the Bank and Fund agreements because of their special privilege clauses (compared to other specialized agencies), which would undermine the authority of the UN. Norway, home to the then UN Secretary-General Trygve Lie, also voted against the draft agreements between the UN and Bretton Woods institutions, but only got the support of the Soviet Union and Byelo-Russia. Other western countries in practice allowed the Bank and Fund to decide the premises for relations between the two sets of institutions, and by November 1947 the Bretton Woods twins formally became (very special) specialized agencies of the UN. The agreement, however, left little doubt about the independence of the World Bank, starting out as it did in the following way: 'By reason of the nature of its international responsibilities and the terms of its Articles of Agreement, the Bank is, and is required to function as, an independent international organisation.'[17]

Also in the more practical aspects of the final agreement, Bank independence loomed large. UN representatives were only allowed to attend (the very general) meetings of the board of governors. The UN was given no privilege with regard to obtaining information from the Bank, and the Bretton Woods institutions agreed only to give 'due consideration' to the inclusion in their agendas of items proposed by the UN. Full autonomy was also given to the Bank in all matters pertaining to budgetary and financial arrangements.

This power demonstration by the Bretton Woods twins and their supporters, and the protracted negotiations that preceded it, contributed to a tense relationship between the two sets of institutions for decades to come. Secretariats of UN bodies, and UN member states (particularly from less developed parts of the world) time and again tried to influence Bank matters, but such infringements were effectively fended off by Bank management by reference to the 1948 agreement. ECOSOC, its commissions and sub-commissions, and the early expert groups appointed by the UN Secretary-General, tended to be severely critical of the World Bank. The Bank reciprocated, by regarding the UN and its subsidiaries as 'busybody empire-builders or do-gooders, blind to the realities of international finance, bent on jeopardising the Bank's standing on Wall Street, agitating for more development finance than could be used productively, and sending out survey missions that should have been organised by the Bank and would have been better if they had'.[18]

Many more examples could be given of Bank/UN tensions during the first post-war decades, and an important controversy is touched in the SUNFED discussion of the previous chapter. The main point here, however, is to show how the independent status of the World Bank vis-à-vis the UN and other intergovernmental organizations influenced the terms under which it operated, and (in all likelihood) made it better placed than UN-type organizations to handle operational challenges. The following comparison of Bank and UN features illustrates how the relative strengths of the Bank were judged by the authors of the first quarter-century of World Bank history:

> '*The structural and organisational differences extend beyond the Bank's budgetary autonomy and include the absence of Communist countries (other than Yugoslavia) from its membership roster, its system of weighted voting, its ties to finance ministries and treasuries rather than to foreign offices or functional ministries (such as agricul-*

*ture or labour departments), and its greater freedom to
hire personnel without reference to their country of origin.
The effect of these features of the Bank is a different
balance of power within the organisation between the
more and the less developed countries, an ability to pay
higher salaries to its staff, and an ability to say "no" to
more governments without jeopardising the re-election of
the chief executive or the adoption of his budget. These in
turn have encouraged the Bank to consider itself more
competent, more independent, more non-political, and
better prepared than other agencies to promote the true
welfare of its clients.'*[19]

Challenges and Constraints on the Conservative, Effectiveness-Oriented Approach

The previous sections have indicated possible reasons why the period
under scrutiny here (1948–58) saw the foundation being laid for
several decades of solid Bank growth, and in fact a unique position in
the global finance and investment community. Crucial, in relation to
our main thesis, was the fact that the (business-like, effectiveness-
oriented) governing structure of the Bank matched its main functions
far better than was the case with the operative part of the UN.

This early period was also soon to demonstrate the limitations of
the conservative lender approach, however. As early as in its annual
report in 1950/51, the Bank conceded that 'increasingly, it was called
upon to provide advice or assistance without reference to any immediate financial operation'.[20] To be further explored in the next section
(1958–68), this seemingly successful approach was almost immediately challenged by *an apparent lack of 'bankable projects'* and
increasing demands for a comprehensive Bank role in loan preparation. Implications were the need for tight dialogue with borrower
countries on development priorities, evolving pressures on the Bank
to provide services beyond 'conservative banking' and related
demands for more flexible and softer financing (leading to the establishment of the IDA in 1958).

A range of features demonstrated emerging/looming strains
between operational effectiveness as judged by Wall Street standards,
and the complex politico-economic world that Bank management had
to face and adapt to:

- The lack of easily bankable projects and the need for solid project preparation work, including that of feasibility studies and the building up of supportive institutional frameworks in borrowing countries.
- The increasing demand to develop projects in softer development areas such as health, sanitation and education, and in order to satisfy such needs to open up soft loan windows.
- The rapidly evolving debt problems of developing countries like India and Pakistan, who had problems in serving even limited debts to the World Bank. This, as shown in a major study published in 1956, demonstrated the need for a more comprehensive approach to economic interaction than delimited project loans.

TOWARDS A DEVELOPMENT AGENCY (1958–68)

By 1960, the World Bank was established as an important player in international development-related finance and investment. Annual amounts of loans and credits were approaching US$700 million (which was high in a comparative perspective at the time), and the sound track record throughout the 1950s had convinced world financial markets that the Bank deserved its triple A rating. Hence, markets were also willing to go along with much greater, and 'softer', development orientation in the Bank's mode of operation. Focus was allowed to shift, therefore, more and more to the developing world. This was evident, not least, in the founding in 1960 of the IDA, the soft loan arm of the IBRD, a creature that Wall Street and conservative US policy-makers advised strongly against only five years earlier. The IDA also complemented an organizational growth that had seen the set-up of the Economic Development Institute (EDI), aimed to train public officials from developing countries, in 1955, and the IFC, targeted at private sector development, in 1956.

The launching of the IDA reflected an acknowledgement that developing the former colonies and other underdeveloped areas was a more complex and demanding task than envisaged by the Bank's founding fathers. From the very beginning, the rate of Bank (IBRD) lending was limited by the creditworthiness of potential borrowers and by the rate at which viable projects could be brought forward. Its involvement in European reconstruction was long gone, and the Bank was already starting to wind up comprehensive and successful engagements in Japan and Australia. At the same time, big potential lenders such as India and

Pakistan had already started foundering under unmanageable debt burdens. The outlook in 1960 for an agency equipped only to make loans at close-to-commercial rates of interest to countries unable to borrow elsewhere would have been bleak indeed. The IDA had to be invented to respond to the needs of the bulk of its clients, and there-fore also to keep the Bank up front in what was emerging as an increasingly competitive market for multilateral agency services. In many ways, its creation was *a watershed* in the evolution of the World Bank group, signalling the transformation from something that initially resembled a private, international bank towards what was to become more and more of a development agency.[21]

External Factors

While the Bank's governing board counted about 40 governments in 1947, towards the end of this period (1970) it was approaching 120. This dramatic increase in member countries and thus borrowers (virtually all newcomers were borrowers) grossly complicated Bank operations. The 'newcomer impact' did not challenge the decision-making system as profoundly as in the UN, however, due to their significantly different governing (voting) structures. The build-up to the paralysing NIEO-decade also went largely unnoticed in Bank circles, dominated as they were on both developing and developed country sides by ministries of finance.

This was also a period of development optimism, and an era of belief in state planning that also immersed the World Bank – even though to a lesser extent than in UN fora. The Bank, for instance, supported five-year plans in many countries. Throughout the 1960s and the early 1970s, sustaining development meant increasing invest-ment levels as the main force of development. Another important development was the foreign exchange crises of many poor countries around 1960, among them India, which served to underline the need for cheaper loans and for donor cooperation in helping them out – in which the Bank was given a crucial role.

The Bank in the 1960s – Still Wedded to Big Infrastructure and Project Loans

The above must not move attention away from the fact that the bulk of Bank lending in this period was primarily for large-scale infrastructure projects: electricity, transport, ports, telecommunications. Approximately two-thirds of Bank resources went into basic infrastructure, while an increasing proportion, particularly of IDA funds, was invested in agriculture (from 1963 and onwards). As in the previous decade, basic infrastructure was seen as the most promising niche for a publicly governed/commercially run financing institution that was not to compete with private banks. Hence, the primary functions of the Bank did not deviate significantly from the purely operative functions we have earlier stated that it was designed for. Or in other words, there was still no conspicuous move towards the left on the continuum of functions described in Chapter 1. This also holds for the main part of IDA projects, even if the soft character of IDA financing (virtually interest-free loans, but still loans) stretched the competence and imagination of traditional bankers far beyond what they were trained for.

Concentration of Activities

Seen in one perspective, the Bank achieved its (in many regards impressive) results throughout the 1960s by way of its ability *to concentrate*: more than two-thirds of the resources went into economic infrastructure, and most of it was invested in electricity and transport. It was also able to concentrate, despite continuous pressures in the opposite direction, quite large proportions of lending on a limited number of countries. For instance, between 30 and 40 per cent of Bank lending and credits between 1945 and 1970 went to five countries: Colombia, Brazil, Pakistan, India and Thailand; and in the 1950s, as mentioned above, Japan had proved an important 'learning ground'. Colombia alone received 49 loans and credits worth US$900 million from 1949–71. Of Colombian loans, 40 per cent went into electric power and 25 per cent to highways.

A Highly Centralized Organization

In tandem with concentration went *centralization*; also a feature making it stand out very clearly from UN agencies. Neither the increasing focus on development issues in the developing world, nor the related need to diversify the range of activities beyond conventional handling of big loans (feasibility studies, TA, institution building, cooperation with UN agencies and bilateral donors), convinced Bank management to delegate decision-making from headquarters to regional or country levels. All stages of the project cycle were managed from Washington, and field operations basically handled by short-term missions – which also provided inputs to country economic reports that in other regards were prepared by Washington. Even in the countries and areas in which the Bank had permanent representatives, headquarters held these on a very short leash. The 11 country/regional missions that existed by 1970 were generally small (one or two persons in each), and their functions limited to economic reporting and to preliminary project identification. They had been established on an ad hoc basis, and there existed no policy as of 1970 concerning conditions justifying resident missions, their size, role or relations with the Washington headquarters.

Arguments often used in favour of continued centralization ran as follows:

1 maintaining full administrative control and substantive consistency in an already complex international organization;
2 interdependence of all stages in the project cycle, which militated against delegating key functions to field offices;
3 independence from pressures wielded by host country governments – the freedom to give unpleasant advice;
4 it made it possible to recruit the best people, and to ensure critical mass with regard to the broad range of qualifications and competence required to fulfil the Bank's mandate.

Many would hold that these features contributed to the World Bank's relative success over the first couple of decades. Continuous growth increased the pressure on all major functions of the organization, but tight and centralized management ensured control and avoided the functional and organizational disintegration that might otherwise have resulted from the dynamic growth process.

TA and Institution Building

Some perspectives have been suggested on how the Bank coped with the transformation from conventional investment banking (to the extent that that was ever Bank reality) to the complex challenges of a development agency. In the period in question here, few significant adaptations in working procedures were made, and the strains put on the Bank were, with few exceptions, manageable. Still, the scarcity of bankable projects, and the cumulative experience of working with

and aiming to influence decisions of (often weak) recipient governments, resulted in a general broadening of the Bank's scope of action.
Throughout the 1960s, therefore, more and more resources were
used on TA in various shapes, mainly justified as needed in order to
develop bankable projects. In the words of a World Bank official in
1970, 'Experience has demonstrated that we do not get enough good
projects to appraise unless we are involved intimately in their identification and preparation.'[22]

While TA is not mentioned in the Bank's charter (the Bank was
seen, fundamentally, as an investment agency), by the early 1960s it
was deeply involved in the following categories of TA:

- TA that is not connected with an immediate investment project,
  for example assistance to a ministry to improve its functioning;
- TA related to the pre-investment stage of a project or programme,
  for example assistance in project identification or preparation,
  feasibility studies or sector studies;
- TA that is connected with a specific loan or credit and is identifiable as a type of TA, for example inclusion in a loan of funds for
  the employment of foreign consultants to help launch the project;
- TA that is inextricably interwoven with the making or supervis-
  ing of a Bank loan or IDA credit and therefore is not separately
  identifiable.

The fully separate TA projects, which started proliferating with the
emergence of the IDA in 1960, were more 'visible' than those
integrated in larger investment operations. From scrutinizing the IDA's
early TA portfolio, we see, for instance, that the Bank launched its
first education projects in 1962 – through support for secondary
schools in Tunisia. The Bank's growing competence in 'softer' TA areas
also made it a frequent consumer of the free sources of pre-investment funds available through the newly founded UNDP. Ironically,
the TA agencies of the UN proved poorly equipped to serve as execut-
ing agencies for the UNDP. The Bank, on the other hand, was already
well prepared to deliver required services such as pre-investment
surveys with cost-benefit data, market information, estimates of
capital requirements, rates of return on capital and other important
inputs to investment decisions. Therefore, while many UN agencies
probably viewed the increasing UNDP/World Bank interface with
suspicion and institutional jealousy, it contributed to an overall
improvement in working relations between the two systems. The new
situation created a favourable situation for the Bank, by simultane-

ously strengthening its position in the emerging hierarchy of international development machinery and lengthening the pipeline of projects suitable for Bank and IDA investments.

Though less conspicuous, the bulk of the Bank's TA was firmly embedded in its regular loan and credit operations. Such TA early (late 1940s) evolved out of the Bank's interest in finding and financing projects that it could regard as technically sound, economically viable and of high priority to the development of the borrowing country. The Bank's emerging focus on development programming was therefore not the beginning of its TA activity as much as it was a further reflection of its interest in financing 'good' projects – by ensuring a better economic policy-setting for, and relationship between, potential investment projects in development countries. A large proportion of TA activities in the period in question was a continuation of the institution building started in the previous decade.

The Bank played a crucial role in building and sustaining industrial finance corporations, agricultural credit banks, power authorities and a range of similar institutions – as concomitants of its investment projects. At the same time, strong alliances were built with ministries of finance and planning in client countries, also seen by the Bank as crucial building blocks for their investment operations. One strategy to forge such alliances was the establishment in 1955 of the EDI, which was set up to enhance economic management capabilities of active or prospective government officials in developing countries. Attendees were trained in activities ranging from specific project appraisal and evaluation to various economic policy issues pertaining to the societal context of Bank investment projects. By the end of the period in question here, more than 1000 officials had participated in EDI courses generally extending from three to six months.

Towards a Fully-Fledged Development Institution?

Although being a continuation of developments dating 20 years back, by the late 1960s the gradual increase in spending on TA and institution building was about to transform the Bank into a development institution. Indicators of a broader development mission were:

- the acknowledgement of the need and capacity for more comprehensive loan portfolios – regarding volumes as well as the number and character of instruments used;

- important institutional developments, like the creation of the IDA, the EDI and the IFC, with a related growing focus on TA and institution building;
- a broadening engagement in industry, agriculture and education;
- significant increases in local expenditure financing;
- the development of the Bank into an important player in the growing international aid community, including significant leadership and coordination responsibilities, for example, in connection with the India and Pakistan aid consortia of the late 1950s.

Still, in 1968 Robert McNamara took over an institution that was still geared towards conventional project lending: two-thirds of the Bank's lending went into basic infrastructure. Comparatively scant attention was paid to the impact of loans on income distribution, social development and political stability. The concern with country performance was limited to policies and practices related to the growth of GNP. Ideologically, the Bank was firmly placed within the capitalist world view of major shareholder governments, with little spillover from the emerging North/South confrontation in the UN.

McNamara's Drive Towards Poverty Orientation (1968–80)

External Factors

This period came to imply the end of development optimism, and tough North/South tensions in the UN and elsewhere. The oil shock of 1973 had major implications for the sense of unity and solidarity forming among developing countries, with a widespread belief in cartel power in the wake of OPEC's apparent success. These developments clearly influenced policy formulation in various UN fora, as spelt out above. The World Bank, however, was left largely untouched by the political earthquakes, although its policies and project portfolio came to be heavily influenced by the economic impacts on poor oil-importing countries of the two oil shocks in 1973 and 1979. Again, the shielding of the Bank from UN-type NIEO ramifications had much to do with OECD country influence as dominant shareholders (who never really believed in the NIEO gospel), the dominance of finance ministries at both lender and borrower sides of the table and the predominance of western-educated economists and engineers in the staff.

The end of development optimism combined with strategic cold war thinking and bad conscience-driven motivation to help out former colonies, all contributed to a phenomenal increase in development assistance during this period. So it was not only the Bank's scope of action that expanded so markedly in this period – it was really the heyday of aid transfers from rich to poor countries

Increase in the Volume of Lending

In line with the general increase in North/South transfers in this period, World Bank lending increased from under US$1 billion in 1968 to over US$12 billion in 1981 (at current prices; a more than fourfold increase in real terms.[23] This is more than twice the growth foreseen (and considered very ambitious) for this period by Bank planners around 1970. IDA funding went up from US$300 million to US$2.5 billion in the same period, sustaining the Bank's ability to engage in TA and cover in more comprehensive ways the poorest developing countries – and thus to focus more on poverty. The numbers for 1970–80 for the IBRD and the IDA (commitments) respectively are shown in Figure 3.3. It should be noted that amounts are given in *fixed* US$ billions (1990).

A Radical Shift Towards Poverty Orientation

With the emergence as Bank president in 1968 of the controversial Robert McNamara, focus was increasingly targeted on poverty alleviation and related and formerly ignored issues such as unemployment, family planning and the welfare of rural populations. In an interview with Nicolas Stern in February 1992, McNamara saw his first 90 days (back in 1968) as being the period where he established his view that the role of the Bank should change from being a bank for infrastructure projects to being *a development agency*. He had seen this change as both basic and necessary, and regarded his rejection of 'trickle down' and his emphasis on the absolute poor as of paramount importance and also revolutionary.[24] The annual meetings of the board of governors were consciously used to spread this message. Consider, for example, McNamara's address to the board of governors in Copenhagen in 1970:[25]

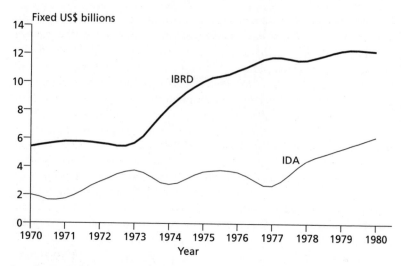

Source: World Bank Annual Reports. Conversion of current prices to constant values has been done by using the US consumer price index (1990=100).

Figure 3.2 *Total World Bank (IBRD and IDA) Loan Commitments 1970–80 (fixed 1990 US$ billions)*

> 'We have made a start at broadening the concept of development beyond the simple limits of economic growth. The emerging nations need, and are determined to achieve, greater economic advance. But ... we believe economic progress remains precarious and sterile without corresponding social improvement. Fully human development requires attention to both. We intend, in the Bank, to give attention to both.'[26]

It is probably fair to say that the Bank was concerned with poverty alleviation also throughout the 1950s and 1960s. Then, however, most analysts – within and outside the Bank, believed in the 'trickle down-effect'; the conviction that strong efforts to encourage economic growth in indirect ways would serve to reduce poverty.[27] This belief was seriously challenged by studies in the 1970s that revealed how hundreds of millions of people continued to live in poverty, lacking such basic facilities as safe drinking water, schools or health clinics. These conditions stifled productivity and kept earning capacity low, resulting in a perpetuating cycle of poverty transmitted from one generation to the next.

But to what extent did actual lending operations reflect these seemingly radical rhetorical transformations? Changes on the ground in this period were, in fact, significant. Poverty was catapulted into the centre of the Bank's activities by the McNamara speeches referred to above.[28] Lending to rural areas and agriculture in particular more than doubled its share to 28 per cent – soaring from US$1.3 billion in the 1960s (cumulative for the decade, current prices) to US$14.8 billion in the 1970s (cumulative). Basic infrastructure, so dominant in the first couple of decades of Bank operations, saw its share of Bank resources fall from 65 per cent in the 1960s to about 35 per cent in the late 1970s. Support for the somewhat vaguely defined concept of human resources development also increased significantly during this period, from 2.3 per cent to 5.4 per cent of Bank lending[29] (a more conspicuous number than it may appear given that no grant money was available to the Bank for these purposes). Add to this the concern with direct measures to reach the poor as embodied in the establishment of the Agriculture and Rural Development Department in 1973, the Urban Development Department in 1975 and the Population, Health and Nutrition Department in 1979. In short, the World Bank dramatically altered the whole thrust of its lending under the reign of McNamara (1968–81).

Towards a Broader Policy Role for the Bank

The Bank started out as a conventional, project-oriented investment bank; forced by Wall Street watchdogs and conservative shareholders (led by the US) to concentrate its attention on sound project management. This narrow project focus was challenged very early, however, by a range of factors described above. The structure of lending clearly changed during the reign of McNamara. Even if project lending still dominated the Bank's portfolio, gradually more resources went into broader programme lending. This partly reflected the increase in IDA operations, which have always been far more flexible and more amenable to programme lending than those of the IBRD, and partly the growing inclination to recycle petrodollars in the form of (IBRD-funded) import/balance-of-payments support schemes, particularly for net oil importers, in the wake of the two oil price hikes in 1973 and 1979 respectively. Short-sighted and even irresponsible as such support schemes appeared when the debt crisis made the headlines from 1982 and onwards, in the 1970s this particular increase in programme lending was clearly demand driven and seen as a valid response to the problems of poor, oil-importing countries severely hurt by OPEC's rise to power in 1973.

The McNamara reign, however, in moving the Bank further towards a leading policy-oriented development institution, was more a consistent continuation of already established developments, than revolutionary change. Interestingly, Gaving and Rodrik argue that 'at least since the mid-1960s, the Bank's name has always been associated with a particular set of ideas about what constitutes important development priorities facing poor countries'. They also aim to explain this emerging role: 'What forced the Bank to enter the business of development "ideas" was the environment in which it found itself operating'... 'Hence, the Bank was required from the very beginning to have ideas about what constituted an appropriate policy context.'[30] Such a view is supported by reference to the Bank's fifth annual report (1949–50), which after reiterating the 'projects only' clause in the Articles of Agreement, goes on to argue that:

> 'criticism of the specific project approach has almost always been based on the assumption that the Bank examines the merit of particular projects in isolation. In fact the Bank does the opposite. The Bank seeks to determine what are the appropriate investment priorities. Consistently with this approach the Bank has encouraged its members to formulate long-term development programmes. The existence of such a programme greatly facilitates the task of determining which projects are of the highest priority.'[31]

None the less, the period saw a considerable growth in the number of areas and subjects that the Bank addressed as part of its regular business, including those of population issues, unemployment and the environment. Although the conspicuous increase in the focus on poverty alleviation was very much driven by McNamara and his associates, these new trends also serve to illustrate the growing pressures and more active policy of shareholder governments and NGOs as to the justification of World Bank business. Such pressures, and the realization that policy and institutional parameters significantly conditioned the relative success of loan projects and programmes, started to move the Bank more and more squarely into the role of a policy adviser; and, to an increasing extent, a norm-creator in economic and social policy. These developments were becoming far more explicit in the following period, but the seeds

were sown for a significant move towards the centre and even left of
our continuum of functions.

Economic Research in Support of Project Performance and Policy Advice

This broadening of the development agenda implied new challenges
for the Bank and other development agencies with respect to
competence and understanding of complex societal processes. It
also implied extensive tasks in terms of economic and social
research, and served to legitimize an increasingly prominent role for
the Bank itself in research and policy analysis. A caption from the
same speech by McNamara illustrates the ambitions of the Bank in
that regard:

> 'We do not want simply to say that rising unemployment
> is a "bad thing" and something must be done about it.
> We want to know its scale, its causes, its impact and the
> range of policies and options which are open to govern-
> ments, international agencies and the private sector to
> deal with it. We do not want simply to sense that the
> "green revolution" requires a comparable social revolu-
> tion in the organisation and education of the small
> farmer. We want to know what evidence or working
> models are available on methods of co-operative enter-
> prise, of decentralised credit systems, of smaller-scale
> technology, and of price and market guarantees. We do
> not want simply to deplore over-rapid urbanisation in the
> primary cities. We want the most accurate and careful
> studies of internal migration, town-formation, decen-
> tralised urbanism and regional balance.'[32]

One asset of being a highly centralized organization, was the ability of
the Bank to build up a strong research and policy analysis unit. The
utility of such a function was appreciated by Eugene Black and the
other early presidents of the Bank. Still, the strength and vitality of
its economic research work is most deservedly associated with first,
George Woods, and then even more so McNamara and the chief
economist during most of his reign – Hollis Chenery.[33] The major
reorientation towards poverty alleviation was reinforced by a comprehensive research effort led by Chenery, who played a pioneering role

in the late 1960s and 1970s in illuminating the crucial role of redistribution issues for any economic growth strategy.[34] McNamara worked very closely with Chenery and his colleagues in what was renamed the Research Department during the major reorganization in 1972. Interestingly, McNamara is renowned for involving his research staff closely in the preparation of key speeches to the board of governors – be they on the need to address poverty in the early 1970s, or the famous 1980 speech on structural adjustment.

Targeted focusing of research on economy-wide conditions for successful investment operations helped to prepare the Bank for the broader policy role described above. Indeed, at the time of McNamara's arrival in 1968, the very purpose of the Bank's research work was seen as providing a well documented and researched economy-wide view, bridging the gap between projects and wider programme priorities. Nicolas Stern quotes a very clear expression of this from McNamara's preface to a 1968 Staff Occasional Paper on the economics of road user charges:

> '*I would like to explain* why *the World Bank Group does research work, and why it publishes it. We feel an obligation to look beyond the projects we help to finance towards the whole resource allocation of an economy, and the effectiveness of the use of those resources.*'[35]

Thanks to the high priority given to economic research by the Bank's top management, it has grown into an important player in terms of understanding the economics of development. Although less famous for the creation of new ideas than for catalysing, disseminating and adapting academic economics into operational policy advice, World Bank operations have long been founded on a robust in-house knowledge production.

> '*On any given subject there are usually people outside the Bank who are more distinguished than those inside, but what the Bank does have is an assembly of people with expertise in a number of areas from micro, to sectoral, to macro, and close knowledge of particular countries. It is the combined application of this collection of competence on various aspects to solve pressing practical problems that characterises the areas where the Bank is likely to have an intellectual comparative advantage.*'[36]

The Bank currently employs around 800 professional economists, and has a research budget of around US$25 million a year. Its annual World Development Report, initiated by McNamara in 1978, is clearly the most widely read document in development economics (average distribution of 120,000). These resources dwarf any university or research institution working on development economics. The weight of the number of development economists, the research budget and the leverage from its lending means that the Bank's potential influence is profound, and that it cannot be seen as just one of a number of fairly equal actors in the world of development economics.

A POLICY REFORMER WITH INCREASING STRAINS ON PROJECT QUALITY (1980–90)

This is an exciting period with regard to our main thesis. The Bank is moving considerably towards the left on our spectrum of functions, getting far more comprehensively involved in policy advice and agenda setting through its sectoral and adjustment lending: 'The Bank adapted the low-conditionality program loans it had made to a few key countries in the 1960s and 1970s to current conditions – and started making structural adjustment loans tied to policy reform.'[37] This period also saw the strengthening of shareholder government demands that the Bank integrate environmental and other 'soft concerns' squarely into its lending policy. In doing that, they (not least the Nordic countries) served to move the Bank closer and closer towards issues and areas formerly considered the prerogatives of UN, bilateral and NGO assistance. At the same time, concern was increasing over the quality of the Bank's project portfolio, as it became more and more difficult to maintain high-level technical competence across the ever-widening number of thematic areas. Figure 3.3 shows total Bank lending from 1980 to 1997 in *fixed* US$ billions (1990), while Figure 3.4 illustrates the growth in Bank lending for human development from the 1960s to the 1990s and a radical shift in the late 1980s (*current* US$ millions).

The Debt Crisis

The debt crisis that unfolded with Mexico's default in 1982 had major implications for Bank and other aid and financing organizations' developing world strategies. Private capital to a large extent withdrew from

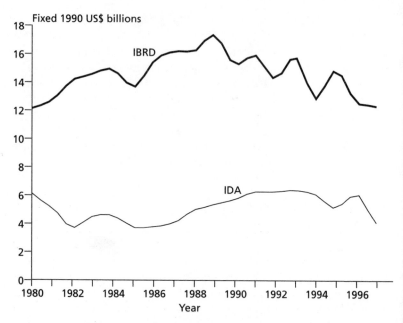

Source: World Bank Annual Reports. Conversion of current prices to constant values has been done by using the US consumer price index (1990=100).

Figure 3.3 *Total World Bank (IBRD and IDA) Loan Commitments 1980–97 (fixed 1990 US$ billions)*

most developing countries other than East Asia, leaving bi- and multilateral aid institutions as the main source of development finance in the 1980s. The debt crisis and the factors that caused it demonstrated that previous development strategies with strong donor support had failed or had at least not served to ensure a sustainable basis for national economic development. At least up to a point, the financing of trade deficits by MDBs and other donors were underwriting poor investments and policies that could lead to debt problems down the road. Once the crisis was evident, this acknowledgement helped to convince the Bank to develop tough conditionalities on the large financial inputs that were required to save poor (particularly African) countries from an unmanageable debt burden.

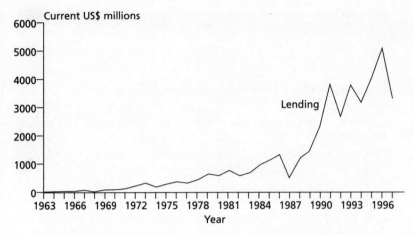

Source: Supporting Human Development: Progress and Challenges World Bank
Annual Reports 1993–97.

Figure 3.4 *World Bank Lending for Human Development
(Population, Health, Nutrition, Education and Social Sector)
(current US$ millions)*

The Reagan/Thatcher/Kohl Era Effect

The debt crisis thus had major ramifications for World Bank action in
this decade, in providing a decisive impetus for (already initiated in
1980) structural adjustment lending (SAL). Mounting debt problems
focused attention on internal rather than external structural causes of
misery for developing countries. In that sense it went well along with
the more consistently rightist policies of three major policy-makers
who made their strong imprint on this decade: Reagan, Kohl and
Thatcher. Most observers, including Nicolas Stern (1993), identify a
relatively clear policy shift at the departure of McNamara and
Chenery in 1981 and the arrival of Clausen, the new president and
his chief economist, Anne Krueger. More market, less central
planning; increased focus on 'getting the prices right' and reduced
focus on targeted poverty reduction strategies. The concern with the
impacts of adjustment on inequality and poverty was de-emphasized
in the years from 1982–87. Instead, the Bank became a prominent
champion of the many of the central tenets of the 'neo-classical'
resurgence – exemplified, for example, through the dominant focus
of the World Development Reports of 1983, 1985, 1986 and 1987 on

issues such as the importance of careful price, trade, tax and institutional reforms to increase the efficiency of resource allocation and domestic investment.

Towards a More Demanding World Community

Increasing concern with environmental and social issues was to have major implications for the Bank. These trends are also interesting in a more generic sense, exemplifying a trend of stronger pressures on the Bank to comply with ideological currents in international society. Even if claims of the Bank as arrogantly fending off external criticism were exaggerated, changes concerning openness to the outside world from the mid-1980s and onwards are identifiable. Steadily increasing lobby efforts by the NGO community may be one of the forces behind these developments, working as they are on both national government Bank policies (eg on the US Congress) and on Bank management.[38]

Increasing Strains on Project Quality

A salient feature of the 1980s was the perceived, and probably real, phenomenon of declining project quality. From 1950 and far into the 1970s, the Bank's mastery of project management was virtually undisputed, and constituted perhaps *the* main indicator of the perception of the World Bank as a success story. The Bank's Operations Evaluation Department (OED) evaluated more than a thousand projects implemented throughout the 1970s (many of which were designed in the 1960s), involving more than US$22 billion in Bank loans and US$67 billion in total investments. The review found that 86 per cent of all projects (90 per cent by value) appeared to have achieved their major objectives and were judged to have been worthwhile, with the rate of return (where applicable) averaged at about 18 per cent.

Over the next decade, however, evaluations of Bank projects, as determined by periodic OED findings, declined and became a subject of much analysis. The critical examinations culminated with the Wappenhans report of 1992, and an internal study revealing that the quality of economic analysis in projects throughout the 1980s was poor in 13 per cent and barely acceptable in 25 per cent of the projects subject to cost-benefit analysis. What was particularly embarrassing for the Bank was that serious performance problems were revealed in areas that constituted its core of infrastructure lending, and where it had built its strong reputation over the previous decades: power, transport, major irrigation systems, water and sewage, and telecommunications.

The reasons behind this trend of decline in project quality from the late 1970s and onwards are diverse. Judgement is also rendered difficult by the lack of clear criteria according to which Bank performance can be judged. Whether 2/3 success and 1/3 failure (as identified in the 1992 Wappenhans report) is good or bad depends crucially on expectations as to what is fair and achievable for an institution like the World Bank. Suffice it here to mention some broad categories of explanatory factors:

- the rapid growth in lending and the increasing pressure on World Bankers to disburse;
- the rapid growth in member countries and the increasing exposure in poor countries with declining overall economic performance;
- the decreasing ability of recipient governments to handle macro-economic policy frameworks and maintain a minimum level of institutional strength and autonomy;
- the pressure from member countries to continuously take on new priorities within new project areas ;
- the 'politeness' vis-à-vis borrowing country governments facing tough external shocks, for example due to the debt crisis.

The Drive Towards Policy-Based Lending

The debt crisis and the political trends just described provided what we may call 'external' justifications for policy-based lending in the form of structural adjustment and sector loans with strong conditionalities. At the same time, pressures had long been built up for reforms in this direction from within the Bank itself. Part of the story has already been told in the previous sections, for instance with respect to the increased focus on (non-project specific) TA, soft loans, donor coordination and sector studies and strategies. Rather then representing something completely new, therefore, what McNamara's 1980 speech to the board of governors meant was a radical shift from soft to hard conditionality, reinforced by a considerable increase in fast-disbursing programme loans/balance-of-payment support. It was preceded by the first SAL in February 1980 and followed up through making 'adjustment' the main topic of the 1981 World Development Report. According to Stern, these developments were 'fundamental in drawing the attention of many in the development community, policymakers and academics alike, to the magnitude of the challenge of adjustment'.[39] The Bank had made a major change in both its actions and its words, and appeared in the case of structural adjustment as a leader of the profession of economists. What was particularly new and conspicuous was

> '*the co-ordination of the various macro, sectoral and micro elements into a single programme with a view to immediate implementation. It was this form of economy-wide approach together with the emphasis on the process of change itself, the asking of just how a country was to move from an earlier set of policies to a new set of policies, that constituted innovative aspects of structural adjustment from the academic perspective.*'[40]

The major impetus for change was acknowledgement that a substantial part of the Bank's growing portfolio of projects failed or performed worse than expected because of faulty policy environments. A 1981 Bank study, called the Berg report, concluded from a review of external and internal factors affecting Africa's performance that policy-induced distortions were so severe in many countries that projects could not be expected to succeed no matter how well designed.[41] One important blend of criticism against the Bank was that it did not anticipate the scale of such problems at an earlier stage, but continued to expand lending – apparently believing that this (active recycling of petrodollars) would at least help improve conditions and counteract some of the negative effects of bad policies. Thus,

> '*between 1974 and 1982, the Bank's view of borrowing was influenced by the need of the global economy to respond to the large current account imbalances which originated with the vast terms of trade changes of the oil price shock of 1973/4, and exacerbated by the second shock, in 1979. In this context, whilst the growth in debt indicators for many countries were recognised, borrowing was seen as an essentially beneficial component of the global adjustment process... In 1977, McNamara felt that "the major lending banks and major borrowing*

countries are operating on assumptions which are broadly consistent with one another"... He concluded that "... we are even more confident today than we were a year ago that the debt problem is indeed manageable, and need not stand in the way of desirable rates of growth for the developing countries..."[42]

It is widely recognized today that the international banking community, including the World Bank, failed fatally in anticipating what was happening. For instance, in a mere two years, 1980 and 1981, total (private and public) bank exposure nearly doubled over the level of 1979 in the major debtor countries. But, finally, with Mexico's default signalling the start of the debt crisis in 1982, the lesson sank in. Apart from aiming to quell criticism over its failure to read the writing on the wall, the World Bank turned the attention on the need for adjustment and policy-based lending in order to correct the 'failures' that threatened developing countries in both Africa and Latin America to go bust.

THE CHALLENGE OF THE 1990S – NEW CONSTRAINTS AND BANK RESPONSES

Well into the second half of the 1990s, the World Bank is facing an up hill battle. While the '50 years is enough' slogan did not represent very deep currents of opposition, the situation as the Bank entered the second half of the centennium presented many difficult challenges. Its support base in the US has always been vulnerable, and James Wolfensohn, the current World Bank president, has an even tougher job than most of his predecessors in convincing Congress of the urgency of the Bank's mission (Clausen's problems in the early Reagan era may be an exception). A significant policy change towards increasing openness and accountability is starting to make imprints on the Bank's hitherto negative image in NGO communities and in world opinion in general, but this particular journey has just begun. Concerns about project quality still run deep following the revelations by the Wappenhans report. Project performance is further challenged by the donor- and NGO-induced addition of new conditionalities and a further proliferation of areas subject to World Bank action. A radical reorganization was launched in 1997 as a means to cope with increasing tensions, creating a high level of organizational turbulence that may prove difficult to handle.

Moving Further Towards the Left on the Continuum of Functions

The 1990s has seen a further movement of the World Bank's span of activities towards the left on our continuum of functions. McNamara's transformation of the Bank into a development institution in the 1970s was consolidated throughout the 1980s not least through the comprehensive venture into sector and structural adjustment lending. The failure of individual projects due to policy anomalies, and the failure of entire economies due to unmanageable debt problems, convinced management and governors alike of the salience of a broad and economy-wide role of the Bank.[43] The high level of structural adjustment and sector-based lending adopted in the early 1980s continues into the 1990s, implying a relative decline in direct project lending (2/3 project lending and 1/3 SAL/sector lending in the late 1980s, a slight decrease in SAL/sector lending in the 1990s). Increasingly, policy advice and building of domestic institutional capacity have been added on to SAL/sector loan packages, in response to criticism that such capacity has been seriously lacking with negative impacts on the sustainability of such lending.

Its expanding mandate in the environmental field is a good illustration of the continuation of the trend towards the centre and even (norm-creation) left of our continuum of functions. By 1998, the World Bank is clearly the leading international institution when it comes to handling environmental challenges in developing countries. This holds for the number of environmental experts employed by the Bank (3–400 by 1997, depending on definitions), as well as the number and size of environmental projects.[44] Moreover, the Bank's environmental mission has gradually moved towards policy advice and norm-creation. More than 50 developing countries have developed so-called National Environmental Action Plans (NEAPs) under World Bank auspices. The Bank's governing board demanded in the early 1990s that further IDA loans would be made conditional on the completion of a NEAP. Other World Bank moves pointing in similar directions are leadership in the development of environmental assessment methodology, a range of widely distributed publications on topical environmental issues (including the 1992 'environmental' World Development Report), and a range of seminars and large-scale conferences – including an annual big 'sustainable development' event. This is not to say that the Bank's record in environmental capacity building and norm-creation is uncontroversial, but by any standard it is the world leader (among international institutions) in terms of support for sustainable development in developing countries. As such it completely dwarfs UNEP, the main UN body geared towards many of the same policy goals.

Proliferation of Tasks and Functions

The expanding role of the World Bank in the environmental field (from 7 to more than 300 environmental experts) is but one example of the proliferation of functions taken on by the Bank. Its widening functional scope (into policy advice/dialogue, capacity building, institutional support) has got a strong impetus from the expansion of thematic focus, particularly for 'soft' issues such as health, education, governance and the environment. The MDBs' increasing role (both in absolute and relative terms) in the health sector is illustrated in Figure 3.5. Figure 3.6 shows the rapid growth of the share of Bank lending going to 'human development'.

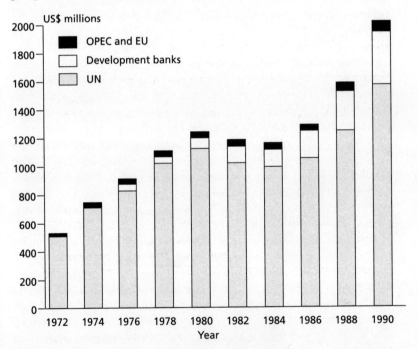

Source: Michaud & Murray: *Aid Flows to the Health Sector in Developing Countries: A Detailed Analysis 1972–1990*, Harvard, 1993.

Figure 3.5 *Multilateral Disbursements for the Health Sector*

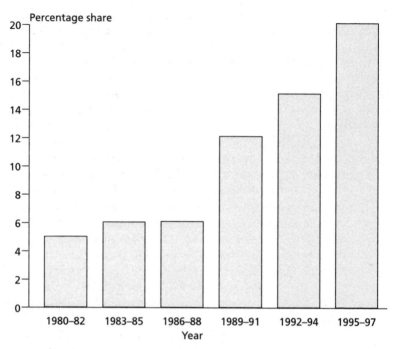

Source: *Poverty Reduction and the World Bank: Progress in Fiscal 1996 and 1997* World Bank, 1997.

Figure 3.6 *Share of Total World Bank Lending for Human Development*

Also, an interesting feature in an historical perspective is that almost 50 years since it gave up 'post-war reconstruction' as a separate business area, the Bank is returning forcefully to this field in a number of African and Asian countries.[45] Contributing to this trend of proliferation is the steadily increasing availability of 'free money' through trust funds and similar sources, which presently (1997) make up an annual US$2 billion. Such grant funds, naturally, make it far easier for the Bank to broaden its thematic and functional agenda, than if it had to rely on money raised in conventional capital markets (like in the good old days) or through capital replenishment with policy requirements from donors.

Thematic and functional proliferation, and the gradual shift of attention towards the left on our continuum of functions, are direct responses to demands from the governing board and other parts of the Bank's external policy environment. Many see these developments as positive evidence of the ability of the World Bank to adapt to changing external demands on the institution.[46] Others, however, are growing increasingly concerned that issue proliferation comes at a high price, with the Bank's ability to concentrate on its alleged comparative advantages as a main victim. The scholars at the Brookings Institution who have spent five years since 1992 in writing up a major two-volume history of the World Bank definitely belong to the critical voices in this respect:

> *'The Bank's dilemma by the middle 1990s was that its span of substantive attention – its list of program priorities – had been stretched almost beyond recognition. There were all kinds of add-ons, among them, population, gender, governance, and probity, education, and commodity trade. The institution was wide open to substantive proliferation. New subjects were worthy, and the dynamism of technical and social change kept raising them. In terms of public and parliamentary relations, the Bank was running scared; it felt driven to take on new subjects as major owners and such major "stakeholders" as the NGOs so demanded. And the Bank's outreach to new subjects was animated also by an element of superciliousness about the generalist components of the United Nations. The latter (in part, it should be noted, because of poor industrialised country support) were seen to be falling short. Many in the Bank felt it was part of being the "world's leading development agency" to reach into one new field after another.'[47]*

These developments, according to the Brookings Institution scholars, were qualitatively different from the response of the Bank to comparable pressures back in the 1970s:

> 'As already noted, there was a tendency toward the proliferation of goals and subjects back in the 1970s also. *But it was held better in check.* The World Bank was certainly not dysfunctionally meek at that time. But its style was to cast itself as a major player in behalf of a *new purpose only if and when the institution had developed a comparative advantage in the new field.* The 1990s bank in its subject choices urgently needed to regain at least a measure of such restraint *[our emphasis].*'[48]

World Bank Responses: Policy Change and Organizational Reform

At the mid-1990s it was generally agreed that the effectiveness of the Bank was unsatisfactory. However, views differed on which relationship existed between proliferation and effectiveness and consequently on which avenue of change the Bank should embark upon in order to increase its impact.

The *first* avenue of change, advocated by the Brookings scholars and probably with broad support among 'World Bank traditionalists', would argue that the loss of effectiveness can be traced back to the proliferation of subjects and broadening of its mission. This expansion of objectives and activities has resulted both from pressures working internally in the organization facilitated by soft budget constraints and in its external environment (owners/governments and NGOs/civil society). The Bank's reputation for effectiveness was first and foremost based on being a specialized organization dealing with a specialized agenda and clearly defined activities, which were not internally conflicting. It is different from a nation-state, which theoretically has an unlimited number of purposes, but it is also different from a private firm, which, at least in theory, pursues one single goal (ie profit-seeking). This approach acknowledges that the Bank must have several goals, but argues that the balance should be struck closer to the firm than to the nation state in terms of number of purposes (*a functional multilateral*). The gradual proliferation undermined the Bank's effectiveness in two different ways: it became impossible to retain its principal strength, namely the 'depth of its specialised expertise', and an increasing number of goals led to an increased possibility for internally conflicting goals.

The recipe for regaining some of the past effectiveness is thus, as a minimum, to exercise a much larger degree of selectivity when deciding upon new goals and purposes for the Bank and preferably to return to more traditional avenues of World Bank action, with IBRD-type lending for high priority projects (eg infrastructure) that prove to be close to being competitive in market terms but still too risky for traditional private investors. This would probably imply working closely with the private sector, perhaps with an increasing role for the IFC and MIGA. According to these sources, this is where the Bank commands a comparative advantage, or termed otherwise: where the Bank's governing structure and organizational design can be meaningfully fitted to functions it is expected to take on.

A *second* diagnosis of unsatisfactory Bank effectiveness is represented by the US Task Force on the MDBs which published its report in September 1997. This approach argues that the remedy should be to move even more explicitly towards becoming the world's major development agency, with increasing focus on funding, capacity building and policy advice for 'reducing poverty alleviation, stimulate broad-based economic growth and promoting environmental sustainability ...'.[49]

The report lists the different functions of the MDBs:

- the banking function (channelling funds to potentially financially viable projects and creditworthy countries),
- aid function (channelling funds to uncreditworthy countries and to projects with potentially high social, economic and environmental returns),
- technical advice function,
- policy change function (supplying financing to support policy change), and
- meeting place and consensus-building function.

Though the report identifies the tendency of the MDBs 'to acquire a proliferation of functions without resolving conflicts among them, setting priorities and relinquishing unsuitable roles ...'[50] as a weakness, it does not specify which functions are outdated. Rather, it specifies how, for example, the Bank could improve the performance of both its traditional and new functions.

Hence, according to this approach:

1 The Bank should take into account that private capital flows have rendered the banking function necessary in fewer countries and projects than before and that new lending should be limited to countries where policy conditions support programme objectives.
2 The aid function of the Bank should be revised and carried out with other means than the present large loan prepared by headquarters staff and where checks on implementation are too reliant on the borrowing government.
3 The technical advice function should be improved through attaining in-depth local knowledge and include a wider variety of disciplines.
4 The function of promoting policy change presently lacks relevance because it is based on general policy prescriptions disregarding local conditions and without involvement of local groups and actors except maybe top government officials.

5   The Task Force report emphasizes the more active role, which the MDBs should play in bringing together diverse groups within and among countries. The Bank (and other MDBs) is seen to have a unique range of contacts and thus well suited to bring different interests together and facilitate common solutions. Similarly, the Bank should expand its role as a consultative forum for countries on regional problems.

This approach, therefore, implies a consolidation of the present wide variety of functions ranging from traditional banking to consultative and consensus-building fora. Selectivity is first of all taken to mean fewer countries and that the Bank should pay closer attention as to where, when and how to perform any of the functions assigned to it.

When it comes to sectors or themes (as distinct from functions) which the Bank should take on, this approach likewise advocates a broad agenda. Infrastructure should still be a priority, environment, natural resources, population, private sector, social sector, institution building, financial sector, women and minorities, participation, macro-economic and sector reform, empowerment, human capital – few, if any, of the key words, or fashions, in the evolving development debate in the last decades are left out.

A special case is made on the need for MDB financing of activities aimed at 'non-physical results'. Such projects, while vital for poverty reduction and economic development, are unlikely to attract private funding. MDB efforts for such projects (eg capacity building and institutional development) are therefore most important.

The present top management in the Bank may be seen to represent *a third approach* trying to correct two serious weaknesses simultaneously: unsatisfactory quality and effectiveness of Bank-funded projects and decreasing relevance of the Bank stemming from a stagnating or even declining lending volume. The current president, James D. Wolfensohn, undoubtedly recognized that the Bank was under severe pressure on both fronts with resulting doubts about the legitimacy and justification of the Bank as he took over just after the fiftieth anniversary when criticism of the Bank peaked.

Even though it was felt that the Bank was ripe for change even before Wolfensohn took over, the diagnosis and prescriptions have not been entirely clear and consistent in the years after. The bottom line has, however, remained the same: effectiveness, defined as tangible impact on poverty and development in the field of Bank-funded projects must improve. Unless greater effectiveness is achieved, the legitimacy of the Bank is likely to be questioned by broader groups in important owner countries, and declining legitimacy would pose a threat to the long-time survival of the organization.

There was also a sense that the *relevance* of the Bank was on the decline. Private capital flows to developing countries increased rapidly in the first half of the 1990s and more countries preferred private sources to IBRD loans due to the higher total costs of the latter (see Figure 3.7). The demand for Bank products declined. The increased flow of private capital could undermine the very raison d'être of the Bank: to lend money to countries unable to attract private capital for otherwise profitable projects. A key response to these challenges was to launch the 'Strategic Compact' as an attempt to renew the Bank and improve effectiveness.[51] In return for the members' continued support they would see a new, vitalized and more effective Bank – striving to be *'the premier global development institution'*.[52]

Traditionally the Bank's effectiveness was seen as a result of a combination of *centralized organization* with effective chains of command running from the top down through the system, and *concentration* or selectivity in terms of goals and areas of operation. Unlike the followers of the first approach described above, the current top management of the Bank rejects this view and argues the opposite: rather than promoting effectiveness, concentration and centralization have hampered effectiveness.

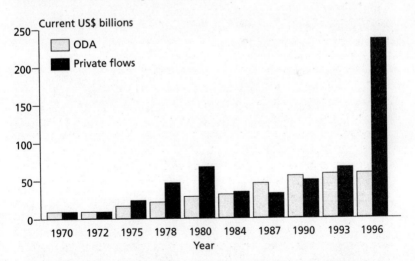

Source: OECD, *DAC Development Cooperation Report*, various years.

Figure 3.7 *ODA and Private Flows to Developing Countries, 1970–96 (current US$ billions)*

Concentration

Though starting out with the notion that the Bank needed to sharpen 'its focus on the issues (it is) tackling', it was apparent that a narrow agenda was rejected:

> 'For me the big lesson from a review of our history and from my travels is that there is no single solution. I have seen how interlinked the pieces of the development puzzle are. Each part of the puzzle poses different problems, and imposes different demands on capacities – both financial and managerial. What I have seen has brought home to me the complexity of development, and the benefits that can be realised when all the pieces fall into place. Solutions must be systemic. I see the Bank's central role as helping to bring all this together in a systemic approach to development: the ideas, the financing, the people – and a knowledge of all these components and of a successful development programme.'[53]

Thus, according to this approach, focusing on one or a few pieces of this puzzle will have little impact. Concentration on, for example infrastructure projects, without due attention to the rest of the puzzle (equity, institutional development, good governance, sound policy environment, population growth, human capital, cultural issues, etc) will not be sustainable. A narrow approach will lead to failures in two different ways: either a road project will fail on its own terms (poor maintenance due to eg weak institutions), or the benefits of the road project could easily be undermined through the social erosion or breakdown resulting from lack of attention to social and political development issues.

Thus the Bank's comparative advantage is, in its current own eyes, that it is 'the only global institution *working in all spheres of development*'.[54] The emphasis on a broad, integrated approach to development is however paralleled with statements on the 'need to sharpen the focus on the issues the Bank is dealing with', and that 'the Bank is focusing on much greater selectivity in order to target those areas where it has the greatest leverage'.[55] Practical evidence for these efforts is hard to find, and is also contradicted by another of the present top management's drives: a client-oriented Bank.

Centralization

The centralized character of the Bank had produced a donor-driven loan portfolio. What was needed to improve effectiveness and secure Bank relevance was a client-oriented portfolio. Centralization had produced ignorance of local conditions and inappropriate conditionality from which both Bank effectiveness and attractiveness was suffering. Centralization had produced excessive red tape and a slow, static organization, which had become less and less attractive to those countries which, could turn to alternatives (private capital). Centralization in Washington had reduced the ability to check on implementation and take corrective measures. It had produced an inward-looking culture where loan approval was the success-criterion rather than the quality and results of the projects. No wonder effectiveness was suffering.

A client-oriented Bank able to take individual countries' needs better into account requires radical organizational changes: A first requisite is greater geographical proximity to its clients, and Bank staff have been deployed in the field. In his 1997 Annual Meetings speech, Mr Wolfensohn could boast of 18 country managers out of 48 having been deployed to the field offices in their respective countries. It also requires new expertise with greater country-specific knowledge of the social underpinnings of economic development. Hence, sociologists and anthropologists will constitute a larger share of total staff. The Bank's clients are countries, and countries have specific needs and characteristics, therefore money and responsibility are shifted from sector departments to operational country departments. A client-oriented Bank must respond quickly, therefore the bureaucratic procedures have to be simplified. Project preparation before board approval has been speeded up. Client orientation requires steady renewal of products, so new projects such as single-currency loans (a country may now have its loan denominated in one currency, not in a set of various currencies as previously), debt reduction packages and loans for innovative projects are now offered.

It is impossible to argue that the Bank should *not* be client-oriented and demand-driven. A Bank seeking to take this beyond rhetoric will, unless proper mechanisms for retaining focus are established, be wide open to new items being added on the agenda. Even if there is a positive relationship between client orientation and effectiveness, there might also be a negative effect through overextended agendas and conflicting objectives. However, mechanisms of constraint are not addressed in the Strategic Compact.

The Bank's present leadership also rejects the notion that a certain degree of insulation from the external environment has freed the Bank from side-constraints and promoted goal achievement. Rather, the current view is that the technological revolution facilitates cooperation and partnering where the potential gains clearly outweigh possible losses. Thus, the Bank will enter into significantly expanded partnerships with the UN system, other regional development banks, NGOs and civil society and the private sector. The grand vision is

> '*a modern, responsive, highly professional institution which operates through partnerships, which provides a unique set of high-quality services to its clients, which serves as a catalyst for public-private collaboration*, a connector among development agencies, and a builder of capacity and knowledge for the entire development community'.[56]

The possibility remains, however, that the efforts to realize this vision will further increase the pressure on the Bank's agenda and functional dispersion.

Although there are important parallels between this and the second approach described above, there are also important differences. One refers to the lending volume of the Bank. While the second approach argues that the Bank should concentrate lending to countries which are unable to attract private capital and step back in countries that are, part of the rationale for the Bank's Strategic Compact is the flat demand for Bank loans and declining income: 'we are not lending as much as we could – even with financial terms that are the best in the market; in fact, our lending has declined in real terms since fiscal year 1995. At the same time, ... income (is) on a declining path – putting at risk our financial flexibility.'[57] This negative trend will be countered by allowing increased lending to large creditworthy countries.[58]

A drive towards higher lending volumes to defend the Bank's relevance and income could easily put improved quality at risk. The key document on the Strategic Compact does not at all discuss the potential trade-off between the two. While at times stressing the need to put quality ahead of quantity, the president in his Annual Meetings speech in 1997 seemed to resolve the issue simply by equalling them: 'We have improved the quality of our portfolio, and as a result our disbursements reached a record level last year of $20 billion.'[59]

It could be argued therefore, that the stagnating demand for Bank loans forces the Bank to find new outlets for its capital, either through geographical expansion (increased lending to middle-income countries) or through further functional and sectoral proliferation labelled and justified as client orientation, or possibly both. There is a striking parallel to the Bank's response to the scarcity of bankable projects in the 1960s and 1970s. If history and organizational dynamics provide any guidance, it would be that the third approach remains the likeliest outcome.

Chapter 4

The UN and the World Bank: Comparing their Current Predicament

'There's no success like failure'

Bob Dylan

We can now return to our framework of analysis and the hypotheses developed at the end of Chapter 1 in order to investigate whether the empirical findings in Chapters 2 and 3 correspond to our ideal type IGOs and our propositions concerning the relationship between functions and governing structure. On this basis, we shall compare the present situation of the UN and the World Bank.

THE UN DEVELOPMENT SYSTEM: WHICH IDEAL TYPE?

As pointed out by veteran observers like Jackson and Bertrand, the UN system is unique in its complexitiy and comprehensiveness. It is therefore highly questionable whether the entire system can be subsumed under any one of our ideal types. It is not our intention to identify *the* category of organization to which the UN belongs. Our purpose here is to characterize the UN in terms of functions and governing structure in search for the main features of the world organization as a development institution.

Normative Functions

The UN started out after World War II with a broad and elusive mandate and few, if any, clear guidelines as to future functions. Given its original role as a world-wide political forum and its universal aspirations ('we, the peoples of the United Nations'), it was the natural platform for the emerging new states in the early post-war period, where they could speak out for their causes, first decolonization, later redistribution of wealth, development assistance and new economic order. The West also used the UN from an early stage to express its concerns and political objectives, as witnessed in the decade long debates over human rights.

We have seen above how the UN has adapted and proliferated its development agenda from decade to decade, beginning with economic growth and social progress in the 1950s and 1960s, adding alleged inequities in the world economy in the 1970s, turning to 'sustainable development' in the late 1980s and early 1990s to end up with 'good governance' and an 'enabling environment for sustainable development' by the late 1990s. The latter slogan, in one stroke of eloquence, combines at least three separate agendas.[1]

So, throughout this 50-year period the UN has been a forum for competing agendas, a meeting place where governments have voiced their grievances and presented their arguments hoping to win support from the community of states. The proponents of an idea, an ideology or a concrete cause have frequently failed to make progress. They have reiterated their case year after year, thus setting their mark on the UN agenda, without achieving much else. The futile call for a new economic order that dominated UN politics for a decade is a telling example. When such controversy runs high, the UN remains stuck with the agenda setting function, easily receding into frustrating, repetitive exercises. This was also the case with the human rights debate in various UN fora almost for a generation, from the late 1940s to the middle of the 1970s with argument against argument in constant recrimination. In contrast to the new order debacle, in the field of human rights the pressures built up over the years gradually led to wider support, at least at the rhetorical level, for the principles introduced on the UN agenda with the Universal Declaration of 1948. Consequently, UN activities slowly expanded into the more ambitious normative functions, standard setting and monitoring. Disagreement over the proper human rights agenda has not disappeared (and probably never will), but this has not precluded the expansion of functions to the current situation where UN bodies regularly negotiate new standards, monitor state performance and provide advice and assistance to governments on request. Their operative tasks within human rights are innovative and significant in many respects, but remain marginal compared with the weight of the normative functions.

At times, the UN has succeeded in going beyond agenda setting in the overall development discussion. There can, for example, be little doubt that the process leading up to UNCED promoted broad understanding for the sustainable development approach, but it did not go much further in terms of our functions. Agenda 21 – the main outcome from the Rio Conference – is too vague and general to be called standard setting and, as a consequence, monitoring of national implementation has turned out to be very complicated and cumbersome.

In the field of climate change, the UN has contributed significantly to define the international agenda, to promote joint understanding through the IPCC, to set broad standards first in the Framework Convention, later and more specifically in the Kyoto Protocol and to monitor national performance through the secretariat to the Convention. In many ways this example illustrates what Kofi Annan calls the 'convening power of the United Nations'.[2] By taking advantage of its universal participation, the UN can imbue such a process with a legitimacy that no other IGO can, both in its political and scientific aspects.

The large specialized agencies have since the early post-war period performed both agenda, standard setting and monitoring functions within their respective mandates. UNICEF's initiative for a World Summit for Children and subsequent monitoring shows how a UN fund can effectively undertake several normative functions and mobilize political energy for its purposes.[3]

The analysis in Chapter 2, as illustrated by these examples, demonstrates that the UN development system has taken up all the normative functions on our spectrum. It seems fair to conclude that its main preoccupation has been agenda setting, often resulting in little more than words, but sometimes prodding governments and other actors towards better understanding of each others' positions and of the issues involved, which has in turn laid the basis for agreement on standards and subsequent monitoring. Numerous problems have reached the agenda setting phase, fewer have been codified into international standards and very few are subject to systematic monitoring under UN auspices.

Operative Functions

As shown in Chapter 2, various UN bodies very soon after 1945 started taking up operative functions by raising funds and defining their own projects. Over time this tendency has proliferated throughout the entire system, involving almost every fund, programme or agency in some kind of operative work. Even if the volumes are small in comparison with other ODA channels, not to speak of private transfers, being in the 'development business' through their own operations is considered of crucial importance to most UN funds, programmes and agencies. So, after 50 years operative functions are regarded as an integral part of current activities and essential to the image the organization communicates to the outside world. In the words of its former chief executive UN 'efforts in the service of humanity' include 'to help the afflicted and the suffering; to oppose war, violence and intolerance; to promote the rights and dignity of every individual; and to help bring about the economic, social, political and environmental conditions for long-term human progress'.[4] The UN system is definitely not content with just defining the agenda and promoting political agreement. One of its comparative advantages and 'core competencies' is seen to be translating consensus into norms, integrating it into national plans and supporting implementation by UN operations.[5] In presenting his reform programme in July 1997, Secretary-General Kofi Annan underlined this notion of the unique position of the UN: 'the United Nations has no peer among international organisations in identifying novel issues on the policy horizon *and devising plans of action for dealing with them*'. He, furthermore, stressed the link between normsetting and operations: '(I)n some key areas, such as development cooperation, the United Nations' normative capacity is linked directly to assisting national policy and is further supported by its own operational activities.'[6]

So, as far as functions are concerned, the UN development system does not fit neatly into either of our ideal types. From the outset, it had mainly normative functions, but over time it has sprawled all over the entire spectrum.

UN Governing Structure

As we pointed out in the beginning of Chapter 2, the UN was from its very inception based on the principle of formal equality among states. This was never in line with real world distribution of resources, but has, for this very reason perhaps, been carefully guarded by the majority of developing countries. At times, they have taken advantage of their numerical superiority by forcing controversial issues to a vote. This was particularly evident during the 'new order' debacle of the 1970s. Despite rhetorical victories, this tactic produced very little in terms of tangible benefits. Consequently, decision-making in the 1990s has become more and more consensus oriented, which means that on major occasions, like the grand world conferences, the main state actors will do their utmost to reconcile positions and, whenever necessary, remaining disagreements will be papered over or deferred to subsequent meetings.

A corollary to the preoccupation with formal equality is wide participation. On paper, participants with equal rights could agree to establish a system based on representative, but small and selective decision-making organs to which power is delegated from bodies with participation. In practice, in the UN system such arrangements are difficult and fragile. There is a strong push for wide participation by governments in every decision-making body, in particular those with access to funding, that is those parts of the system with operative functions. Proposals for more selectivity, as forwarded in the Gardner report (small negotiating groups under ECOSOC) and the Independent Commission on Global Governance (replacing ECOSOC with a smaller and more powerful Economic Security Council) have fallen on stony ground, as they run counter to the logic of the governing structure of the UN.

In addition to wide state participation in all aspects of decision-making, the UN system has since the late 1980s opened up its procedures to non-governmental actors in ways that would have been inconceivable 20 years ago. With the UNCED preparations, the 'stakeholder' approach, involving everyone with a legitimate interest regardless of formal status, won general acceptance, despite grudging disapproval in some diplomatic quarters.[7] Since then, participation by NGOs and private industry has come to be seen not only as a necessary part of UN deliberations, but increasingly as a major asset, giving new life to the ambition inherent in 'we, the peoples of the United Nations'.[8]

Another important feature of the governing structure of the UN system is staffing. From the outset, secretariat positions were seen to be one of the benefits to be distributed among governments. With the emerging developing world majority this tendency became even more pronounced. Since the 1950s, winning staff positions is not only important in itself, but also as a means to future influence. This is not unique to the UN system among IGOs, but in most other organizations this attitude is kept under control by requiring technical competence from would-be staff members. Within the UN such controls seem to have been very lax for a very long time, if we are to take seriously the devastating criticism levelled at recruitment practices and staff morale by such veterans as Childers and Urquhart, which echoes similarly critical assessments made by Jackson and Bertrand decades earlier.[9] There seems to be little disagreement that this tendency has had a negative impact on the professional standard of the UN development apparatus. However, the wide distribution of secretariat positions to nationals from across the world reinforces the representative, universalist nature of the UN system.

Functions and Structure

The upshot is that as for the governing structure, the main features of the UN development system are consistent and unambiguous; formal equality, wide participation in process and staff, little delegation of powers, consensus as the overriding decision-making principle and incorporation of ever new actors. In other words, *a structure ideally suited for a normsetting IGO*, which was, probably, what the founding fathers had in mind back in 1945. This, however, is definitely not what the UN development system is today, as we have shown above.

So, here is a clear discrepancy between the functions of an organization and its governing structure. According to our hypotheses, this state of affairs should produce serious malfunctions to which the IGO will respond with never-ending reform. In the case of the UN, performance problems have been adequately and regularly documented over the last 30 years with focus on the unwieldy and ungovernable character of the system. Report after report has pointed to the lack of coordination and the absence of a decision-making centre that can produce the 'coherence of effort and unity of purpose' that Kofi Annan has called for.

The coordination problem with all its ramifications is, in our judgement, not a coincidence but a logical consequence of the governing structure. It is very difficult, if not impossible to achieve operative effectiveness within a decision-making system that resents hierarchy, balks at delegating authority, constantly includes new concerns and new actors and prefers representativeness to technical competence in its recruitment. However, it is precisely because of its non-hierarchical, inclusive structure that the UN has, from time to time, been fairly successful in its normative functions. It has adapted to the changing agendas of its changing majorities; it has opened up to a range of new issues and incorporated a whole new world of actors.[10] In short, it has been very good at reflecting inconsistencies in its environment, in terms of changes in geopolitics, in development agenda and in stakeholders. So, the strength of the UN is also its weakness. The structure that is well adapted to normative functions is ill suited for the operative ones.

The UN development system has tried to handle this dilemma by promising improvement in the future, in line with our 'never ending reform' hypothesis. As we have described in Chapter 2, there is very little new in the debate over UN reform. The Jackson report, written almost 30 years ago, is as valid and useful today as it was then. Kofi Annan's grand scheme of 1997 reiterates the main themes and even points to the same solutions in important respects, thereby underlining how little has changed in the meantime. The UN reform debate appears as a textbook example of how an organization of this kind can and *should* respond, meeting criticism of dissolution and lack of coordination with reform proposal after reform proposal, as if a solution lies around the corner. The root cause of the problem is, however, the governing structure, which the dominating actors do not want to change and which serves the normative functions of the organization well. Hence, the reform processes are bound to be futile, and it is worth asking if they were ever intended to succeed. If, in the purely hypothetical case, a solution were to be found and implemented and the UN emerged as a hierarchical, business-like organization with unity and coherence – 'streamlined' in diplomatic jargon – such a governing structure would soon erode its normative functions.[11] So, our interpretation is that the reform process is not really meant to succeed in conventional terms – by producing and implementing a blueprint for effectiveness. In order to succeed it must fail, because failure leads to new reform proposals and new decades of discussion of reorganization and coordination. In this way, the reform debates have turned out to be a highly successful mechanism for handling the insoluble dilemma that the reform schemes purport to solve. Fortunately, they never do, as the UN experience so vividly illustrates.

The question then arises: isn't failure to reform after so many attempts a serious threat to the legitimacy of the UN? If students of organizations are right, no: failing organizations, in general, stand a much better chance of survival than their successful counterparts, because 'solutions normally last for a much shorter time than insoluble problems'. The UN system and its supporters can seek comfort in the fact that the 'organizations that have survived the longest are universities, churches, and nation states – all of which are good at reflecting inconsistencies' and, we should add, have gone through reform processes that last centuries, not decades.[12]

The key to legitimacy for these long-lived 'creatures' lies in incorporating the environment to the extent that outside groups will perceive their own values to be dependent on the survival of the organization. If this is a widely held view, the organization becomes legitimate by definition.

One serious problem remains, however, for the UN development system – the gap between rhetoric and resources. The proliferation of UN functions across the entire spectrum that began as early as the 1950s and was completed in the 1970s is founded on a relatively weak and, as the 1990s have shown, unpredictable resource base. The funding available to UN development assistance is in no way commensurate to the high aspirations and lofty ambitions expressed by its political masters, that is government representatives, often at the highest level, in the General Assembly and at the whole series of world conferences.[13] They repeatedly promise to eradicate hunger, poverty, illiteracy and the like, while protecting the natural riches of the earth for future generations. The result is a credibility problem, to which the UN system can respond by repeating or recycling rhetoric and/or extend its activities into new areas, which require even more resources. The account we have given in Chapter 2 indicates that both kinds of response are frequently found. The problem is that both of them tend to reinforce the credibility gap they were intended to bridge; more rhetoric raises expectation of more action – further expansion spreads resources even more thinly.

We shall return, in Chapter 5, to this issue which is decisive to the future of the UN development system. Let us first see whether its main competitor has fared any better the last 50 years.

THE WORLD BANK

As demonstrated in Chapter 3, the World Bank began its life with a straightforward mandate, providing loans for clearly defined projects within industry and public infrastructure. As early as the 1960s, management received warnings that such confinement of its projects from society at large was problematic given the circumstances in developing countries, as opposed to reconstruction in Europe. During the 1970s Bank management gradually realized that this approach was too narrow and in the 1980s the shortcomings could not longer be concealed; whether the Bank failed or succeeded hinged not only on selection, design and implementation of its projects as such, but on a number of external issues. The fate of a power plant turned out to be more than a question of concrete and money, as it depended on electricity prices and a host of other factors, both macro-economic and institutional.[14] The response, most markedly in the 1980s, was structural adjustment and policy-based lending. During the 1990s the Bank has, again, extended the range of relevant factors into formerly uncharted territory, taking into account such unpredictables as political rights and the role of civil society in recipient countries. Its current agenda covers the whole spectrum of political and social issues that have stifled development in large parts of the developing world over the last generation; corruption, rent-seeking, inequity, oppression of opposition, weak legal institutions and the like.[15] So, its agenda is now cast wide open; 'our role ... is to ... get a justice system ... a system of property rights ... to stop street crime',[16] which is a world apart from financing airlines and ports.[17] Today, there is hardly a slogan in the international development debate that is not a World Bank concern, whether it is environment, gender, health, children, corruption or good governance.

This expansion of agenda is the result of continuous pressures from both governments and NGOs since the 1970s, and it goes beyond rhetoric. As we have shown in Chapter 3, the Bank has stepped up lending for so-called soft sectors very rapidly since the late 1980s.

A New Paradigm

The Bank's basic mission still sounds like McNarama's heyday – '(P)overty reduction remains at the heart of everything we do'[18] – but the current management has recognised that 'development' is a complex and multifaceted affair, to which there is no single solution. In Wolfensohn's jargon it is a 'puzzle' that involves the interplay of numerous factors – macro-economics, private investment, environmental protection, human capital, to name a few. He has also taken care to underscore the role of people and the societal underpinnings of development. 'Social, cultural and institutional factors are key to success and sustainability.'[19] This recognition lies behind the Bank's new approach to participation and its new development paradigm:

'The lesson is clear: for economic advance, you need social advance – and without social development, economic development cannot take root. For the Bank, this means that we need to make sure that the programs and projects we support have adequate social foundations... I see this as ... *the* critical challenge before us.'[20]

Not only are such issues more demanding than the confined projects the Bank was set up to deal with, the main trouble is that they tend to raise questions to which there are no easy answers and, even worse, include problems that may turn out to be 'essentially insoluble, or have defied solution for thousands of years'.[21] Even with the large research capability of the World Bank and its long experience, there is good reason to ask whether its experts will ever come up with answers to questions like; what is the best system of property rights in an African rain forest? Which legal system can promote development in Bangladesh? How can street crime be eradicated in Lagos?[22]

Changing Functions

In tandem with its expanding agenda, the Bank has gone through a remarkable transformation in terms of functions. This process began as early as the 1970s under McNamara's reign and has been completed by current president Wolfensohn. The Bank started out with a clear focus on financing projects. As it moved into developing countries with limited administrative capacity it took on increasing responsibility also for project preparation and follow-up. Even if formally the recipient government was responsible for implementation on the ground, the Bank in practice undertook much of the management function to the right on our spectrum.

Following a better understanding of the importance of framework conditions for individual projects, the Bank as early as the 1960s began to offer advice to its counterparts on appropriate policies. During the 1970s and 1980s, its functions expanded to cover not only policy advice, but also to set clear cut standards of performance in the form of conditionalities tied to sector or structural adjustment loans and subsequent monitoring of recipient performance. These functions brought the Bank into heated controversies with governments of developing countries and pro-development NGOs in the West. In the 1980s, environmental NGOs joined the battle. Faced with such wide criticism, Bank management and its major shareholders could not simply respond by referring to its formal statutes of non-interference in politics. The Bank needed to build a larger constituency for its approach to development and its position as a leading development institution. This was to have a profound impact on both its functions and its structure.

With regard to the former, the Bank has over the last 15–20 years had a strong ambition to influence the overall development agenda, through such measures as the World Development Report, large-scale conferences, annual meetings with high media profile, general PR efforts and the like. It has also devoted considerable resources to promoting understanding for its view of development through documentation and research, dissemination of results and best practices and training programmes. By carefully cultivating such normative functions (agenda setting and promoting understanding) the Bank has attained intellectual leadership in the international development debate and continuously reinforced its position as number one in the 'market for ideas'. In this way, it has achieved a political leverage that far exceeds its financial resources.

In terms of our framework of analysis, the World Bank has moved consistently and systematically from its original purely operative mandate across the entire spectrum of functions to the point where it now covers 'all spheres of development'.[23] Its ambition is to be the premier global development institution, which is a world of difference from being a bank where 'only economic considerations shall be relevant to (its) decisions'.[24]

Governing Structure

During its first generation, the structure of the Bank was unequivocally business-like. Control over decision-making was in the hands of top management and the limited group of large shareholders, to a large extent detached from the outside pressures. The staff, consisting mainly of economists educated in the Anglo-Saxon world, was homogenous and technically highly competent. The whole operation was run in a centralized fashion from Bank headquarters in Washington DC. Since the 1980s and especially in the 1990s, this structure has undergone important changes:

- The Bank has opened up its processes and procedures to the outside world in an attempt to make its operations more transparent. It has taken pains to include a much larger group of stakeholders in its discussions, treating NGOs, and industry, as legitimate participants, though without making formal changes in access to decision-making. Its rhetoric is more than ever geared to the needs of its clients, which in current parlance number not some 150 governments, but 4.7 billion people.[25] Even if it is open to argument how much real impact these changes have had on Bank operations, they have set in train a process of openness and transparency that is most likely to be irreversible.[26]

- The Bank has slowly begun to decentralize parts of its operations to regional and country offices, again in order to get closer to its clients.
- Even if the predominance of economists remains, the Bank has started recruiting larger numbers of specialists from other disciplines in order to deal with its much wider agenda. It has, for example, more professional expertise in the field of the environment than any other IGO.

Which Ideal Type?

There can be little doubt that the World Bank from its inception and at least well into the 1960s had the main features of our ideal type of an operative IGO with a clearly confined mandate and a business-like, hierarchical structure. Over the last generation it has expanded into normative functions, which means that at present it fits into neither of our ideal types. It has tried to adapt its governing structure to its comprehensive functions and all-encompassing agenda, grudgingly in the 1980s, apparently enthusiastically in the 1990s. But the trouble is that it is now trying to be two very different things at the same time, both a bank and a development institution. As a bank it is required to be precise and effective, both in decision-making and implementation. In Wolfensohn's words: 'To get the biggest bang from our scarce resources, we must be absolutely tough-minded... We have to promise only what we can deliver and deliver what we promise.'[27] In other words, to act like an operative IGO.

At the same time, the Bank intends to be the 'premier development institution' in the world, which would include, in our view, setting and propagating an agenda that is generally acceptable, incorporating new issues as they arise and new actors as they emerge. In a recent study this was aptly referred to as the tendency to 'satisfy multiple masters'.[28] This requires a governing structure that is open to the outside world and reflects changing and conflicting demands in the environment. In practice this entails consensus orientation, time consuming processes with wide participation and considerable patience on the part of all participants. In other words, to work like a normsetting IGO.

In trying to cover the entire spectrum of functions simultaneously, the World Bank puts heavy stress on its governing structure as it faces this kind of cross pressure. If it retains the old characteristics of a bank, it will be seriously constrained in its efforts to incorporate the larger agenda and the broader environment. If it makes the decisive transition to a development institution, its structure can no longer be as effective and as efficient as would be expected from a bank. At present, the Bank is determined to undertake both normative and operative functions and to be *the* premier development institution on the eve of the twenty-first century. It is not clear, however, whether its governing structure has been successfully adapted for such grand intentions. Some observers hold that in practice Bank staff are largely unaffected by the rhetoric, continuing to disburse money in much the same way as they did 20 years ago.[29] Others underline that the widening agenda with all kinds of add-ons is taken seriously and that this has negative ramifications on its performance as a bank.[30] If the former view is correct, Bank structure and functions are clearly incompatible. If the latter is closer to reality, the problem is not incompatibility between functions and structure, but confusion arising from inconsistent and irreconcilable demands on the governing structure.

In either case, we can conclude that the current predicament of the Bank is well in line with our overreach hypothesis. By expanding its functions far beyond the original mandate, it imposes significant strain on its governing structure, which was established for different purposes and does not change overnight. This creates increasing inconsistencies between words and deeds and among different parts of the organization.[31] In response to such a dilemma an IGO can, according to our fourth hypothesis, either retreat to where it came from, its original mandate or venture reform. World Bank management has chosen the latter option. Wolfensohn's 'Strategic Compact' is apparently intended to solve the entire spectrum of overreach problems in one operation, taking the best out of the 'old' Bank and merging it with the aspirations of the 'new'. Whatever the outcome of the reform process, the tension between normative and operative functions and the structures needed to take care of each of them will continue to haunt the World Bank. This is a consequence of the inconsistent norms and the ever widening agenda the Bank intends to accommodate and the intransigent, at times insoluble, nature of its new development paradigm. If our interpretation of its current predicament is not beyond the mark, the Bank will not succeed in riding the two horses at the same time. It will have to make a choice, either be a good development institution or be a good bank.

PARTNERS OR COMPETITORS ?

The UN development system and the World Bank have evolved over these 50 years to become more and more alike along all important dimensions:

- functions;
- development approach;
- openness in decision-making;
- decentralization.

Functions

Starting out from opposite sides of our spectrum, they have converged towards the same pattern as both endeavour to cover the entire range. The UN from an early stage expanded into the operative side, which led to its first clash with the World Bank over access to funding in the aborted SUNFED initiative in the 1960s. Even if the UN system has long been well established as an operator with its own funds, it lags far behind the Bank in attracting resources. IDA alone has, ever since the early 1970s, normally attracted more funding that the entire UN development system, as illustrated in Figure 4.1.[32] If we add the bulk of Bank commitments through IBRD, the resources available to the World Bank for development purposes are at least four times those of the UN as a whole.[33]

The UN system has, despite limited funding, taken on operative tasks in all fields of development. The World Bank, for its part, has systematically encroached on what used to be UN turf – setting the development agenda, promoting common understanding among governments and setting standards for development policy. Both provide policy advice in almost every field to governments across the world, insisting on the links between the consensus they have forged and national strategies.

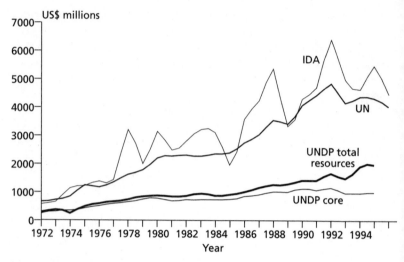

Source: UN A/48/940: Funding Operational Activities for Development within the UN System, May 1994, and UNDP Resource Mobilization Department. OECD/Development Assistance Committee (DAC) Annual Reports.

Figure 4.1 *Contributions to IDA, UN and UNDP, 1972–95 (current US$ millions)*

Development Approach

In the 1970s and 1980s the development agenda and the discussions taking place in the UN and in the World Bank had recognizable and predictable differences, the former dominated by developing world concerns over 'new order' and inequities in the world economy, the latter by economic liberalism and structural adaptation as preached by the West. Since then, a remarkable ideological convergence has taken place. Within the UN, little is now heard of developing world rhetoric of the traditional kind. In the Bank, the magic of the market is no longer the answer to most problems. Both have embraced the sustainable development notions of the early 1990s and the good governance/social development agenda of the latter part of the decade. Following this shift, the World Bank, for its part, has extended a large share of its operations into soft sectors that used to be UN 'territory'. Today, the speeches given by Bank President Wolfensohn on the 'people first' approach to development could have been written in UN headquarters.

Openness in Decision-Making

The UN development system used to be dominated by the majority of governments from developing countries, the Bank by a combination of professional managers and large shareholders. In both cases, decision-making took place within systems that favoured insiders and the established influential actors, at times in a club-like manner. Again, a remarkable convergence has slowly taken place in the course of the 1990s. Today, both the UN and the World Bank have opened up their processes to include a much wider group of stakeholders, from large multinational companies to small grassroots NGOs. They both eagerly seek moral support from a variety of non-governmental actors and acknowledge their own dependence on civil society in delivering services on the ground.[34]

Decentralization

While the UN system has long had a ubiquitous presence in developing countries, the World Bank has only recently followed suit in an attempt to get closer to its clients. Still, a substantial difference in the degree of centralization remains, as demonstrated in Figure 4.2.

Given this convergence in functional scope, development approach, thematic coverage, inclusion of previous outsiders and organizational structure, there is little wonder that the UN and the World Bank have come to appear more and more openly as competitors vying for the same sources of funding and the same sources of political and moral support. Both underline their assumedly comparative advantages when addressing the world, often in barely concealed reference to the other. The UN, for example, tends to emphasize its unique link to the political and security side of the world organization, while the Bank stresses its record as a business-like, product-oriented institution. The more similarities that develop between the two organizations, the more emphasis on what remains of comparative differences.

As the World Bank and the UN both attempt to be best at both normative and operative functions, the rivalry between them seems bound to intensify – perhaps to a point where either one of them retreats to its original functions or competition makes one of them superfluous. In Chapter 6, we shall return to assess what future role they can be expected to play. Before we can proceed to that assessment, we need to clarify an important premise for the future of

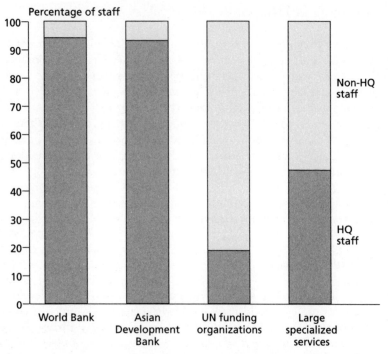

Source: CSIS Task Force: *The United States and the Multilateral Development Banks. Final Report*, Washington DC: Center for Strategic & International Studies, 1997; and Joint Inspection Unit: *Strengthening Field Representation of the United Nations System*, Geneva: United Nations, 1997.

Figure 4.2 *Distribution of Staff in UN and World Bank*

MDIs: which common goods are in demand at the turn of the century, and to what extent are MDIs needed to provide them?

Chapter 5

Global Goods and Bads

It has long been conventional wisdom that the world is becoming ever more interdependent and the world economy increasingly globalized. As a consequence, 'goods' and 'bads' flow across borders with increasing speed and volume, apparently creating more and more intractable common problems for governments. Even large countries and powerful governments face severe constraints on their ability to apply unilateral solutions to problems arising from the international arena. Hence, the much repeated need for intergovernmental collaboration in order to overcome such barriers. The rhetoric – and the literature – on such needs is all but endless. Our intention here is, first, to clarify the fundamental question: which are the important common goods that can only be realized at the global level, or the common bads that must be handled by the international community on the verge of the twenty-first century? And, second, which role can IGOs, and more specifically the UN and the World Bank, play in providing such goods or in preventing such bads?

The role of IGOs depends on whether problems can be solved by governments acting alone or in small coalitions. We assume that if the states concerned can cope with a problem without IGO involvement, they will be inclined to do so, rendering multilateral cooperation superfluous. Such cases fall outside the category of common goods of concern to us. We are interested in the issue areas where unilateral or 'minilateral' measures are meaningless or insufficient and solutions require close to universal participation, in other words the problems that require response at the global level.

Not all questions that are placed on the international agenda under the assumption of being of global concern, qualify as 'common goods' in the analytic sense we want to apply here. We shall reserve the term for issues that have the following characteristics:

1 they affect people across a large number of borders;
2 they cannot be provided unless a significant number of governments contribute to solutions; and
3 once provided, they are available to everybody, regardless of
   contribution (they are indivisible).

These points need some elaboration. We shall start out with a rather
general review and then concentrate on a few issues within social and
economic development.

Affectedness

For a good to be 'common' it must be of interest if not to all, at least
to a large number of countries in the sense that if the good is not
provided they (that is their leaders and/or their peoples) will be
negatively affected either in physical or ethical terms. In the former
instance the welfare of the population suffers in a tangible manner as
a result of a degradation or absence of the common good. If, for
example, the ozone layer is seriously depleted, the population of
North America and Europe will be exposed to health hazards, which
they would avoid if the common good is protected. In case of ethical
affectedness the impact is more diffuse as it relates to intangible
values: if Africans suffer from poverty or oppression, Europeans and
Americans are negatively affected to the extent that their sense of
values (human dignity, cross-border compassion) are touched upon.
The more they care, the more they are affected – and the more likely
that their governments will somehow react.

Participation

Whether common goods are preserved or jeopardized is often the
result of the behaviour of an indefinite number of actors, governmental and non-governmental, across the world. Whether the good is
upheld or replaced by a bad depends on their ability to coordinate
their actions. The larger the number of actors, the more complex the
coordination. Even if the goods of interest to us do not necessarily
require universal participation, their provision hinges on the actions
of numerous governments and other actors in all parts of the world.

Indivisibility

Goods of this kind are indivisible in the sense that once they are provided, they are available to everyone, whether they have contributed or not. The distribution of the good cannot be controlled by those who bear the costs, which stimulates free-riding behaviour.

GOODS AND MEANS

For analytic purposes we distinguish between common goods, as a state of affairs, and the means necessary to achieve them which is where MDIs can, or cannot have a role to play.

The most important common goods at stake in international relations by the end of the 1990s can be summarized in the text that follows and in Table 5.1.

Ecological Balance

People around the world depend on the global, life-supporting ecosystems, such as the ozone layer, the global climate and biological diversity. This includes physical affectedness – like vulnerability to extreme weather conditions or sea level rise in the case of climate change – or ethical concern, like empathy for endangered species. It needs to be underlined that a large number of environmental issues are *not* global in scope and therefore fall outside our definition. We are only concerned with the common environmental goods that affect the globe as a whole. The means to preserve (or restore) such goods are normally emission reductions, world-wide or in the countries that contribute most to the problem, but it can also be more indirect measures such as population policies that over time reduce the burden on global environmental resources.

Stability in Trade and Communication

When trade or travel is constrained or interrupted, countries that depend upon exports and imports and international communication suffer, mostly in material terms: income and jobs are lost, goods not delivered. But cross-border communication also affects wider interests connected with cultural and interpersonal contacts. In order to maintain stability in these areas internationally respected rules of conduct are essential.

Cultural Heritage

We are affected as 'citizens of the globe' not only by the extinction of natural species, but also when parts of our man-made cultural heritage disappear, like historic monuments and other structures that carry significance to people across borders. Appropriate countermeasures in this case are site protection of various kinds.

Health

This is normally a private good that belongs to an individual, but since some diseases are easily transmitted, depending on circumstances, a healthy environment in the sense of absence of contagious disease belongs to our category of common goods. Correspondingly, epidemics that move across borders with large-scale implications for human health, such as the classic pests like tuberculosis and the modern pandemics like AIDS, are typical examples of global bads.

Counter measures include action that either contains the epidemic at source or its dissemination across borders.

International Peace and Security

Whether peace is indivisible, is a question that has defied agreement for a very long time. We shall therefore simply note that to the extent that armed conflict spills over from one state to another, the absence of war is a common good and war is a common bad, at least for the countries directly involved. Security in the international arena can be promoted in a large number of ways, depending on one's definition of the term 'peace' – another endless discussion from which we abstain. In this context, civilian measures, that is, social and economic development that reduces the conflict potential within or between states is clearly relevant.

Social Cohesion

A fractured society with deep cleavages affects its members negatively in two ways: by creating tensions and relegating the lowest strata to misery. Poverty affects society at large through tensions leading to higher crime rates and to the extent that the non-poor feel that it touches on their conscience.

Whether social cohesion is a common good at the global level is also a matter of dispute. When poverty and deprivation spill over into cross-border conflict, the absence of social cohesion in one society affects other countries and arguably the larger international community. This is frequently invoked to justify development assistance to poor countries, that is, the resources provided are seen as a means to reach a common good, social cohesion inside as well as across borders.

However, it can also be argued that both war and deprivation in distant countries either do not affect states on the other side of the globe or, if they do, they can take preventive measures to protect the interests at stake on a unilateral basis without seeking cooperative solutions aimed at securing what is purportedly a common good.

Democracy and Human Rights

These can be considered common goods in themselves in the sense that if some people are deprived of their liberty, others feel the pinch, as soon as they learn about it. Again, whether these values constitute common goods across borders is basically a question of perception: to the extent that people care about oppression on the other side of the globe, human rights qualify as a common good in our usage of the term, at least along the affectedness dimension.

The upsurge in concern with good governance in the post cold war development debate indicates that human rights define values, which are widely, if not universally shared. In addition to being of value in itself, this set of issues is also increasingly seen to be linked to the broader development problematique. Good governance is, thus, of intrinsic importance as well as a means to promote development.

To summarize, in terms of affectedness these global bads (and the corresponding goods) fall into two separate categories, those that have a material or physical impact on a large number of people in countries across the globe and those that have primarily an impact on their values (which we term ethical affectedness). The scope of the impact

Table 5.1 *Common Goods and International Measures to Promote Them*

Common goods	Corresponding bads	International measures
Ecological balance	Pollution	Environmental protection, emission reductions, population policies
Cultural heritage	Site destruction	Site protection
Stability in trade and communication	Trade war	International rules
Healthy environment	Epidemic disease	Preventing or containing epidemics
Peace and security	War	Peacekeeping, conflict prevention
Social cohesion	Poverty	Poverty reduction
Democracy and human rights	Oppression	Promoting good governance

in geographic terms is largely the same in the two cases. The difference lies in the nature of the consequences for those who are affected; is the impact concrete and tangible on their pocketbook or physical well being, or is it primarily a question of their conscience?

THE SHORT LIST

In the first category that comprises material affectedness we find, following the reasoning above, only a handful of global bads: degradation of specific global environmental resources, epidemic disease, trade wars and military conflict on a global scale. Of these the latter two fall outside the scope of this study, which leaves us with a short, strictly confined list of global bads of relevance to social and economic development. These are the matters where governments across the world have a common material interest in finding joint solutions, as they are all, or at least most of them, affected in a manner that is if not unequivocal, at least much less ambivalent than is the case with ethical affectedness. Despite scientific uncertainty that looms large around some of these global bads, in particular the environmental ones, it is in principle possible to uncover the direct, tangible impact on different countries if the goods in question are not preserved.

The best example of such issues is probably depletion of the ozone layer; as the physical impacts in different regions were, not without resistance, documented, understood and accepted, a sense of material affectedness emerged strong enough by the late 1980s to provide the basis for effective international measures to curtail emissions of ozone depleting substances. This also included an innovative fund for transfer of resources, which we shall use as an illustration in Chapter 6.[1]

The other two most prominent cases of global environmental threats, climate change and biodiveristy loss, are at present not so well understood in terms of physical impacts and hence perceptions of affectedness are much more ambiguous. This does not, however, alter the thrust of our argument, as we assume that over time the effects and consequences of these environmental threats can be documented in a way that might, in turn, produce a sense of physical affectedness not unlike the case of ozone depletion. This is why we have included all of these global environmental issues in our short list.

The final example of a global bad that belongs to this category of direct affectedness is the AIDS epidemic. If not contained, it spreads easily across borders with tangible impacts on the population.

Even if all of these cases involve physical or material affectedness, this does not mean that the road to effective international cooperation is short and easy.[2] The main problem that needs to be tackled in all of them is related to our other two defining characteristics of common goods: participation and indivisibility. In order to prevent the common threats arising from these global bads, wide, if not universal, participation is required. If a minority of states whose activities are important for any one of these issues (ozone depletion, climate change, biodiveristy loss and the spread of the HIV virus) refuse to cooperate, whatever actions are taken by other states may turn out to be meaningless as attempts to solve the common problem. The indivisible character of these global goods reinforces this difficulty. Once the ozone layer is preserved, climate change averted, biodiversity saved and the AIDS epidemic contained, the goods achieved are available to everyone, regardless of contribution. Those who have paid the price cannot control the distribution of the good. So, the temptation to free ride is prevalent.

The Long List

In the second category, we find all the other issues that are purportedly of concern to 'the international community', not because they pose any material threats, but because they somehow touch upon or challenge values that are considered common property among civilized people. Here, we find such widespread phenomena as poverty and oppression of fundamental civil and political rights in addition to local and regional armed conflict. The basic question confronting us as analysts here is simply whether human misery, whatever its cause, is a global bad. Does it really affect the affluent on the other side of the globe?[3] As stated above, there is no clear cut answer to this question. Ethical affectedness is, like other moral questions, in the eyes of the beholder. Whether people feel affected by misery, suffering or oppression in distant countries, is a moral issue, which is by its nature unpredictable. Simply declaring that there is such a link between the fate of the poor and the feelings of the rich, as is often done by political leaders, does not in itself make much difference. If such proclamations do not find resonance in popular sentiment, they will have scant influence beyond the immediate rhetorical effect. The only way to find out whether ethical affectedness has any impact, is to look at resource flows, to which we return in the next chapter.

Implications for MDIs

We shall summarize this argument by pointing out the difference this categorization makes for MDIs like the World Bank and the UN development system.

If we assume that there is no such thing as ethical affectedness, the list of common goods (or bads) at the global level, remains confined to the few issues on our short list. Under these circumstances, the need for IGOs operating within social and economic development under the motivation of promoting common goods would be very limited. Only a small selection of IGOs with a mandate carefully defined for these purposes would be in demand. If we compare this with the ambitions expressed by Kofi Annan and James Wolfensohn, as cited above, there is very little left to do for both the UN and the World Bank.

If, on the other hand, we accept the argument underlying the notion of ethical affectedness the list of global goods and bads becomes very long, indeed, including the entire sustainable development and good governance agendas. As we have documented above, these are virtually without limits – and keep expanding. In addition, these endless agendas fit the current ambitions of our two MDIs perfectly. Consequently, their room for manoeuvre is critically dependent on how the concept of common goods requiring global solutions is defined. This in turn depends on perceptions and attitudes, primarily in the western countries since these states are expected to come up with the resources necessary for international problem solving. It makes little difference if only the states or the populations that suffer from poverty or deprivation define their misery as a global problem. In our final chapter, we shall therefore turn to donor governments in order to clarify their priorities for the funding of MDIs and the implications for the UN and the World Bank.

Chapter 6

Donor Support – Implications for the Future of the UN and the World Bank

We shall round off this study in this final chapter by reviewing the support these two multilateral institutions have been able to attract in recent years from their major donors and what this implies for their position in the 'development business'. We shall assess the level of support in relation to our short and long list of common goods, as elaborated above in Chapter 5, and return to the fundamental question of which roles the UN and the World Bank can play within the new development paradigm that is now in vogue, given these financial constraints. Finally, we shall give our recommendations of what the major donors can and should do to reform the multilateral development system, based on our interpretation of the lessons of the past and the challenges of the future.

SUPPORT FOR MULTILATERAL ASSISTANCE

As we have shown in Chapters 2 and 3, ODA rose very rapidly from the middle of the 1970s throughout the 1980s and peaked in the early 1990s. From 1994 to 1996 official statistics showed a decline of almost 3.7 billion dollars and from 1992 to 1996 a decrease in real terms by 16 per cent.[1] The 'development dividend' that was expected after the cold war never materialized. In fact, if it had not been for the dramatic emergencies in the former Yugoslavia, which attracted large amounts of bilateral and multilateral aid, the figures would probably have shown a gradual, systematic decline in ODA since the very beginning of the 1990s.[2] Furthermore, as large recipients like

China and Israel disappear from the OECD approved list of countries eligible for ODA, the downward trend in development assistance figures becomes even more pronounced.[3] The marked decrease in the 1990s confirms that with the end of the cold war, a major motivation for providing assistance to developing countries has gone. In addition, many donor governments are under strong pressures to reduce their budget deficits and aid is a tempting target for such cuts.[4]

The main pattern of support for the UN and the World Bank follows the same trends as ODA in general. In both cases donor contributions peaked in 1992 and have since shown gradual decline.[5] This decrease is larger for the Bank's IDA than for the UN as far as contributions are concerned, with a fall for IDA of 1.3 billion dollars from 1992 to 1996.[6] As for disbursements, IDA remained on the increase in the middle of the 1990s, while the UN experienced a decline of 800 million dollars, or 13 per cent, from 1993 to 1996.[7] World Bank loan commitments including both IBRD and IDA, which are probably the best measure of its financial weight, have declined systematically since the late 1980s (in fixed prices and since the early 1990s in constant dollars).[8]

The relative share of multilateral agencies in relation to total ODA has remained around 30 per cent since the late 1980s. The UN share of ODA has been equally stable at 7 per cent, while IDA contributions have shown more fluctuation, but have converged over time to a corresponding level.[9]

Relative Importance of MDIs

The resources available to MDIs have fallen not only in absolute, but also in relative terms in the 1990s, as private resource flows to developing countries at market terms have rapidly surpassed ODA. In 1988, official aid stood at 47.6 billion dollars and net private transfers at 36.4 billion dollars. Eight years later, the corresponding figures were 58.2 to 234. In other words, in this period private flows grew by 650 per cent and ODA by 22.[10] As shown in Figure 6.1, the relative importance of multilateral institutions has fallen from 16 to 8 per cent of total net financial flows with the shrinking share of ODA. By 1996 the entire UN development system and IDA together accounted for 4 per cent of these flows to developing countries.

Adding the bulk of World Bank funding channelled through the IBRD does not alter this picture significantly; IBRD commitments by 1996 stood at 12.5 billion dollars which is no more than 6.4 per cent

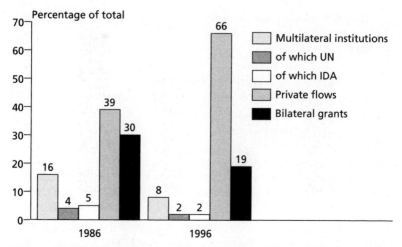

Source: OECD (1998), *Development Cooperation: Efforts and Policies of the Members of the Development Assistance Committee*, 1997 report.

Figure 6.1 *Share of Total Net Flow of Financial Resources from DAC Countries to Developing Countries and Multilateral Organizations (percentage)*

of total net financial flows from DAC member states to developing countries and multilateral organizations and a mere 4 per cent of total net resource flows.[11] (See Figure 6.2.)

So we can conclude that the financial weight of both the UN and the World Bank as development institutions is in a process of long-term decline. This stands in notable contrast to the Commission of the European Communities (CEC), which has strengthened its position as a channel for development assistance significantly since the middle of the 1980s. NGOs have likewise recorded remarkable progress and have been able to retain a level of support well above that of both the UN and IDA.

As mentioned in Chapter 2, the resources available to the UN for development purposes – and to IDA – are also very modest compared with the major bilateral agencies (Figure 6.3).

Distribution of Resources Within the UN

The main pattern in the distribution of resources for operational activities within the UN is illustrated in Figures 2.7 and 2.8. The total

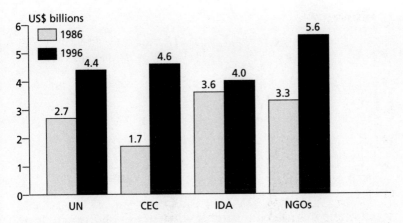

Source: OECD (1998), *Development Cooperation: Efforts and Policies of the Members of the Development Assistance Committee,* 1997 report.

Figure 6.2 *The Total Net Flow of Financial Resources from DAC Countries to Multilateral Organizations and NGOs (in billion US dollars)*

showed an increase from 1991 to 1995 from 4.8 to 5.5 billion dollars, of which the bulk was accounted for by cost sharing and government counterpart contributions to UNDP. This covered large contributions from a number of Latin American governments to UNDP-sponsored projects in their countries. Even if these make resources available for development purposes in the region, this can hardly be considered support for the multilateral development system in its efforts to solve global problems. If we disregard these contributions, which in 1995 amounted to approximately 500 million, the stagnation in contributions to the UN becomes as visible in UN statistics as in those of DAC.[12]

Another critical feature of UN finance in the 1990s is the decline in core funding and a rapid increase in contributions earmarked for specific purposes by donors. We have shown this trend for UNDP at the end of Chapter 2, cf. Figure 2.11. If we take core funding for the three largest UN funds and programmes, a similar pattern emerges. While core funding has shown gradual decline from the early to the middle of the 1990s, other contributions have almost tripled as demonstrated in Figure 6.4.

As for the specialized agencies, their extrabudgetary funding, that is the resources they have available for operative activities, also seems to be in a long-term decline.[13] Compared with the UN total, these

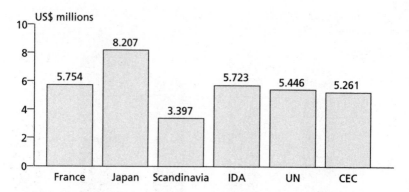

Source: OECD (1998), *Development Cooperation: Efforts and Policies of the Members of the Development Assistance Committee*, 1997 report. These figures are not directly comparable to Figure 6.2, as the latter refers to contributions to MDIs.)

Figure 6.3 *Resources Available to Selected Bilateral and Multilateral Agencies (net disbursements 1996, in million dollars)*

agencies have a very modest position, claiming less than a fifth of the funds contributed to the UN development system in 1995.[14]

Two Groups of Donors

We shall review the relative level of support for the World Bank versus the UN, by dividing the major donors into two groups – the large countries that belong to the Group of 8 (G-8) – France, Germany, Italy, Japan, the UK and the USA[15] – on one hand, and the small countries with large contributions, The Netherlands and Scandinavia,[16] on the other. In this way we can gauge the connection between the size of the country and its willingness to support these two MDIs. In total the ten countries included in our two groups of donors account for 75 to 90 per cent of the resources for most international development purposes. With very few exceptions, they normally constitute what is often referred to as the 'international community' as far as willingness to pay is concerned.[17]

As for the UN, the large countries in 1996 accounted for just over half the contributions (54 per cent) and the small ones more than a fourth of the DAC total. In the case of the World Bank the G-8 governments stood for almost 80 per cent of the funding and the other group 10 per cent. The difference is illustrated in Figures 6.5 and 6.6.[18]

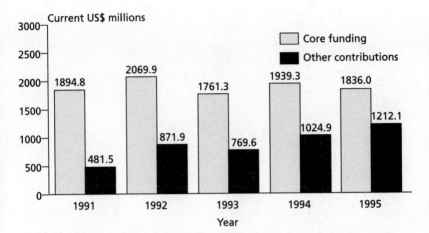

Source: ECOSOC (1997), Operational Activities of the United Nations for International Development Cooperation: Follow-up to Policy Recommendations of the General Assembly.

Figure 6.4 *Contributions to UNDP, UNDP Administered Funds, UNFPA and UNICEF, 1991–95 (million current US dollars)*

Another way of exploring variations in donor support for the multi-lateral system is to look for core contributions. As these are not tied directly to national political or commercial interests, they can be taken to indicate the willingness of different governments to provide support for general development purposes through MDIs. In the case of the UN, the UNDP, UNFPA and UNICEF depend on such core funding for the overall level of their activities. As for the World Bank, contributions to IDA should be a good proxy measure for the kind of support that reflects general trust in the organization. In order to assess long-term support we shall use accumulated contributions in this case (see Table 6.1).

The overall pattern is reinforced by the figures shown in Table 6.1; the committed contributors in Northern Europe make a disproportional effort in maintaining core funding for the UN (43 per cent of DAC) by taking on an even larger share than in their general contributions to the world organization. In the case of IDA the burden is much more evenly shared in proportion to population and national economy, with the small countries accounting for 11 and the large 85 per cent of accumulated contributions from 1990 to 1996.[19] This underlines that the governments of the large western powers are much more willing to provide funding for the World Bank than for

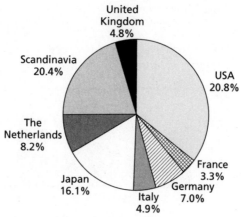

Source: OECD (1998): *Development Cooperation: Efforts and Policies of the Members of the Development Assistance Committee,* 1997 report.

Figure 6.5 *Percentage of Total DAC Contributions to UN Agencies in 1996 for Selected Countries*

the UN, which is most likely closely linked to their dominating influence in Bank decision-making. In the case of the latest (eleventh) replenishment of IDA for 1997–99, the pattern is roughly the same; even if the share of the G-8 governments of total funding has fallen to 68 per cent, they remain the predominant donors. (See Appendix Table A.12.)

Table 6.1 *Relative Contributions to UN Core Funding (UNDP, UNFPA and UNICEF) 1995 and Accumulated Contributions to IDA 1990–96*

	UN (%)	IDA (%)
France	3.6	9.5
Germany	11.7	15.7
Italy	4.1	4.9
Japan	14.5	25.5
The Netherlands	11.9	4.4
Scandinavia	30.7	6.4
United Kingdom	4.7	7.3
USA	17.9	22.2

Source: OECD, *Development Cooperation: Efforts and Policies of the Members of the Development Assistance Committee,* volumes 1991–97 (Paris: OECD).

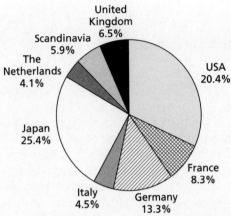

Source: OECD (1998): *Development Cooperation: Efforts and Policies of the Members of the Development Assistance Committee*, 1997 report.

Figure 6.6 *Percentage of Total DAC Contributions to the World Bank 1990–96 Average*

Another way to illustrate the same point is to calculate contributions on a per capita basis, which is shown in Table 6.2.

Again, the gap between large and small countries is striking; the Scandinavian MDI contribution relative to population is, for example, ten times that of the US. It is also noteworthy that the difference

Table 6.2 *Per Capita Contributions to Multilateral Institutions, 1996 (dollars)*

	All multilateral institutions	of which UN agencies	of which the World Bank
France	29.1	2.5	8.2
Germany	37.4	3.8	14.3
Italy	27.9	3.8	7.6
Japan*	32.4	5.9	18.5
The Netherlands	62.7	23.0	17.9
Scandinavia	90.9	48.2	15.9
United Kingdom	24.0	3.6	5.7
USA	9.3	3.4	3.0

* 1995 figures for Japan, as the 1996 figures are exceptional.

Source: OECD (1998), *Development Cooperation: Efforts and Policies of the Members of the Development Assistance Committee*, 1997 report (Paris: OECD). Fridtjof Nansen Institute calculations.

between the two groups in per capita support is much wider in the case of the UN than for the World Bank. Again, the figures reveal the large powers' confidence in the Bank.

GENERAL VERSUS SPECIFIC PURPOSES

If we return now to the short and long list of common goods that we elaborated in Chapter 5, we can attempt to compare the level of donor support for specific and general development purposes. Within the short list of common goods based on physical affectedness, we shall briefly focus on donor contributions to two examples of multi-lateral efforts to raise funds to avert what are commonly perceived as serious *global* threats to the human condition – depletion of the ozone layer and other environmental degradation on a world scale.

The Multilateral Fund for the Implementation of the Montreal Protocol

This fund was established in 1990 to provide financial and technical support for developing countries that joined the Montreal Protocol on substances that Deplete the Ozone Layer. Its initial budget for 1991–93 was agreed at 240 million dollars. It has since been replenished twice, for 1994–96 with 510 million and for 1997–99 with 540 million. So, by the end of the decade, donors will have contributed 1.3 billion dollars for this fund.[20] There is little doubt that this level of funding has played a major role in bringing the developing countries, in particular large states like India and China, into the emerging international regime to deal with ozone depletion. The size of the fund has demonstrated that governments of industrialized countries are willing, in this case, to deal with the equity issue that continues to haunt global environmental politics. Burden sharing among donors was decided by using the scale of assessments that defines general contributions to the UN budget, which means that the largest developed countries pay most of the bill. These are also the ones that have contributed most to the problem to be solved, accumulated production of ozone depleting substances.[21] The actual distribution of contributions among donors as shown in Table 6.3. further demonstrates that burden sharing between large and small countries is pretty fair also in per capita terms in this case.

Table 6.3 *Agreed Contributions to the Multilateral Fund for the Implementation of the Montreal Protocol*

	Average annual contributions 1991–97 ($ million)	Per capita contribution ($)	Share of budget (%)	Share of DAC population (%)
France	8.6	0.15	7.3	7.1
Germany	12.7	0.16	10.8	10.0
Italy	6.2	0.11	5.3	7.0
Japan	18.1	0.14	15.4	15.4
The Netherlands	2.2	0.14	1.9	1.9
Scandinavia	3.4	0.18	2.9	2.3
United Kingdom	7.1	0.12	6.0	7.2
USA	30.4	0.11	25.8	32.5

Source: The secretariat of the Montreal protocol. OECD (1998), *Development Cooperation: Efforts and Policies of the Members of the Development Assistance Committee*, 1997 report (Paris: OECD). Fridtjof Nansen Institute calculations.

The Global Environment Facility

The Global Environment Facility (GEF) was established in 1990 for a three-year pilot phase with a budget of 1 billion dollars for the purpose of counteracting four global environmental bads – climate change, biodiversity loss, ozone depletion and pollution of international waters. The basic idea behind the Facility was that the richest states in the world should bear the costs of environmental protection of a global character, as these are the only ones who can afford and are willing to pay for what most other governments consider ecological 'luxury'.[22] After a major review and arduous renegotiations, GEF entered its second phase, 1994–97, with a trust fund of 2 billion dollars, based on pledges from 28 countries.[23]

We shall leave aside the otherwise fascinating question of control over GEF decision-making[24] and concentrate on the issue of concern in this context – burden sharing among donors. Table 6.4 shows that the large countries in the West have born nearly three-fourths of the costs, which is almost proportional to their share of population in the western parts of the world. The ten countries we have selected for scrutiny here together account for 81 per cent of the funding. Per capita contributions are still markedly higher among the smaller countries, with Scandinavia four times the level of the US and twice the level of Japan, but the gap in this regard is much smaller than in the case of the UN.

Table 6.4 *Agreed Contributions to the Global Environment Facility (GEF)*

	Average annual contributions 1991–97 ($ million)	Per capita contribution ($)	Share of budget (%)	Share of DAC population (%)
France	35.8	0.61	7.1	7.1
Germany	60.0	0.73	11.9	10.0
Italy	28.7	0.50	5.7	7.0
Japan	103.6	0.82	20.5	15.4
The Netherlands	17.8	1.15	3.5	1.9
Scandinavia	22.2	1.67	4.4	1.6
United Kingdom	33.6	0.57	6.7	7.2
USA	107.4	0.40	21.3	32.5

Note: Scandinavia only includes Sweden and Norway.

Source: GEF secretariat. OECD (1998), *Development Cooperation: Efforts and Policies of the Members of the Development Assistance Committee*, 1997 report (Paris: OECD). Fridtjof Nansen Institute calculations.

DONOR SUPPORT: CONCLUSIONS

If we put together the pieces assembled above the following broad picture emerges:

1   There are items on the short list of global goods that have obtained substantial funding on a fairly equal footing from both large and small donor countries. The experience with both the Montreal Fund and the GEF demonstrates that the major western powers which are essential for any global effort of this kind, are willing to contribute their share of resources, roughly in relation to population and size of economy, once the purpose is clearly defined and decision-making is not beyond their control.[25] Following the support from the large countries in the West, these funds have been able to attract resources of considerable magnitude at least compared with MDIs with wider objectives. By the middle to late 1990s, the GEF had annual commitments of

around 500 million dollars and the Montreal Fund disposed of 180 million, both of which compare very favourably with, for example, UNDP core funding of around 900 million for a much wider scope of activities. In a telling contrast, UNDP's major follow-up to UNCED and the sustainable development agenda, an institutional development programme entitled Capacity 21 has not been able to attract more than some 60 million dollars (which are to be distributed in over 35 countries).[26] Donors have not been willing to contribute more than a third of the amount for such a comprehensive objective than they are prepared to spend for the specific purpose of protecting the ozone layer.

2   The large donors clearly favour the World Bank over the UN development system, probably because they have much more influence in the Bank, but also, in our judgement, because they have more confidence in the effectiveness of Bank spending. The importance of these factors seems, however, to be in decline. As shown in Table 6.5, the large countries, the ones that have dominated the Bank from its inception, have cut their share of IDA funding considerably, from 85 per cent in the first half of the 1990s to 68 per cent in the latest replenishment covering 1997 to 1999. We take this as a strong indication that even among G-8 governments with their long standing preference for the Bretton Woods institutions, support for general development funding, including the World Bank, is definitely losing ground.

Table 6.5 *Contributions to MDIs from Large and Small DAC Countries (percentages)*

	Large countries	Small countries
UN, general development funding, 1996*	54.1	28.6
World Bank average 1990–96*	79.4	10
IDA 1990–96*	85.1	11
IDA 11th replenishment*	68.2	8.6
UN core (UNDP, UNFPA, UNICEF)**	56.5	42.6
Montreal Fund**	70.6	4.8
GEF**	73.2	7.9
(Share of OECD population)	79.2	3.5

* share of DAC total.
** share of total budget, including non-DAC contributors.

Sources: Tables 6.1, 6.3, 6.4, Figure 6.6 and Appendix Tables A.5 and A.12. Percentages do not add up to 100 as other donors than the ten listed above are not included.

3   As for the common goods on our long list, the body language of the large majority of donor governments is unequivocal. Whatever the rhetoric on 'poverty eradication' might mean, the willingness to support general development efforts through both the UN and the World Bank (via the IDA) has always been limited and is now clearly falling. The gap between the resources available to these (and other) MDIs and the solemn declarations emanating from the never-ending series of world conferences is undeniable. The relative importance of MDI funds compared with private resource flows is minute and shrinking from year to year. Within ODA, donors seem to favour channels closer to their influence (or their hearts), like bilateral programmes, the Commission of the European Communities in the case of European Union members and NGOs.

In our judgement, this demonstrates that there is either no widespread sense of ethical affectedness that makes poverty a global bad or, if there should be such a sentiment, there is no confidence in MDIs as we now know them as the right means to take on the challenges of world development. The only exceptions to this conclusion are the Scandinavians and the Dutch. Their governments make contributions to multilateral development that signifies that they are concerned about poverty as a global bad and that they have confidence in MDIs, even in the United Nations. If in the purely hypothetical case that the large western countries had followed their example, funding for MDIs would have been entirely different, as indicated in Table 6.6. Their contribution would then have been 31 billion dollars, an increase by a factor of six from current levels. If that were to happen, the world organization would indeed stand a chance of matching words with deeds in promoting development. However, the prospects of such support for the UN from the large countries in the West have always been slim. Today they are nil. The outlook seems no better for the smaller donors not included here and the potential contributors among the newly rich countries in the world. So, we are left with the inescapable fact that only a tiny minority of governments are willing to make available the financial resources that would enable the UN and the World Bank to play a major role in providing the global common goods on the long list we have outlined above. The rhetoric on 'sustainable development' and 'poverty eradication' remains intact, but it has become increasingly clear that deeds simply do not follow words.[27]

Table 6.6 *Hypothetical Contributions from Large Countries if Following Scandinavian Level of Per Capita Funding (million dollars)*

	All multilateral institutions	UN agencies	The World Bank
France	5306.7	2813.5	926.3
Germany	7442.9	3946.0	1299.1
Italy	5224.0	2769.6	911.8
Japan	11,440.7	6065.5	1996.9
The Netherlands	1408.0	746.5	245.8
United Kingdom	5343.1	2832.7	932.6
USA	24,139.4	12,797.9	4213.4
Total	60,304.8	31,971.7	10,525.9

Source: OECD (1998), *Development Cooperation: Efforts and Policies of the Members of the Development Assistance Committee*, 1997 report (Paris: OECD). Fridtjof Nansen Institute calculations.

IMPLICATIONS FOR THE UN AND THE WORLD BANK

We can now return to the questions raised in the introduction to this book: Given the trend in financial support that is forthcoming from donors, which roles can and should the UN and the World Bank play as development institutions? Given the historic experience elaborated in Chapters 2 to 4, which functions – normative and operative – can they constructively undertake? We shall conclude this study by offering three overall recommendations to both donors and the organizations themselves under the following headings; promote specific purposes, cultivate pluralism and scale down rhetoric. Based on our analysis above, these express our interpretation of the current predicament of the two MDIs and our view of which direction they should take to avoid further marginalization.

Promoting Specific Purposes

The thrust of our concluding argument is that both the UN and the World Bank should give up their ambitions to cover all functions and to implement integrated strategies for all aspects of development. This is based on two key premises – the new paradigm and the changing pattern of donor support.

As mentioned in Chapter 4, the new development paradigm that has emerged in the late 1990s – often referred to as 'people centred, participatory development' – is much more complex and multifaceted than earlier predominating schools of thought, whether they belonged to neo-classical economics or to its radical counterparts.[28] Development under the new (or rediscovered) paradigm is perceived as a *'learning process [that] is essentially undetermined and open-ended, ie, there is no advance blueprint'*.[29] For MDIs, this entails, in our view, that the days of the grand designs are over. There is no use pretending there is a widely shared vision and strategy for development, when that is not the case. If social and economic development is an unpredictable process that is poorly understood and cannot be designed in any advance blueprint, a predetermined strategy is most likely to fail. The alternative is development by trial and error. From the donors' point of view, this could easily lead to complete disillusionment; why bother to fund development efforts, if we don't know how to do it? But this is not the only way out of the fundamental rethinking that is currently taking place. The alternative, which we recommend, is to look for much more limited, more specific tasks within the comprehensive new paradigm, where donors and recipients have common interests in finding concrete solutions to a larger problematique. Slogans like 'sustainable development' and 'poverty eradication' will no longer suffice to bring the two sides together in joint efforts. The grand ideas must be 'decomposed' to attract the confidence and funding of the donors and the practical commitment of recipients. This means going the opposite way from the 1990s where one complex agenda has been added to another in the futile hope that this would make everybody happy.[30] In practice, this is more likely to produce 'overload, disappointment by member governments, disrepute and failure'.[31]

From a moral point of view, one may deplore that there is so little support among donors for the concerns on our long list of common goods. Instead of just bemoaning this lack of compassion we recommend a pragmatic and selective approach to the short list. The challenge is to search for common ground among donors and recipients in areas where both see a need for joint action, without invoking the worn-out slogans of the 1990s. We are convinced that if there is a political basis for international development Cupertino and for MDIs in the post cold war era, this is where to find it.

For the UN and the World Bank such a selective approach means that they should concentrate on the functions and tasks where each of them has if not a unique position, at least comparative advantages.

In the case of the UN, this entails concentration on normative functions where the world organization has at critical junctures in the post-war period clearly shown its value as a forum for agenda setting and promoting understanding of emerging issues. As we pointed out in the conclusions to Chapter 2 and in Chapter 4, the trouble arises when the UN takes on ambitions to proceed from the conference hall into the field. We have concluded that the UN system is, with few exceptions, organizationally ill equipped for such tasks. We don't know if donor governments agree, but most of them have voted with their money as if they do, by cutting down on core contributions. The result is the glaring discrepancy between UN ambitions as propagated in innumerable 'action plans' and quite a few 'special action plans' and the resources at its disposal which are a trifle compared with the problems purportedly to be solved through UN initiatives. This is not to say that the UN should henceforth abstain from all operative functions. Our point is (i) that the UN can play a very valuable normative role in promoting international collaboration on development issues *without* having any ambition to take on operative tasks and (ii) that if UN agencies are to play an operative role they must be able to attract funding in a highly competitive market. There is no longer any convincing reason for donors to give money for UN operations if the agencies involved cannot prove by their results on the ground that they deserve it.

For the World Bank, our selective approach is equally challenging. As we pointed out at the end of Chapter 3, the Bank currently faces a serious overreach problem. Its attempt to integrate everything into a new paradigm is apparently in keeping with the notion of development as social learning. But to adapt a large, hierarchical, centralized, Washington-based bureaucracy to the idea that development is undetermined and open-ended and therefore must be adaptable to local circumstances in thousands of localities, is indeed a daunting task.[32] There is every reason to question whether such a transition is possible. Whatever their motives, the Bank like the UN is facing increasing scepticism, even among its traditional supporters, as witnessed in shrinking contributions. In our view, its current efforts to attempt more of everything, across issue areas and across functions, is not tenable. If the Bank is to maintain its financial and political support, it must make a tough choice in either of two directions.

One alternative is to specialize its operations in fewer areas where it has a competitive edge, either in relation to other MDIs and bilateral agencies or in comparison with private capital.[33] It would then be business-like and effective in its specialities, but less comprehensive and ambitious than its current leadership wants it to be. In principle, it would then revert to its earlier, more confined role as a source of finance for clearly defined purposes. It could fund schools and hospitals instead of ports and highways, but relinquish its objective to be the leading policy-making forum.

The other alternative is the very opposite – to concentrate on being the world's 'premier development institution' in a normative sense, which entails forging a common agenda on the major issues in the new paradigm and be in the forefront of development as a learning exercise. This could build on its strong professional expertise, complemented by experience and knowledge from various quarters in order to improve the understanding of governments, NGOs and industry of the unpredictable and intricate connections between social and economic development. In this way, the Bank could become the authoritative source of expertise of development as social learning and the main producer of consensual knowledge in this contested field, which is clearly in line with the goals of its current leadership. The question is whether this is compatible with its equally strongly held ambition to carry out its own operations in every aspect of development. As follows from our conclusions in Chapters 3 and 4, we believe it is not, as the two ambitions – premier development institution and large-scale operator – require qualitatively different governing structures, the one emphasizing equal participation and open, time-consuming processes, the other requiring hierarchical order and effective decision-making.[34]

Our point here is not to recommend one or the other course of action, but to underline the necessity of making a choice.

Cultivating Pluralism

The upshot of our first recommendation is that in response to faltering confidence in general purpose organizations, both donors, recipients and MDIs should seek to identify specific objectives where they have common interests in international development collaboration. Core contributions to MDIs will continue to decline to the point where the very existence of UN and other multilateral agencies is at stake. This is bound to intensify the scrambling for shrinking funds.

The response of UN leadership to funding problems and to recurrent criticism of waste and inefficiency has been to promise 'coordination' through organizational reform – 'unity of purpose and coherence of effort' in the words of Kofi Annan.[35] We have pointed out in Chapter 2 that all previous efforts along the same lines have consistently failed and there is, in our judgement, no reason to expect a different outcome this time.[36] At this point, we shall take the argument one step further; is coordination through UN reform not only infeasible, but also undesirable?

If we are right in assuming that (i) funding for general purposes is declining, (ii) donors are becoming more selective and (iii) the most attractive option is purpose specific cooperation, then there is no reason to 'coordinate' UN activities from a decision-making centre. Nor is there any need to seek 'functional rationalization' between the UN system and the World Bank.[37] On the contrary, under these circumstances, the more diversity the better. The most attractive analogy is simply to envisage development Cupertino as a market place where donor money and recipient needs can meet and set up jointly beneficial schemes, which could be bilateral, 'minilateral' or multilateral depending on the task at hand.

Such a market-like environment would have number of advantages:[38]

- It would fit the trial and error approach that follows from thinking of development as social learning. Coordination from the top could easily stifle initiatives on the ground that could bring out new ideas and interesting experience if allowed to be tested out. The more uncertainty about the 'best' development strategies, the higher the risk of central control.
- It would allow a diversity of donors with different priorities to seek out MDI partners that suit their purposes.
- It would expose all operative MDIs to competition, among each other, with international and local NGOs, with bilaterals and with private industry. The inefficient agencies among MDIs will after a while simply whither away for lack of funding, like any other obsolete product or firm. Nobody will need to take a controversial decision to close them down. It will just happen when there is no longer any demand for their services.
- As a consequence, the necessary reform of UN agencies in particular will come as a result not of compromise decisions from above, but *of pressures from below*. MDIs that want to stay alive will be forced to use their money as efficiently as possible. If this entails coordination at country level, they will probably find practical solutions in the form of common premises and the like without orders from above. If not, why should such agencies be kept alive?

At first sight, this may seem tailor made for donors only, but in our view it is also a long step forward for recipients, whether state or non-state actors in developing countries. They will also have the opportunity to operate in this market place for projects and ideas, and they will have a number of different, competing MDIs to approach.

On the other hand, there is no denying that this kind of pluralism can and should be encouraged primarily by the largest donor governments. They have an interest in getting more value for their money, which is more likely in a competitive environment. They should therefore promote pluralism and competition not only as far as UN agencies are concerned, but also between these and the World Bank. The increasing overlap between the two largest MDIs thus becomes not a liability, but an asset. This goes not only for the operative functions, but also for the normative ones. There is no good reason why the UN system and the World Bank should not compete for the position of the 'premier development institution' on the basis of the differences in their history, their political standing in different quarters and their professional expertise.

This pluralistic approach is already being pursued by some of the main donors by stressing the link between contributions and expected output. The most visible example, so far, is the policy of 'active multilateralism' adopted by the Danish government which has chosen to publish not only its strategies for the multilateral development system, but also its objectives for individual organizations and its assessment of their performance. In this way the government makes its preferences clear to other donors and the IGOs involved, thereby hoping to encourage improvements in efficiency[39] and more responsiveness to its policy goals.[40]

Two counter arguments to this line of reasoning deserve consideration; first, our approach can be taken to undermine the general position of the UN and, second, this way of thinking is purportedly 'undemocratic'.

The answer to the first argument is that we do not foresee that all UN agencies should be entirely market based. There will never be sufficient 'demand' for the normative activities carried out within the UN development system, broadly defined. Donors should nevertheless continue to fund them as fora for discussion of competing agendas, hopefully proceeding over time to the more constructive normative functions (understanding and monitoring). Our argument is primarily directed to the operative functions of the UN – and for that matter the World Bank. For the agencies with both operative and normative functions, this means the core funding should only be applied to the latter. The former should be exposed to competition. Consequently, we argue that there is no *intrinsic* value in an operative task being carried out by a UN (or any other MDI) agency. If it is more efficiently carried out by an NGO, a national agency or a local business, we cannot see why donors should channel the money through an MDI. It is often said, as a counter argument, that one cannot have a 'UN a la carte'. If you want the good courses, you also have to put up with the less tasty ones. We disagree. If donors want to, they can retain the essential items on the menu of UN activities and discard the superfluous. There is no reason why a reduction of UN operations, if that were to happen as a result of the policies we advocate, should undermine support for essential normative functions. The connection, we believe, is rather the opposite; inefficient operations can easily erode confidence in the entire UN system, thereby undercutting also its valuable normsetting tasks. Even if it is not necessarily intended, the 'a la carte' argument serves to cover up dead wood and waste.

The second counter argument is more difficult to deal with, as it appeals at a more fundamental level to international justice: the 'haves' in the world have a moral obligation to make transfers to the 'have nots' and these resources should be distributed in representative, democratic bodies where all members are equal.[41] The easiest response to this position is that it is unrealistic. As we have pointed out, the large majority of donors are no longer willing to provide funding for the UN as a kind of international public service institution (if they ever were). This is the political side of the argument. On the moral side, we will maintain that if funds for development purposes are used more efficiently (with less waste) in a competitive environment, this should primarily benefit recipients, that is the communities in developing countries that are involved in a project or a programme. They will get more development services for the same amount of money, if our argument on the effects of competition is correct. This can hardly be considered undemocratic and certainly not anti-development. If current MDI channels of aid are as efficient as potential competitors, competition will not lead to any major shift in funding, and recipients will be no worse and no better off than today.

We also question the democratic content of UN decision-making. Most of the diplomats and politicians that meet in UN bodies can hardly be said to represent democratic governments in any meaningful sense of the term. Open and fair elections, civil rights and the rule of law are the exception rather than the rule among UN member states. As long as this is the case, the majority of delegates have a poor moral case when they invoke democratic rights in dealing with donor governments, which are for the most part democratically elected. One cannot on moral grounds impose on others a duty which one is not willing to respect oneself.

Scaling Down Rhetoric

The gap between both UN and World Bank rhetoric and the reality of the resources they have at their disposal is evident. Nevertheless, shrinking funding and faltering confidence seem to be met with more and more demanding declarations of ambition from the management of both MDIs to the point where it is reasonable to ask if their words are to be taken seriously. Surely, Kofi Annan cannot really mean that the UN with its access to 1 dollar of ODA per developing world inhabitant can make 'the hopes and dreams of all the world's peoples' reality.[42] In the same manner, James Wolfensohn is probably sincere in saying that the World Bank's job is to 'improve the human condition', but is this a realistic statement of what it can actually achieve with 4 dollars per capita recipient? Given the resource constraints we have described in this chapter, there is ample reason to question the value of these and numerous similar expressions of rhetoric from UN and World Bank fora. Such statements seem to work like drugs – larger and larger doses are required to maintain the same effect, and in the end the impact is cancelled out.

We strongly believe such overblown ambitions do both organizations and their management a disservice. Every time they make an empty promise – like eradicating poverty – their credibility suffers, on both sides of the world. As a consequence, they risk ending up with less money from donors and less commitment from recipients. UN and World Bank managers, as well as some of the political leaders on their governing bodies would do well reminding themselves of Churchill's famous adage: 'You can fool some of the people some of the time, but not all the people all of the time.'

The need to scale down rhetoric is particularly acute for the time being for two reasons:

1   The uncertainty surrounding development as social learning, if taken seriously, implies that all actors should be careful about promising quick and tangible results.

2   The increasing scepticism among donors can easily backfire on MDIs that promise what they cannot deliver.

In our view, realistic ambitions and corresponding official rhetoric are imperative in order to maintain confidence in the role of MDIs in general and the UN and the World Bank in particular. The alternative to the overblown statements of the kind referred to above is to admit that these organizations can *never* make our dreams come true and should *not* be expected on their own to improve the human condition, but they still have essential practical roles to play in promoting international development cooperation:

- They can give governmental and non-governmental actors the fora they need to express their concerns.
- They can help them understand and appreciate the positions of others and to craft agreements that are mutually beneficial.
- They can provide advice and technical support for such agreements.
- They can pool resources for specific purposes on the ground, whenever donors and recipients have sufficient common interests.
- They can bring politicians, experts, diplomats, activists, businessmen and people closer to each other in their joint efforts to understand the mysteries of development.

It is by recognizing that they will not and should not be the dynamos of development that they can avoid the fate of the dinosaurs.

Appendix

Table A.1 *Total ODA, Multilateral ODA and Donor Contributions to the UN and IDA 1960–96 (current US$ millions)*

	1960	1961	1962	1963	1964	1965	1966	1967	1968
Total ODA	4718	5217	5539	5889	6018	6076	6293	6690	6400
of which Multilateral	658	842	668	362	375	452	513	736	682
of which									
UN				185	226	183	194	262	281
IDA				130	130	216	151	277	140

	1969	1970	1971	1972	1973	1974	1975	1976	1977
Total ODA	6707	6840	7718	8672	9408	11,317	13,585	13,665	14,696
of which Multilateral	1007	1124	1287	1905	2253	3060	3770	4161	4612
of which									
UN	309	368	431	637	651	831	1197	1153	1303
IDA	339	289	284	573	642	1121	1190	1359	1414

	1978	1979	1980	1981	1982	1983	1984	1985	1986
Total ODA	19,986	22,375	27,266	25,540	27,731	27,590	28,738	29,429	36,663
of which Multilateral	6863	6461	9157	7345	9297	8963	9048	7512	10449
of which									
UN	1584	1697	2171	2227	2260	2243	2302	2335	2685
IDA	3155	1993	3101	2433	2766	3146	3010	1948	3555

	1987	1988	1989	1990	1991	1992	1993	1994	1995	1996
Total ODA	41,596	48,114	45,741	52,960	56,678	60,850	56,472	59,152	58,894	55,485
of which Multilateral	11,580	14,959	12,782	15,814	15,425	19,601	17,126	17,863	18,299	16,347
of which										
UN	2998	3468	3430	4046	4368	4732	4119	4302	4260	4372
IDA	4204	5293	3319	4222	4708	6302	4970	4605	5405	3986

Source: OECD DAC Annual Reports 1960–98.

Table A.2 *Multilateral and UN Aid as Percentage Share of ODA.*
UN and IDA Shares of Multilateral Aid 1960–96

	1960	1961	1962	1963	1964	1965	1966	1967	1968	1969
Multilateral as % of ODA	13.9	16.1	12.1	6.1	6.2	7.4	8.2	11.0	10.7	15.0
UN as % of ODA				3.1	3.8	3.0	3.1	3.9	4.4	4.6
UN as % of Multilateral				51.1	60.3	40.5	37.8	35.6	41.2	30.7
IDA as % of Multilateral				0	0	35.9	34.7	47.8	29.4	37.6

	1970	1971	1972	1973	1974	1975	1976	1977	1978	1979
Multilateral as % of ODA	16.4	16.7	22.0	23.9	27.0	27.8	30.5	31.4	34.3	28.9
UN as % of ODA	32.7	33.5	33.4	28.9	27.2	31.8	27.7	28.3	23.1	26.3
UN as % of Multilateral	5.4	5.6	7.3	6.9	7.3	8.8	8.4	8.9	7.9	7.6
IDA as % of Multilateral	20.5	33.7	25.7	22.1	30.1	28.5	36.6	31.6	32.7	30.7

	1980	1981	1982	1983	1984	1985	1986	1987	1988	1989
Multilateral as % of ODA	33.6	28.8	33.5	32.5	31.5	25.5	28.5	27.8	31.1	27.9
UN as % of ODA	23.7	30.3	24.3	25.0	25.4	31.1	25.7	25.9	23.2	26.8
UN as % of Multilateral	8.0	8.7	8.1	8.1	8.0	7.9	7.3	7.2	7.2	7.5
IDA as % of Multilateral	46.0	30.8	33.9	33.1	29.8	35.1	33.3	25.9	34.0	36.3

	1990	1991	1992	1993	1994	1995	1996
Multilateral as % of ODA	29.9	27.2	32.2	30.3	30.2	31.1	29.5
UN as % of ODA	25.6	28.3	24.1	24.1	24.1	23.3	26.7
UN as % of Multilateral	7.6	7.7	7.8	7.3	7.3	7.2	7.9
IDA as % of Multilateral	35.4	26.0	26.7	30.5	32.2	29.0	25.8

Source: OECD DAC Annual Reports 1960–98.

Table A.3 *World Bank (IBRD and IDA) Loan Commitments 1970–97 (1990 US$ millions)*

	1970	1971	1972	1973	1974	1975	1976	1977	1978	1979
IBRD	542	5805	574	5631	8113	9949	1078	11671	11,451	12,067
IDA	1954	1788	2919	3716	2761	363	3585	2649	4344	5217

	1980	1981	1982	1983	1984	1985	1986	1987	1988	1989
IBRD	1207	12,644	13,959	14,463	14,858	13,631	15,399	16,063	16,089	17,148
IDA	606	4998	363	4339	4445	3635	3669	3946	486	5148

	1990	1991	1992	1993	1994	1995	1996	1997
IBRD	1518	15,762	14,191	15,531	12,688	14,638	12,447	12,095
IDA	5522	6051	6133	6188	5872	4924	5827	3849

Source: World Bank Annual Report 1970–97.

Table A.4 *Donor Contributions to IDA and UN (current US$ millions)*

	1972	1973	1974	1975	1976	1977	1978	1979	1980
Contributions to IDA	573	642	1121	1190	1359	1414	3155	1993	3101
Total contributions to UN	637	651	831	1197	1153	1303	1584	1697	2171
Total contributions to UNDP	268.4	317.4	264.5	467	546.4	608.4	681.5	790.4	837.4

	1981	1982	1983	1984	1985	1986	1987	1988	1989
Contributions to IDA	2433	2766	3146	3010	1948	3555	4204	5293	3319
Total contributions to UN	2227	2260	2243	2302	2335	2685	2998	3468	3430
Total contributions to UNDP	804.8	824.1	879.1	828.6	839.4	964.2	1090.3	1198.7	1203.8

	1990	1991	1992	1993	1994	1995	1996
Contributions to IDA	4222	4708	6302	4970	4605	5405	3986
Total contributions to UN	4046	4368	4732	4119	4302	4260	4372
Total contributions to UNDP		1344.5	1351.7	1564.9	1426.1	1849.2	1897.8

Source: UN and IDA: OECD/DAC Annual Reports 1960–98. UN A/48/940: Funding Operational Activities for Development within the UN System, May 1994, and UNDP Resource Mobilization Department. Conversion of current prices to constant values has been done by using the US consumer price index (1992=100).

Table A.5 *Main Donor Contributions to the World Bank, CEC and UN Agencies (US$ millions)*

	World Bank			CEC			UN agencies		
	1987	1990	1996	1987	1990	1996	1987	1990	1996
France	–	318	481	–	764	845	–	145	146
Germany	397	524	1170	497	784	1355	209	284	313
Italy	240	340	438	240	435	551	157	261	216
Japan	1192	1168	136	–	–	–	359	484	702
The Netherlands	226	194	277	167	192	245	211	248	357
Scandinavia	313	310	294	55	68	189	648	865	893
United Kingdom	226	310	333	363	587	707	158	196	210
USA	958	1119	806	–	–	–	590	724	910
EU members	–	–	3090	–	4374	4600	–	–	2140
DAC total	–	4734	4353	–	2975	4600	–	3973	4372

Source: OECD (1988, 1991, 1998), *Development Cooperation: Efforts and Policies of the Members of the Development Assistance Committee*, 1987, 1990 and 1996 reports (Paris: OECD).

Table A.6 *Main Donor Contributions to the UN (US$ millions)*

	1990	1991	1992	1993	1994	1995	1996	Annual average	% of total DAC 1996
France	145	146	187	168	164	113	146	153	3.3
Germany	284	360	358	339	287	310	313	322	7.2
Italy	261	314	323	185	190	148	216	234	4.9
Japan	484	649	602	593	678	744	702	636	16.1
The Netherlands	248	242	292	266	280	306	357	284	8.2
Scandinavia	865	912	1007	726	750	817	893	853	20.4
United Kingdom	196	232	313	198	155	192	210	214	4.8
USA	724	655	904	961	1135	976	910	895	20.8
Total DAC	3973	4366	4736	4025	4302	4260	4372	4291	100
EU members	–	–	–	–	1810	1894	2140		

Source: OECD, *Development Cooperation: Efforts and Policies of the Members of the Development Assistance Committee*, volumes 1991–97 (Paris: OECD). Fridtjof Nansen Institute calculations.

Table A.7 *Main Donor Contributions to the World Bank (US$ millions)*

	1990	1991	1992	1993	1994	1995	1996	Annual average 1990–96 Million dollars	% of total DAC 1990–96
France	318	436	460	440	445	493	481	439	8.3
Germany	524	524	648	622	704	751	1170	706	13.3
Italy	340	19	595	233	21	19	438	238	4.5
Japan	1168	1168	1283	1603	1763	2323	136	1,349	25.4
The Netherlands	194	179	250	189	194	247	277	219	4.1
Scandinavia	310	338	333	313	279	320	294	312	5.9
United Kingdom	310	384	379	350	314	336	333	344	6.5
USA	1119	1034	2175	1106	746	594	806	1083	20.4
Total DAC	4734	4797	7018	5308	4995	6004	4353	5316	100
EU members	–	–	–	–	1988	2559	3090		

Source: OECD, *Development Cooperation: Efforts and Policies of the Members of the Development Assistance Committee*, volumes 1991–97 (Paris: OECD). Fridtjof Nansen Institute calculations.

Table A.8 *Main Donor Contributions to CEC (EEC to 1992) (US$ millions)*

	1990	1991	1992	1993	1994	1995	1996
France	764	951	905	835	915	984	845
Germany	784	1225	1179	1133	1413	1578	1355
Italy	435	632	583	566	613	634	551
The Netherlands	192	248	250	247	279	327	245
Scandinavia	68	83	82	93	95	205	189
United Kingdom	587	743	683	708	746	856	707
Total	2975	4374	4285	4097	4709	5481	4600

Source: OECD, *Development Cooperation: Efforts and Policies of the Members of the Development Assistance Committee*, volumes 1991–97 (Paris: OECD). Fridtjof Nansen Institute calculations.

Table A.9 *Contributions from Governments and Other Sources for Operational Activities of the United Nations System: Overview, 1991–95 (current US$ millions)*

	1990	1991	1992	1993	1994
Contributions to United Nations Funds and Programmes					
1 Contributions to UNDP (a)	1192.9	1240.0	1481.8	1318.3	1516.1
2 Contributions to UNDP administered funds and trust funds (b)	128.5	103.3	283.8	126.9	177.5
Subtotal (1–2)	1321.4	1345.3	1765.6	1445.2	1693.6
3 Contributions to UNFPA (c)	227.8	272.6	293.8	265.1	340.7
4 Contributions to UNICEF (d)	785.7	781.6	918.5	793.7	937.6
5 Contributions to other United Nations funds and programmes (e)	66.8	62.3	73.5	55.0	78.3
6 Contributions to WFP (f)	1029.1	1404.6	1722.4	1421.1	1515.8
Subtotal (1–6)	3430.8	3866.4	4773.8	3980.1	4566.0
Contributions for Operational Activities of Specialized Agencies					
7 Assessed contributions to regular budgets (g)	216.5	272.1	219.4	345.8	280.0
8 Extrabudgetary contributions	604.9	676.2	649.5	706.5	651.2*
Subtotal (7–8)	821.4	948.3	868.9	1052.3	931.2
Grand total	4252.2	4814.7	5642.7	5032.4	5497.2

* UNRWA data not available

Contributions to IFAD and the World Bank Group					
9 Contributions to IFAD	129.0	194.6	336.3	32.4	97.8
10 Contributions to IDA	3478.6	4850.1	4034.0	3977.6	5098.2
11 Capital subscription payments to IBRD	511.6	118.3	1085.2	127.1	198.4
12 Capital subscription payments to IFC	167.1	74.2	76.0	253.2	238.3
Memo Items Explanatory Items					
Cost-sharing and government counter-part contributions to UNDP	292.5	293.8	421.6	687.2	714.9
UNICEF greeting cards	69.6	95.2	95.1	113.4	132.0
Government 'self-supporting' contributions to organizations and agencies	64.5	77.7	72.2	72.3	80.7

Source: Financial Statements of United Nations Funds and Programmes and of WFP; IFAD.

Notes for Table A.9

(a) Includes cost-sharing and government cash counterpart contributions.
(b) Includes the Capital Development Fund, the Special Fund for Land-Locked Developing Countries, the Revolving Fund for Natural Resources Exploration, the Special United Nations Volunteer Fund, the United Nations Fund for Science and Technology for Development, the United Nations Development Fund for Women and the Trust Fund for Sudano-Sahelian Activities; and other funds, accounts and trust funds of the UNDP including trust funds established by the Administrator, and contributions for the Junior Professional Officers programme. Includes cost-sharing contributions to these funds.
(c) Includes contributions to trust funds and 'special population programmes' of UNFPA.
(d) Includes net profit from the sale of greeting cards, which resoources are then used in operational activities.
(e) Constitutes regular budget and extrabudgetary contributions, including government self-supporting contributions, in relation to the United Nations, and its regional commissions, UNCHS, UNCTAD and UNDCP. See also the annual UNDP document on UN system regular and extrabudgetary technical cooperation financed from sources other than UNDP.
(f) Includes contributions to the International Emergency Food Reserve and extrabudgetary contributions. Core and other resources are not available at this time.
(g) That is, the imputed share of regular budget financing of technical cooperation expenditures in relation to the distribution of assessments among member states.

Table A.10 *Accumulated Contributions to IDA 1990–96*

	Total contributions (million dollars)	Share of budget (%)	Per capita (dollars)
France	2981	9.5	51.1
Germany	4910	15.7	60.0
Italy	1543	4.9	26.8
Japan	7978	25.5	63.4
The Netherlands	1370	4.4	88.4
Scandinavia	1996	6.4	107.7
United Kingdom	2293	7.3	39.0
USA	6962	22.2	26.2

Source: OECD, *Development Cooperation: Efforts and Policies of the Members of the Development Assistance Committee*, volumes 1991–97 (Paris: OECD).

Notes: *Share of budget*. Budget indicates the funding from DAC countries.
Per capita figures are Fridtjof Nansen Institute calculations, based on the 1996 populations.

Table A.11 *Distribution in Core Funding for UNDP, UNFPA and UNICEF, 1995*

	UNDP $ million	Share of budget (%)	UNFPA $ million	Share of budget (%)	UNICEF $ million	Share of budget (%)	Total $ million	Share of all budget (%)
France	19.8	2.3	0.7	0.2	32.7	6.0	53.2	3.6
Germany	94.1	10.9	32.6	10.9	47.7	8.7	174.4	11.7
Italy	18.6	2.2	1.3	0.4	41.7	7.6	61.6	4.1
Japan	105.1	12.1	51.8	17.4	58.9	10.8	215.8	14.5
The Netherlands	103.1	11.9	38.8	13.0	35.1	6.4	177.0	11.9
Scandinavia	249.8	28.8	91.1	30.6	116.1	21.2	457.0	30.7
United Kingdom	38.7	4.5	16.3	5.5	15.2	2.8	70.2	4.7
USA	114.7	13.2	35.0	11.8	116.1	21.2	265.8	17.9

Source: ECOSOC (1997), *Operational Activities of the United Nations for International Development Cooperation: Follow-up to Policy Recommendations of the General Assembly.*

Table A.12 *Contributions to the Eleventh Replenishment of the International Development Agency (IDA) (1997–99)*

	Basic contribution ($ million)	Share of budget (%)	Supplementary contributions ($ million)	Total contributions ($ million)	Per capita ($)
France	538.4	7.0	21.5	559.9	9.6
Germany	843.7	11.0		843.7	10.3
Italy	333.7	4.4		333.7	5.8
Japan	1434.3	18.7	99.7	1534.0	12.2
The Netherlands	253.1	3.3		253.1	16.3
Scandinavia	409.6	5.3		409.6	22.1
United Kingdom	471.7	6.2		471.7	8.0
USA	1600.0	20.9		1600.0	6.0

Source: The World Bank. Fridtjof Nansen Institute calculations.

Notes

INTRODUCTION

1 *Renewing the United Nations: A Programme for Reform* (A–51–950).
2 Kofi Annan at press conference at UN Headquarters in New York, 16 July 1997.
3 Quoted in the *Financial Times*, 17 July, 1997.
4 Wolfensohn 1997.
5 Nor did the architects that designed the UN headquarters in New York.

CHAPTER 1

1 These concepts and the following argument builds on Brunsson 1989: pp1–39.
2 Ibid: p2.
3 Ibid: p18.
4 Ibid: p4.
5 Ibid: p23.
6 Ibid: p24.
7 Decisions are defined as 'talk important enough to warrant classification as a separate category' (ibid: p26).
8 Ibid: p27. Brunsson calls this organizational hypocrisy, which we believe is an unnecessarily pejorative term, as it is not a question of deliberate deception.
9 Ibid: p31, our emphasis.
10 Jønsson, Kronsell and Søderholm undated: p2.
11 A classic example is the framing of autoimmunodeficiency syndrome (AIDS) at an early stage before it reached the headlines: Was it a medical, a development or a human rights issue? For elaboration, see Jønsson et al, undated.
12 Ibid: p8.
13 For elaboration on the role of secretariats, see Sandford 1994.
14 In the best of cases, this will lead to 'consensual knowledge' and mutual learning among the participants, see Haas and Haas 1995.
15 In principle, this can also be performed by a non-governmental entity, for example a research institution, but the task is normally entrusted to an IGO.
16 For elaboration, see Chayes and Chayes 1991 and Bergesen 1995.
17 Norms are commonly defined as 'mental models or guidelines by which, ideally, we control and evaluate our action and that of others' (*The Social Science Encyclopaedia*, Routledge, London, 1989: p560). Norm-creation

requires agreement on (i) perception of reality, (ii) relevant values and (iii) appropriate behaviour (Norsk samfunnsleksikon, *Norwegian Social Science Encyclopaedia*, Pax, Oslo, 1987: p289).

18 For elaboration see Chayes and Chayes 1991.
19 This definition includes organizational efficiency; that is how well an entity economizes on the use of its resources.
20 Brunsson 1989, pp194–5.
21 For elaboration of this concept and the reasoning behind it, see Stokke and Vidas 1996.
22 Brunsson 1989: p33.
23 This is confirmed by Brunsson's empirical analysis as far as local government is concerned. For a classical overview of combinations of functions in various IGOs see Jacobson 1979.
24 In the study of organizations a whole school of thought has been devoted to organizational behaviour of this kind. The classical text remains Cohen, March and Olsen 1972. For an application of their concepts to IGOs see Jønsson et al undated.
25 Brunsson gives the following account of such use of decisions: 'Under inconsistent norms it is possible for different descriptions of a single decision to be inconsistent; and explanations of the decisions to the public may be inconsistent with the content of the decisions as described in the minutes and records. In such situations it is quite obvious that a decision has been made, but it is not at all clear what exactly it consists of. The decision is both evident and equivocal' (ibid: p189).
26 Ibid: p202.
27 As for the UN system, social and economic development excludes all activities that fall within the mandate of the Security Council.

CHAPTER 2

1 (UN) Joint Inspection Unit, (JIU) 1985: p5.
2 Jackson 1969: p4.
3 For a discussion of the lasting importance of this principle, see Malnes 1996.
4 The views of David Mitrany, on the merits of functional cooperation, as framed by Rosemary Righter (Righter 1995: pp33–35).
5 The following extract provides a clear interpretation to this effect: 'Of course, if governments decided they wanted stronger and more decisive action, then the thing to do would be to centralise the budgets of all the Specialised Agencies – except those of the IMF and [International Bank for Reconstruction, ie World Bank] the IBRD – and bring them under effective co-ordinated control in ECOSOC. Then you really would see opposition to change! *That battle was fought out when I was at Lake Success in the early days and the supporters of the sectoral approach won the day*' (Jackson 1969: pvi, our emphasis).
6 Righter 1995: pp36–7, our emphasis.
7 Goodridge 1960: p264.
8 Asher et al 1957a: p2, with a reference to the UN Charter, Article 55.
9 Righter 1995: p37.
10 Asher 1958: p289.
11 Asher 1958: p289–90.
12 Emil J Sady, in Asher et al 1957a: p856, our emphasis.

13 JIU 1985: p37.
14 Asher et al 1957a: p1075.
15 Asher et al 1957a: pp1074, 1076.
16 'By loading onto the human rights platform every goal of human endeavor espoused by a vocal group, the span of United Nations concern has been broadened excessively. By self-discipline it should be narrowed and deepened' (Asher et al 1957a: p1067).
17 Asher et al 1957a: p1067, our emphasis.
18 Asher et al 1957a: p1068.
19 Kirdar 1966: p9.
20 Mason and Asher 1973: p383, our emphasis.
21 Consider, as an indication of such a strategy, the following description of the Bank by a UN-nominated group of experts of 1951: 'The experts were extremely critical of the World Bank, which they said "has not adequately realised that it is an agency charged by the United Nations with the duty of promoting economic development"' (Mason and Asher 1973: p384).
22 Asher et al 1957a: p239.
23 Asher et al 1958: p301.
24 Asher et al 1957a: p1021.
25 Asher et al 1957a: pp586–7, our emphasis.
26 Asher 1958: p288, our emphasis.
27 Asher 1958: p292.
28 Asher 1958: p291.
29 Righter 1995: p99. Righter provides a telling example of what she calls a typical cold warrior's overreaction, in quoting the then US Secretary of State John Foster Dulles's perception of the emerging concept of non-alignment as 'an immoral and short-sighted conception'.
30 The significance of UNCTAD as vehicle of developing world unity and power will be discussed in the next section (1970–90).
31 Krasner (1985) set out to demonstrate that developing country NIEO deliberations were primarily born out of political power and sovereignty aspirations, and not purely economy driven. Both he and a range of scholars leaning more in the direction of economic explanations, acknowledged that a combination of political power and economic incentive-based motivations were at play.
32 Quoted by Righter 1995: p102 from Mosley 1987: pp25–7.
33 Some of these agencies were reshaped and renamed after 1945 (new names given here), but without significantly changing their mandates.
34 The picture is not necessarily uniform, however. In a critical assessment of specialized agency 'salesmanship' of projects linked to new and fashionable agendas, Douglas Williams states 'the International Telecommunications Union (ITU) – normally one of the more responsible agencies – saw nothing incongruous in circulating posters in Africa proclaiming "International Communications for Rural Health Week"', Williams 1987. In a similar vein, Rosemary Righter tells of a 1982 ITU meeting on the allocation of radio frequencies, where four out of six weeks went into wrangling over a proposal to exclude Israel from its proceedings; Righter 1995: p123.
35 Maurice Bertrand in JIU 1985: p24. He added, in frustration, that 'all the other activities (than those of functional agencies and humanitarian ones) of the World Organisation lie within areas where consensus is either at a very low level or even at variance with the tasks entrusted to the organisation'.
36 Jackson 1969: p11.

37   The Jackson report was very critical of the performance at this level: 'Organisation at the regional level is now so convoluted that the UN development system will need to use it with great care if the capacity of the present operation is not to be prejudiced' (Jackson 1969: p12). It reinforces this message on page 35 in claiming that 'drastic rationalisation of the existing confused pattern of regional represenation is imperative'.

38   Asher et al 1957a.

39   Jackson 1969: piii.

40   JIU 1985: p7. This survey may contain some organizations that were created after 1970, but most of them were already in place at the end of the period discussed here (1970).

41   Jackson 1969: p7.

42   JIU 1985: pp10–11, our emphasis.

43   Quoted from Righter, who sees the following link between the disintegrating international monetary system and the rise of developing world power: 'the "North" gave new edge to the language of resentment. The Western powers could now be presented not only as the manipulators of the international system, but as the incompetent manipulators of an unworkable structure' (Righter 1995: p106).

44   Righter 1995: p107.

45   Righter 1995: p117.

46   Jackson 1983: p159 (quoted by Righter 1995: p116).

47   See Bergesen et al 1982a, for a detailed account and assessment of the rise and fall of NIEO.

48   Bergesen et al 1982a: p231.

49   See below for a more comprehensive exploration of the 'sprawling phenomenon' and its implications for UN performance.

50   Righter 1995: p135.

51   Leonard 1994: p226, our emphasis.

52   JIU 1985: pp12–14.

53   Edgren and Møller 1991: p168, our emphasis.

54   For details in the development of public opinion and environmental organization since the 1970s, see Bergesen and Dahl 1997.

55   For a review of the origins of UNEP and its subsequent development, see von Moltke 1996.

56   The lack of agreement on agenda and the consequences for MDIs are described in Wettestad 1987. For a general overview of the North-South controversy on the environment, see Thomas 1992.

57   This is the essence of the foreword by Gro Harlem Brundtland to the Commission's report, quotes from ppxi and xii. (World Commission on Environment and Development 1987).

58   World Commission on Environment and Development 1987: p43.

59   World Commission on Environment and Development 1987: pp44–5.

60   The contrast to the Brandt Commission is striking; it argued, almost a decade earlier, that rich and poor countries had a common interest in stimulating economic growth by massive transfers from the North to the South, but failed to convince the large donors (Brandt 1980).

61   Peter Haas concludes that 'the Brundtland Commission's manifesto was a polemical success which resonated with the political urgency accompanying the issues at the time' (Haas 1996: p244).

62   World Commission on Environment and Development 1987: p343.

63   See Bergesen and Dahl 1997.

64   For elaboration of the follow-up process and of the way the Commission developed in the first years after its inception, see Bergesen and Botnen 1996.
65   Bergesen and Botnen 1996.
66   Follow-up of Agenda 21 at the national level in developing countries is described by Yamin 1998.
67   IPCC was set up by virtue of a decision by the UN General Assembly decision in 1987; the same session that heard the official end report of the WCED.
68   For a detailed analysis of the early days of the IPCC, see Lunde 1991. For an account of the role of the IPCC after Rio, see Lanchbery and Victor 1995.
69   Quoted in Williams 1987: p54.
70   Williams 1987: p154, quotes a 1979 programme recommendation for S&T stimulation at regional level, which amply illustrates the vagueness in objectives: 'collective self-reliance among developing countries is a multi-dimensional process requiring the adoption of policies and measures that are both bilateral and multilateral in scope, with a view to a strengthening of the internal capacities of developing countries and improving their bargaining position'.
71   Williams 1987: p155.
72   This development is described in Bergesen 1982b.
73   Weiss, Forsythe and Coate 1994: p168.
74   In some cases more than one request from the same government. For details Boutros-Gali 1996: pp318–20.
75   This does not include the protection activities undertaken across the world by the UNHCR.
76   Based on OECD/DAC numbers which vary somewhat from UN figures.
77   The costs to the UN from field representation trebled in the same period from 211 million dollars to 622 million (JIU 1997: pp3 and 7).
78   UNDP 1996/1997 Annual Report. For a review of the proliferation problem ('projectities') in UNDP, see Engberg-Pedersen and Hvashoj Jorgensen 1997.
79   This argument is made, for example, by UNDP Administrator James Gustave Speth, in Speth 1996.
80   DAC 1998: pA4.
81   Wolfensohn 1996: p2.
82   DAC 1998: pA22. For UNDP, see Figure 2.11.
83   For a review of the ups and downs of UNEP, see von Moltke 1996.
84   After the Council was reorganized in 1993, merging its formerly separate secretariat with the central UN secretariat in New York, its set-up has more in common with a functional commission than with a UN fund or programme.
85   JIU 1985: p5.
86   The strategy for the Fourth UN Development Decade was formally adopted by the General Assembly on 21 December 1990 in resolution 45/199.
87   A UN insider uses the term 'an exercise in hypocrisy'. Havelock Brewster, former head of UNCTAD's commodities division, quoted in Righter 1995: p179.
88   Using a wider definition of global conferences, Willetts (1989) puts the number to 147 for the period 1961–85.
89   An anecdotal illustration: The late Norwegian Minister of Foreign Affairs, Knut Frydenlund, recounted how he once discussed with Lord Carrington, then his British counterpart, preparations to the annual session of the UN General Assembly. Frydenlund, among other things, asked how much time the British Minister would spend preparing for this event. The response was straightforward: 'Two hours', which by the Norwegian note-taker was taken to mean 'two hours a day'.

90 The agenda of the General Assembly consisted in 1997 of 168 items.
91 'Interest aggregation' in political science jargon.
92 Urquhart 1987: p108.
93 Urquhart 1987: p120.
94 Urquhart 1987: p108.
95 Urquhart 1987: p352.
96 Childers and Urquhart 1994: p164. The same kind of criticism is expanded and substantiated in the 1985 report from the Joint Inspection Unit (JIU 1985: pp11–14).
97 JIU 1985: p23.
98 The report is entitled 'A New United Nations Structure for Global Economic Cooperation: Report of the Group of Experts on the Structures of the United System', EC/AC.62/9, New York, United Nations, 28 May 1975. Its raporteur was Professor Richard Gardner of Columbia University.
99 JIU 1985: p10.
100 JIU 1985: p54.
101 JIU 1985: p55.
102 The United Nations in Development. Reform Issues in the Economic and Social Fields. A Nordic Perspective, Final Report of the Nordic UN Project, Stockholm 1991: pp55–7.
103 JIU 1985: p63.
104 For details of its analysis and proposals, see Commission on Global Governance 1995: pp263–85. This quote is from p278.
105 This point is strongly underlined by Bertrand in JIU 1985, especially pp15–19.
106 This is the main message in Righter's detailed account of UN development throughout the 1970s and 1980s (Righter 1995: pp155–84).
107 The 'strategies' for the various UN Development Decades are a telling illustration of how political disagreement is cloaked in diplomatic jargon. To the outside observer negotiations over such 'language' are often mysterious and opaque. Righter notes that 'arguments over squared brackets and modifying subclauses have an allure for professional bureaucrats that few politicians, and no layman, can hope to understand' (1995: p255).
108 Jackson 1969: ppiv–v.
109 JIU 1985: pp11–14.
110 Righter 1995, in particular Chapter 6: pp155–84.
111 Jønsson 1996, see also his theoretical paper on the importance of interorganizational factors: Jønsson 1995.
112 Categories taken from Engberg-Pedersen 1991: pp9–10.
113 UN press release, New York, 16 July 1997. 'Renewing the United Nations: A Programme for Reform' was published as UN General Assembly document A/51/950, from which the quotes below are taken.
114 Para 130.
115 Para 137.
116 Para 86.
117 Idem.
118 Para 87.
119 Para 148.
120 Para 153 and 161.
121 Para 160.
122 Para 163, our emphasis.

CHAPTER 3

1 Inspired by Lateef 1995.
2 See Singer 1995, for a fuller description of how the 'Never Again!' sentiment influenced the early thinking on the Bretton Woods system.
3 Singer 1995: p2.
4 In inviting the 44 governments to Bretton Woods in 1944, the US Secretary
   of State described the purpose as being to 'formulate definite proposals for
   an International Monetary Fund and *possibly* a Bank for Reconstruction and
   Development'. Quoted from Mason and Asher 1973: p12.
5 Statement by Sir Roy Harrod, quoted by Mason and Asher 1973: p12.
6 Mason and Asher 1973: p28 our emphasis.
7 By the terms agreed to at Bretton Woods, the member countries having the
   largest number of shares were, in order, the United States, the United
   Kingdom, the Soviet Union, China and France. India took the place of the
   Soviet Union when Stalin decided not to ratify the Articles of Agreement.
8 Quoted from Mason and Asher 1973: p30.
9 Article V, section 5 (b).
10 Article V, section 5 (d).
11 Quoted from Mason and Asher 1973: p33.
12 Mason and Asher 1973: p27, our emphasis.
13 Mason and Asher 1973, p
14 Mason and Asher 1973: p50.
15 The application from Czechoslovakia was withdrawn 'voluntarily' after the
   Soviet-supported coup in February 1948. Poland was a more complex case,
   illustrating the delicate balancing act that the Bank was exposed to between
   economic and political concerns. The Polish executive director was told infor-
   mally that the US would veto Poland's application for a coal industry loan,
   and it was therefore not presented to the board. The kind of compromise
   language used for such difficult occasions is amply illustrated in the following
   quote from its third annual report (1947–48): 'The Bank is fully cognizant of
   the injunction in its Articles of Agreement that its decisions shall be based on
   only economic considerations. Political tensions and uncertainties in or among
   member countries, however, have a direct effect on economic and finacial
   conditions in those countries and upon their credit position.'
16 Mason and Asher 1973: p73. The image of Bank officials as being arrogant
   and remote when approaching less developed country governments was thus
   already established. It was into the 1980s that it first started doing the Bank
   much harm, however, when public opinion in the western world grew increasingly sceptical of World Bank performance.
17 Resolution 124 (II) of the General Assembly.
18 Mason and Asher 1973: p561.
19 Mason and Asher 1973: p564.
20 Quote from Lateef 1994: p19.
21 As described in the previous chapter, IDA can also be seen at least indirectly
   as the rich and powerful's belated response to poor countries' demand
   throughout the 1950s for a sizable grant-based fund for economic and social
   development under UN auspices (the SUNFED proposal) . Even if IDA is
   neither under any form of UN control nor makes grants, and operates by
   weighted voting, it can be seen as a partial victory of the developing
   countries' UN-centred strategy for better terms of financing. Or in the
   words of Mason and Asher (1973), 'as living proof that the "international
   power structure" is responsive to persistent peaceful pressure' (p380).

22 Warren C Baum, 'The project cycle', *Finance and Development*, vol 7, 1970, p6; quoted by Mason and Asher 1973: p308.
23 Lateef 1995.
24 Stern 1993: pp137–9.
25 The speeches in 1972 and 1973 are seen as just as significant in justifying the new poverty orientation.
26 Copenhagen, 21 September 1970, quoted in Mason and Asher 1973: p475.
27 For a survey of the relationship between development theory and policies and practices of multilateral development institutions, see Harboe 1996.
28 Stern 1997: p45.
29 Lateef 1995: p23.
30 Gaving and Rodrik 1995: p332.
31 Quoted from Stern 1993: pp18–19. The 'projects only' clause in the Articles of Agreement, to be more precise, reads as follows: 'Loans made or guaranteed by the Bank shall, except in special circumstances, be for the purpose of specific projects.'
32 Mason and Asher 1973: pp476–7.
33 While until the mid-1960s the Economics Department was small and 'undermanned, a substantial research facility was introduced by President Woods in 1964/65, with Irving Friedman as economic adviser to the President and Andrew Karmack as director of the Economics Department. When Friedman and Karmack departed in 1970, staff in the department had increased six-fold' (Stern 1997).
34 See, for instance, Chenery et al 1974.
35 Stern 1997: p22.
36 Stern 1997: p145.
37 Lateef 1995: p26.
38 For a recent case study, see Kroksnes 1997.
39 Stern 1997: p27.
40 Stern 1997: p36.
41 Lateef 1994: p24.
42 Stern 1997, additional quotes from McNamara 1981.
43 For a study of the Bank's role in the power sector and the impact on sector performance, see Haugland et al 1997.
44 In 1995, the World Bank's active portfolio of loans primarily directed towards better management of environmental and natural resources amounted to US$70 billion (World Bank 1995).
45 In 1997, the Bank published a major strategy paper on post-war reconstruction.
46 For a study of, for example, the Bank's ability to integrate environmental concerns into structural and sectoral adjustment programmes, see Claussen et al 1996.
47 Kapur, Lewis and Webb 1997.
48 Kapur, Lewis and Webb 1997.
49 CSIS Task Force 1997: pxi.
50 CSIS Task Force 1997: pxiii.
51 Many would argue that several key elements of the Strategic Compact were launched well before Wolfensohn took over.
52 World Bank 1997.
53 1995 Annual Meetings speech by Mr James D Wolfensohn, 10 October 1995.
54 World Bank 1997: p5.
55 'The World Bank and the Evolving Challenges of Development', speech given by James D Wolfensohn at an Overseas Development Council Congressional Staff Forum, 16 May 1997.

56   World Bank 1997: p1, our emphasis.
57   World Bank 1997: p4.
58   World Bank 1997: p17.
59   Mr Wolfensohn's Annual Meetings address, 1997.

CHAPTER 4

1   That is, if the following interpretation is correct: 1 'enabling' is the code word for traditional World Bank and western concerns over the prospects for the private sector, that is a market economic approach to development; 2 'environment' gives associations to the conservation agenda of other influential circles in the West; while 3 'sustainable development' caters to the aspirations of developing world elites for economic growth.
2   Annan 1997, para 2.
3   See Laugen 1996.
4   Boutros-Ghali 1996: p1.
5   Speth 1996: p75 and Boutros-Gali 1996: p3.
6   Annan 1997, paras 3 and 10, our emphasis.
7   See Willetts 1996, Conca 1995 and Gordenker and Weiss 1995.
8   A quantitative illustration of the trend towards involving more and more non-state actors, in terms of NGOs in consultative status with ECOSOC, is given in Willetts 1996: p38.
9   Childers and Urquart held that ' a cynicism virtually unknown in the early decades of the organization pervades the working environment... Cronyism has become widely entrenched in secretariats' (1994: p164).
10   This corresponds very well to Brunsson's assumptions: '(A)ny political organisation that wants to grow ... will actively seek to incorporate new ideas in the environment into its own organisation. No group need be left outside its domain. The organisation grows by reflecting an increasing number of inconsistencies' (1989: p23).
11   According to Kofi Annan 'strategic deployment of resources, unity of purpose, coherence of effort, agility and flexibility' are 'the very organisational features that are now most demanded by the United Nations' (Annan 1997, para 23).
12   Quotes from Brunsson 1989: p212.
13   For a review of the World Summit for Children and subsequent follow-up by UNICEF see Laugen 1996.
14   See Haugland, Ingeberg and Roland 1997.
15   For elaboration see World Bank 1994.
16   Wolfenshohn 1997.
17   One of the very first IBRD loans was given to KLM.
18   Wolfensohn 1996, para 36.
19   Wolfensohn 1996, para 38.
20   Ibid: para 41.
21   According to Brunsson 1989, p206, this is typical of public organizations.
22   Teaching the world about stopping street crime from a base in Washington DC is quite a paradox.
23   World Bank 1997: p5.
24   Quoted above from Mason and Asher 1973: p27.
25   Wolfensohn 1997: p2.
26   For a contribution to the 'real impact' debate see Nelson 1995.

27   Wolfensohn 1996, para 48.
28   CSIS 1997: p74.
29   Such views are referred to in CSIS 1997: p109, thus quoting an anonymous World Bank staffer: 'The cognitive dissonance between high-level pronouncements and daily practice is at an all-time high.'
30   Cf. Lewis extensively quoted in Chapter 3.
31   CSIS 1997: pp73–5 and pp104–9.
32   For details see Appendix Table A.4.
33   Appendix Tables A.3 and A.4. The question of donor support is further treated in Chapter 6.
34   For general analyses of these complex interactions and the increasing importance of NGOs, see Willetts 1996, Gordenker and Weiss 1995 and Fisher 1993. For case studies see Christoffersen 1997, Park 1997 and Jønsson and Søderholm 1995.

CHAPTER 5

1   For reviews of the ozone negotiations, see Miller and Mintzer 1992 and Parson 1996.
2   For an analysis of the complexity of the AIDS case, see Gordenker, Jønsson et al 1995.
3   Our argument disregards the case where poverty or conflict causes migration at such a scale that the receiving countries are directly affected. This is more a matter of regional concern, not a question of a global good, at least for the time being. Only if millions of poor Africans began to emigrate to all corners of the world at the same time, would poverty in Africa constitute a global bad belonging to our short list.

CHAPTER 6

1   DAC 1998: ppA37 and 55.
2   In 1993 net disbursements by DAC countries to the states of ex-Yugoslavia amounted to 2.5 billion dollars, in 1994 to 1 billion (DAC 1998: pA54).
3   This was implemented as from 1997, according to a DAC decision. In 1996, these two countries accounted for 6 per cent of total ODA, or 3.3 billion dollars together.
4   DAC reports underline this link between budget balance and aid (DAC 1998: p55).
5   This is shown in Figure 4.1. The increase in contributions to IDA in 1995 is an exception to the trend.
6   See Appendix Table A.4.
7   DAC 1998: pA42.
8   See Figure 3.3 and Appendix Table A.3.
9   Appendix Table A.2. The variation in IDA contributions is due to its replenishment cycles.
10   DAC 1998: pA2, see also Figure 3.7.
11   Appendix Table A.3 and DAC 1998: ppA2 and A4.
12   The main source of UN figures is ECOSOC 1997, cf. pp9–10 and pp11–17.
13   See Appendix Table A.9.

14   ECOSOC 1997: p9.
15   This excludes Canada which is a much smaller donor than the others in this group and, of course, Russia which is not a donor at all.
16   Denmark, Norway and Sweden.
17   Other countries occasionally make significant contributions for particular purposes.
18   For details see Appendix Tables A.5–7. In the case of the World Bank actual contributions vary considerably from one year to the next, which is why we have chosen to use annual averages for the purpose of this comparison.
19   For a detailed analysis of relative support for MDIs, see Ravlum 1997.
20   For a condensed description see the reference section in *Yearbook of International Cooperation on Environment and Development*, Earthscan, London, latest edition.
21   According to this formula the EU is obliged to pay 35, the USA 25 and Japan 12 per cent of the contributions to the fund. For details on this arrangement and evalution of the working of the fund, see DeSombre and Kauffman 1996.
22   For analysis of the ideas behind and the first phase of GEF see Kjørven 1992, for subsequent developments, see Botnen 1997 and Fairman 1996.
23   *Green Globe Yearbook* 1997: p213.
24   See Jorgensen 1997, Botnen 1997 and Fairman 1996.
25   In both cases donors have been willing to share influence in intricate decision-making arrangements with recipients, but the former still retain sufficient control to block funding to which they are opposed. Cf. Fairman 1996 and DeSombre and Kauffman 1996.
26   *Green Globe Yearbook* 1997: p229.
27   A recent example of how poverty eradication is used to underpin arguments in favour of supporting MDIs is the report of the bipartisan US Task Force on multilateral development banks (CSIS 1997).
28   For a review of the changing and competing notions of development in the post-war period, see Harboe 1996.
29   This is how the Development Assistance Committee (DAC) of OECD defines the new paradigm, with due reference to Albert Hirschman's work from the 1950s, with its focus on 'essentially uncoordinated microlevel strategy'. Quotes from DAC 1998: p18, our emphasis.
30   Take, for example, the current notion of 'enabling environment for sustainable development': As a diplomatic compromise, it may work. As a basis for attracting funding and commitment, it probably won't.
31   This is the way Haas and Haas (1995: p277) describe the result of making more and more integrated UN programmes.
32   In line with our conclusions in Chapter 3, DAC points to the 'approval driven culture' of the Bank as 'the source of a deep seated flaw that had become lodged in the way their institutions functioned' (DAC 1998: pp18–19).
33   One example could be to develop measures or institutions to mobilize additional private capital for social or environmental investment, cf. Assenza 1998.
34   On paper, this dilemma could be solved by splitting the Bank into two separate parts.
35   As quoted in Chapter 2.
36   At the end of the fifty-second session of the UN General Assembly (1997–98) the president of this body, Hennadiy Udovenko of the Ukraine,

admitted that after 'almost nine months of further intensive consultations, consuming an enormous amount of time, efforts and conference services, all we can offer is the decision to send a considerable bulk of them (Kofi Annan's reform proposals) for additional consideration during the fifty-third session' (*International Document Review*, 14 September 1998: p8).

37 Kofi Annan has advocated both 'a functional rationalisation in a complementary and co-operative manner between the work of the United Nations and the World Bank' (Renewing the United Nations, part II, para 163) and 'greater system-wide coherence' within the UN, including the specialized agencies (UN Press Release, 12 November 1997, SG/SM/6391).

38 This is in line with what Righter has called the 'discriminate buyers' UN (1995: Chapter 10).

39 See Ministry of Foreign Affairs, undated.

40 According to DAC similar studies have been conducted in other OECD countries – USA, Canada and Australia – but none of them have published their official strategies with such openness and commitment as the Danish government (DAC 1998: pp70–4).

41 This is the main thrust of a report published by a developing world think tank on the occasion of the UN's fiftieth anniversary (South Centre 1995).

42 As quoted in the introduction to this book.

References

Annan, Kofi (1997) *Renewing the United Nations: A Programme for Reform. Report of the Secretary-General*, New York, United Nations

Asher, Robert et al (1957a) *The United Nations and Promotion of the General Welfare*, Washington DC, The Brookings Institution

Asher, Robert, et al (1957b) *The United Nations and Economic and Social Cooperation*, Washington DC, The Brookings Institution

Asher, Robert (1958) 'Economic Co-operation under the UN Auspices', in *International Organization*, vol 12, no 3, pp288–302

Assenza, Gaudenz B (1998) *Mobilizing Private Capital for the Global Environment*, Lysaker, Norway, Fridtjof Nansen Institute

Bergesen, Helge Ole, Holm and McKinlay (1982a) *The recalcitrant rich – a comparative analysis of the Northern responses to demands for a new international economic order*, London, Pinter Publishers

Bergesen, Helge Ole (1982b) *The power to embarrass: The UN human rights regime between realism and utopia*, Paper presented at IPSA World Congress, Rio

Bergesen, Helge Ole (1995) 'A Global Climate Regime' *Green Globe Yearbook*, Oxford: Oxford University Press, pp51–8

Bergesen, Helge Ole and Botnen, Trond (1996) 'Sustainable Principles or Sustainable Institutions? The Long Way from UNCED to the Commission on Sustainable Development', *Forum for Development Studies*, 1, 1996, pp35–62

Bergesen, Helge Ole and Dahl, Agnethe (1997) *Who Runs the Environment*, Lysaker, Norway, Fridtjof Nansen Institute, mimeo

Botnen, Trond (1997) *Funding for the global environment: Determined by national or common objectives?* Lysaker, Norway, Fridtjof Nansen Institute

Boutrus-Ghali (1996) *The 50th Anniversary Annual Report on the Work of the Organization*, New York, United Nations

Brandt, Willy (1980) *North-South: A Programme for Survival*, The Report of the Independent Commission on International Development Issues, London, Pan Books

Brunsson, Nils (1989) *The Organization of Hypocrisy. Talk, decisions and actions in organizations*, Chichester, John Wiley & Sons

Chayes, Abram and Chayes, Antonia H (1991) 'Adjustment and Compliance Processes in International Regulatory Regimes', in Mathews, Jessica Tuchman *Preserving the Global Environment*, New York, W W Norton

Chenery, Hollis B et al (1974) *Redistribution with Growth*, Oxford, Oxford University Press

Childers, Erskine and Urquhart, Brian (1994) *Renewing the United Nations System*, Uppsala, Sweden, Dag Hammarskjöld Foundation

Christoffersen, Leif E (1997) 'IUCN: A Bridge-Builder for Nature Conservation', in Bergesen, Helge Ole and Parmann, Georg *Green Globe Yearbook*, Oxford, Oxford University Press

Claussen, Jens, Stein Hansen, Jørgen Hansen and Henrik Harboe (1996) *Integrating Environmental Concerns into Economywide Policies in Developing Countries: The Role of the Multilateral Development Banks*, Development and Multilateral Institutions Programme. Draft Working Paper no 6/1996. The Fridtjof Nansen Institute/ECON Centre for Economic Analysis

Conca, Ken (1995) 'Greening the United Nations: Environmental Organisations and the UN System', *Third World Quarterly*, vol 16, no 3, pp441–58

Cohen, Michael D, March, James G and Olsen, Johan P (1972) 'A Garbage Can Model of Organizational Choice', *Administrative Science Quarterly*, vol 17, no 1

Commission on Global Governance (1995) *Our Global Neighbourhood*, Oxford, Oxford University Press

CSIS Task Force (1997) *The United States and the Multilateral Development Banks. Final Report*, Washington DC, Center for Strategic & International Studies

DAC (1998) *Development Cooperation*, Paris, OECD

DeSombre, Elizabeth R. and Kauffman, Joanne (1996) 'The Montreal Protocol Multilateral Fund: Partial Success Story', in Keohane, Robert O and Lecy, Marc A (eds) *Institutions for Environmental Aid. Pitfalls and Promise*, Cambridge, MIT Press, pp89–126

Dunlap, Riley E (1994) 'International Attitudes towards Environment and Development', in Bergesen, Helge Ole and Parmann, Georg *Green Globe Yearbook* 1994, Oxford, UK, Oxford University Press, pp115–26

ECOSOC (1997) *Comprehensive Statistical Data on Operational Activities for Development for the Year 1995*, Note by the Secretary-General, E/1997/65/Add.4, 3 June 1997

Edgren, Gus and Møller, Birgitte (1991) 'The agencies at a cross-roads – the role of the UN specialised agencies', in *The United Nations, issues and options*, The Nordic UN Project, Stockholm

Engberg-Pedersen, Poul (1991) *Effectiveness of Multilateral Agencies at Country Level: Case Study of 11 Agencies in Kenya, Nepal, Sudan and Thailand*, The Danish Ministry of Foreign Affairs, Copenhagen

Engberg-Pedersen, Poul and Hvashoj Jorgensen, Claus (1997) 'UNDP and the Global Environment Problems: The Need for Capacity Development at Country Level', in Bergesen, Helge Ole and Parmann, Georg *Green Globe Yearbook*, Oxford, Oxford University Press, pp37–44

Fairman, David (1996) 'The Global Environment Facility: Haunted by the Shadow of the Future' in Keohane, Robert O and Lecy, Marc A (eds) *Institutions for Environmental Aid. Pitfalls and Promise*, Cambridge, MIT Press, pp55–88

Fisher, Julie (1993) *The Road from Rio. Sustainable Development and the Nongovernmental Movement in the Third World*, Westport, Praeger

Gavin, M and Rodrik, D (1995) 'The World Bank in Historical Perspective', *American Economic Review*, pp329–34

Goodrich, Leland M (1960) *The United Nations*, London, Stevens and Sons Limited

Gordenker, Leon, Jønsson, Christer, Coate, Roger A and Søderholm, Peter (1995) *International Cooperation in Response to Aids*, London, Pinter

Gordenker, Leon and Weiss, Thomas G (1995) 'NGO Participation in the International Policy Process', *Third World Quarterly*, vol 16, no 3, pp543–56

Green Globe Yearbook 1997, Oxford, Oxford University Press

Haas, Peter (1996) 'Is "Sustainable Development" Politically Sustainable?', *The Brown Journal of World Affairs*, Summer/Fall 1996, vol III, no 2, pp239–47

Haas, Peter M and Haas, Ernst B (1995) 'Learning to Learn: Improving International Governance', *Global Governance*, vol 1, pp255–85

Harboe, Henrik (1996) *Development Theory and Policies: Contrasting the UN System with the Multilateral Development Banks*, Development and Multilateral Institutions Programme, Working Paper no 4, The Fridtjof Nansen Institute/ECON Centre for Economic Analysis

Haugland, Torleif, Ingeberg, Kjetil and Roland Kjell (1997) 'Price reforms in the power sector', The World Bank's role, *Energy Policy*, vol 25, no 13, pp1041–9

Jackson, R G A (1969) *A Study of the Capacity of the United Nations Development system*, vol 1, Geneva, United Nations

Jackson, Richard L (1983) *The Non-Aligned, the UN and the Superpowers*, New York, Praeger

Jacobson, Harold (1979) *Networks of Interdependence*, New York, Alfred A Knopf

Joint Inspection Unit (JIU) (1985) *Some reflections on reform of the United Nations*, Geneva, (JIU/REP/85/9)

Joint Inspection Unit (JIU) (1997) *Strengthening Field Representation of the United Nations System*, Geneva, United Nations

Jorgenson, Lisa (1997) 'The Global Environment Facility: International Waters Coming into its Own', in Bergesen, Helge Ole and Parmann, Georg (eds) *Green Globe Yearbook*, Oxford, Oxford University Press, pp45–58

Jønsson, Christer (1995) *An Interorganization Approach to the Study of Multilateral Institutions: Lessons from Previous Research on International Cooperation*, Oslo/Lysaker, Development and Multilateral Institutions Programme, The Fridtjof Nansen Institute/ECON Centre for Economic Analysis

Jønsson, Christer (1996a) *The problem of coordination among UN agencies: Experience from AIDS-related assistance programmes*, Oslo/Lysaker, Development and Multilateral Institutions Programme, The Fridtjof Nansen Institute/ECON Centre for Economic Analysis

Jønsson, Christer (1996b) 'From "Lead Agency" to "Integrated Programming": The Global Response to AIDS in the Third World', in Bergesen, Helge Ole and Parmann, Georg *Green Globe Yearbook*, Oxford, Oxford University Press, pp65–72

Jønsson, Christer and Søderholm, Peter (1995) 'IGO–NGO Relations and HIV/AIDS: Innovation or Stalemate?', *Third World Quarterly*, vol 16, no 3, pp459–76

Jønsson, Christer, Kronsell, Annica and Søderholm, Peter (undated) *International Organizations and Agenda Setting*, mimeo

Kapur, D, Lewis, J P, and Webb, R (1997) *The World Bank: Its first half century. Volume 1. History*, Washington DC, Brookings Insitution Press

Kirdar, Uner (1966) *The Structure of the United Nations Economic Aid to Underdeveloped Countries*, The Hague, Martinus Nijhoff

Kjørven, Olav (1992) *Facing the Challenge of Change: the World Bank and the Global Environment Facility*, Lysaker, Norway, Fridtjof Nansen Institute

Krasner, Stephen D (1985) *Structural Conflict: The Third World against Global Liberalism*, Berkeley, University of California Press

Kroksnes, Ingunn (1997) 'Non-governmental organizations and development policies: Identifying and explaining strategies. The case of the World Bank's Narmada dam project', Lysaker, Norway, Fridtjof Nansen Institute

Lanchbery, John and Victor, David (1995) 'The Role of Science in the Global Climate Negotiations', in Bergesen, Helge Ole and Parmann, Georg (eds) *Green Globe Yearbook*, Oxford, Oxford University Press, pp29–40

Lateef, K Sarwar (ed) (1995) *The Evolving Role of the World Bank. Helping meet the Challenge of Development*, Washington DC, The World Bank

Laugen, Torunn (1996) 'Balancing effectiveness and legitimacy: UNICEF's follow-up of the World Summit for Children', in *Forum for Development Studies*, no 1, 1996

Leonard, James F (1994) 'The US policy towards the United Nations', in Roger A Coate, (ed) *US policy and the future of the United Nations*, New York, Twentieth Century Fund Press

Lunde, Leiv (1991) *Science or Politics in the Global Greenhouse*. Lysaker, Norway, Fridtjof Nansen Institute

Malnes, Raino (1996) 'Democracy in the United Nations: For and against', *Forum for Development Studies*, no 1, 1996

Mason, Edward S. and Asher, Robert E (1973) *The World Bank since Bretton Woods*. Washington DC, The Brookings Institution

McNamara, R (1981) *The McNamara Years at the World Bank*, Baltimore, Johns Hopkins University Press

Miller, Alan and Mintzer, Irving (1992) 'Statospheric Ozone Depletion: Can we Save the Sky?', in Bergesen, Helge Ole and Parmann, Georg *Green Globe Yearbook*, Oxford, Oxford University Press

Ministry of Foreign Affairs (Denmark) (undated) *Plan of Action for Active Multilateralism and Strategies for Individual Organizations*, Copenhagen

Mosley, Paul (1987) *Overseas aid: Its Defence and Reform*, London: Wheatshaf Books

Nelson, Paul J (1995) *The World Bank and Non-Governmental Organizations. The Limits of Apolitical Development*, London, Macmillan

Park, Jacob (1997) 'The World Wide Fund for Nature: Financing a New Noah's Ark', in Bergesen, Helge Ole and Parmann, Georg *Green Globe Yearbook*, Oxford, Oxford University Press

Parson, Edward A (1996) 'International Protection of the Ozone Layer', in Bergesen, Helge Ole and Parmann, Georg *Green Globe Yearbook*, Oxford, Oxford University Press

Ravlum, Inger-Anne (1997) *Byrdebærere og gratispassasjerer. Staters oppslutning om de multilaterale bistandsorganisasjonene* (Burden bearers or free riders. States' support for the multilateral development agencies), Lysaker, Norway, Fridtjof Nansen Institute

Righter, Rosemary (1995) *Utopia Lost. The United Nations and World Order*, New York, Twentieth Century Fund Press

Sandford, Rosemary (1994) 'International Environmental Treaty Secretariats: Stage-Hands or Actors?', in Bergesen, Helge Ole and Parmann, Georg *Green Globe Yearbook*, Oxford, Oxford University Press

Singer, Hans (1995) 'Rethinking Bretton Woods: from an historical perspective', in Griesgraber & Gunter (eds) *Promoting development – effective global institutions for the twenty-first century*, London, Pluto Press

South Centre (1995) *For a Strong and Democratic United Nations. A South Perspective on UN Reform*, Geneva, South Centre

Speth, James Gustave (1996) 'The UN, the US and Development Cooperation', in *United Nations Chronicle*, XXXIII, 4, pp72–6

Stern, Nicolas (1997) 'The World Bank as Intellectual Actor', in Kapur, D, Lewis, J P, and Webb, R *The World Bank: Its first half century*, Washington DC, Brookings Institution Press

Stokke, Olav Schram and Vidas, Davor (1996) 'Effectiveness and Legitimacy of International Regimes', in Stokke, Olav Schram and Vidas, Davor *Governing the Antarctic. The Effectiveness and Legitimacy of the Antarctic Treaty System*, Cambridge, Cambridge University Press

Thomas, Caroline (1992) *The Environment in International Relations*, London, Royal Institute of International Affairs

Urquhart, Brian (1987) *A Life in Peace and War*, New York, Harper and Row

von Moltke, Konrad (1996) 'Why UNEP Matters', in Bergesen, Helge Ole and Parmann, Georg *Green Globe Yearbook*, 1996. Oxford, UK, Oxford University Press: pp55–64

Weiss, Thomas G, Forsythe, David P and Coate, Roger A (1994) *The United Nations and Changing World Politics*, Boulder, Westview Press

Wettestad, Jorgen (1987) *Multilaterale bistandsorganer og miljøvernet* (Multilateral Development Bodies and the Environment), Lysaker, Norway, The Fridtjof Nansen Institute

Willetts, Peter (1989) 'The Pattern of Conferences' in Taylor, Paul and Groom, A J R *Global Issues in the United Nations' Framework*, London, Macmillan

Willetts, Peter (ed) (1996) *'The Conscience of the World'. The Influence of Non-Governmental Organizations in the UN System*, London, Hurst & Co

Williams, Douglas (1987) *The Specialised Agencies and the United Nations – the System in Crisis*, New York, St Martin's Press

Wolfensohn, James D (1996) 1996 Annual Meetings Speech, 1 October

Wolfensohn, James D (1997) 'People First' UNDP Paul Hoffman Lecture, New York, 29 May 1997

World Bank (1994) *Governance. The World Bank's Experience*, Washington DC, The World Bank

World Bank (1995) *Mainstreaming the environment; the World Bank's annual environmental report*, Washington DC, The World Bank

World Bank (1997) *The Strategic Compact: Renewing the Bank's Effectiveness to Fight Poverty*, Memo from the President dated 13 February 1997

World Commission on Environment and Development (1987) *Our Common Future*, Oxford, Oxford University Press

Yamin, Farhana (1998) 'The CSD Reporting Process: A Quiet Step Forward for Sustainable Development', in Bergesen, Helge Ole and Parmann, Georg *Green Globe Yearbook, 1998*, Oxford, Oxford University Press

Index

Page references in **bold** refer to figures, tables and boxes